The Routledge Introduction to Qur'ānic Arabic

The Routledge Introduction to Qur'ānic Arabic is an innovative, text-based, language course designed for students interested in acquiring a foundation in Qur'ānic and Classical Arabic.

Focused on enhancing comprehension and vocabulary acquisition, the book contains 40 lessons designed to be covered in about 40 hours of classroom instruction. Starting with the shorter *sūras* of the Qur'ān, such as *al-fātiḥa* and those of the *Juz' 'Amma*, it utilizes their recurring vocabulary and grammatical structures to build a stable linguistic foundation for learners before moving on to more challenging and longer *sūras* such as *Yāsīn*, *Maryam* and *Yūsuf*.

Although the book is primarily designed for classroom use, the vocabulary and structures of the short *sūras*, the accompanying audio recordings, and the activities found throughout the book will also be helpful for independent learners. The only prerequisite is knowledge of the Arabic writing system.

The audio material, which is available on the Routledge website at www.routledge.com/9780415508940, helps learners improve their pronunciation of individual sounds and develop their skills to syllabify Arabic words and phrases correctly in order to approximate that of native speakers.

Written by an experienced teacher, *The Routledge Introduction to Qur'ānic Arabic* is an essential guide for instructors, students and anyone interested in developing their knowledge of Qur'ānic Arabic.

Munther Younes is Reis Senior Lecturer of Arabic Language and Linguistics and Director of the Arabic Program at Cornell University, USA.

The Routledge Introduction to Qur'ānic Arabic

Munther Younes

مقدمة الى لغة القرآن

منذر يونس

Routledge
Taylor & Francis Group

LONDON AND NEW YORK

First published 2013
by Routledge
2 Park Square, Milton Park, Abingdon, Oxon OX14 4RN

Simultaneously published in the USA and Canada
by Routledge
711 Third Avenue, New York, NY 10017

Routledge is an imprint of the Taylor & Francis Group, an informa business

British Library Cataloguing in Publication Data
A catalogue record for this book is available from the British Library

Library of Congress Cataloging in Publication Data
A catalog record for this book has been requested

ISBN: 978-0-415-50893-3 (hbk)
ISBN: 978-0-415-50894-0 (pbk)
ISBN: 978-0-203-10940-3 (ebk)

Typeset in Times New Roman and Geeza Pro
by Graphicraft Limited, Hong Kong

Printed and bound in Great Britain by the MPG Books Group

The Routledge Introduction to Qur'ānic Arabic

Munther Younes

مقدمة الى لغة القرآن

منذر يونس

LONDON AND NEW YORK

First published 2013
by Routledge
2 Park Square, Milton Park, Abingdon, Oxon OX14 4RN

Simultaneously published in the USA and Canada
by Routledge
711 Third Avenue, New York, NY 10017

Routledge is an imprint of the Taylor & Francis Group, an informa business

British Library Cataloguing in Publication Data
A catalogue record for this book is available from the British Library

Library of Congress Cataloging in Publication Data
A catalog record for this book has been requested

ISBN: 978-0-415-50893-3 (hbk)
ISBN: 978-0-415-50894-0 (pbk)
ISBN: 978-0-203-10940-3 (ebk)

Typeset in Times New Roman and Geeza Pro
by Graphicraft Limited, Hong Kong

MIX
Paper from
responsible sources
FSC
www.fsc.org   FSC® C004839   Printed and bound in Great Britain by the MPG Books Group

Contents

Introduction

The Routledge Introduction to Qur'ānic Arabic was inspired by a group of students at Cornell University who asked me to offer a course that would help them understand the language of the Qur'ān, which they had been hearing and reading since childhood with little understanding. The book was designed with such a group of learners in mind.

Since these students are likely to be familiar with the Arabic writing system, the book assumes prior acquaintance with it. And since they are likely to be familiar with the short *sūras* of the Qur'ān through daily prayers and religious instruction, the book starts with them, builds a linguistic foundation by utilizing their vocabulary and grammatical structures, and then moves to longer and more challenging *sūras*. It begins with *al-fātiḥa* and covers all the *sūras* of Part 30 (*Juz' 'Amma*), from Q114 to Q78. These are followed by the three longer *sūras* Q36 (*Yāsīn*), Q19 (*Maryam*), and Q12 (*Yūsuf*), in that order.

This doesn't imply that other groups of learners cannot benefit from the book. The similar vocabulary and structures of the short *sūras*, the accompanying audio recordings, and the activities found throughout the book will facilitate the acquisition of a solid foundation in the most commonly used words and structures of the Qur'ān even without prior acquaintance with its language. The only prerequisite in this case is knowledge of the Arabic writing system, which can be acquired from a variety of sources.

The book is divided into 40 lessons, each with a text of about 200 words, and is designed to be covered in about 40 hours of classroom instruction, or one 15-week semester, with three class meetings a week, plus reviews and testing. For that reason, several of the short *sūras* are grouped into a single lesson, and the longer *sūras* are divided into smaller units. At the beginning of the book, only the text of the *sūra* is presented along with a vocabulary list and a list of "words to remember." More challenging and varied types of activities are introduced gradually and systematically. These consist mainly of grammar and vocabulary-building exercises and grammar explanations, where grammar includes the system of sounds, word formation, and sentence formation.

The book also includes two appendices: the first is a summary of the grammar points presented in the different lessons, and the second is a listing by root of all the words introduced in the textbook.

The texts of the *sūras* are based on the Egyptian edition of the Qur'ān, and the English translations in the vocabulary lists and the cumulative glossary are based on Muhammad Marmaduke Pickthall's *The Meaning of the Glorious Qur'ān* and

Arabic-English Dictionary of Qur'anic Usage by Elsaid M. Badawi and Muhammad Abdel Haleem (Brill 2008).[1]

Two aspects of the textbook that signal a departure from the way the texts of *suras* are presented in standard copies of the Qur'ān, which are based on the Uthmānic script, are the sparse use of diacritics and the use of modern Arabic orthography. The reason for this departure in the two cases is purely pedagogical.

I believe that the book can be a more effective learning tool if words are presented in their basic forms and not surrounded by marks that are for the most part predictable and redundant. For example, in standard copies of the Qur'ān a word like واستغفره (Q 110:3), is written as follows: وَٱسْتَغْفِرْهُ. In addition to the eight letters with which the word is spelled, there are eight diacritics, one accompanying each letter. Some of these diacritics can play an important role in distinctions between words or helping with the correct pronunciation; others are completely redundant. In this book, three diacritics, not eight, are included because they are deemed important for correct pronunciation, as follows: واستَغفِره.

The use of modern Arabic orthography refers mainly to writing the letter *alif* in words where it is not found in the Uthmānic edition, as in صراط instead of صرط (Q 1:7). This modern spelling is commonly used in Arabic instructional materials, such as school textbooks, as well as scholarly essays citing Qur'ānic verses. It is pedagogically more effective, since it shows relationships among words more clearly, particularly in a textbook that aims to build a foundation in Arabic, not just Qur'ānic Arabic. The Uthmānic spelling الكتب, for example, can be read as الكِتاب "the book", or الكُتُب "the books". Distinguishing the two in writing, as is done in all forms of Arabic outside the Uthmānic edition, makes it easier for the learner to distinguish the two forms.

▮ Suggestions for Using the Textbook

Although the book is designed for classroom use, it can easily be adapted to independent study. For a classroom setting, the material can be most effectively mastered if prepared ahead of time. Class time, which is always limited, is then used for practicing material that is already familiar, clarifying points that need clarification after students have tried to understand them on their own, and asking and answering focused questions. The importance of preparing the material before coming to

---

[1] A useful manual of basic information about the Qur'ān, which includes a brief listing of sources and publications, is *The Koran: A Very Short Introduction* by Michael Cook (Oxford University Press 2000). For a more in-depth understanding of the Holy Book, the reader is referred to *The Blackwell Companion to the Qur'ān*, ed. by Andrew Rippin (Blackwell Publishing 2006) or *The Cambridge Companion to the Qur'an*, ed. by Jane Dammen McAuliffe (Cambridge University Press 2006). Each volume consists of a collection of essays on various aspects of the Qur'ān written by leading scholars in the field.

class cannot be overemphasized, and the more this is done on a regular basis, the more the students will be meaningfully engaged in class activities and the more they will learn. They should prepare the *sūra* or the part of the *sūra* assigned for a specific class meeting by reading and understanding the text with the help of the vocabulary lists and grammar explanations. In addition to enhancing comprehension and vocabulary acquisition, listening to the text on the audiofiles will help improve pronunciation of individual sounds and develop the skills to syllabify Arabic words and phrases correctly so pronunciation will approximate that of native speakers.

For the independent user of the book, in the absence of a teacher and a classroom, the key is discipline and follow-through. And for both the student in the classroom and the independent learner, it is important to remember that the texts and activities in the book are arranged in a way that maximizes learning and retention of the material. That is why they should be introduced and studied in the order given. The learner should not move to a new lesson before mastering the preceding ones.

In addition to introducing the learner to the most commonly used words and grammatical structures of the language of the Qur'ān, the book provides a solid foundation in the vocabulary and grammar of Classical Arabic and its modern manifestation, Modern Standard Arabic. Most of the vocabulary presented is still in common use and most of the grammatical structures introduced, explained and practiced, such as the rules of possession, person/subject marking, negation, the case and mood system (*i'rāb*), and the construct (*iḍāfa*), are essentially the same in all these varieties.

▇ Key to transliteration symbols used in the book

Ā	ā	ا
B	b	ب
T	t	ت
Ṯ	ṯ	ث
J̌	j	ج
Ḥ	ḥ	ح
H̱	ẖ	خ
D	d	د
Ḏ	ḏ	ذ
R	r	ر
Z	z	ز

S	s	س
Š	š	ش
Ṣ	ṣ	ص
Ḍ	ḍ	ض
Ṭ	ṭ	ط
Ẓ	ẓ	ظ
	ʻ	ع
Ġ	ġ	غ
F	f	ف
Q	q	ق
K	k	ك
L	l	ل
M	m	م
N	n	ن
H	h	هـ
Ū W	ū w	و
Ī Y	ī y	ي
	ʼ	ء، أ، إ، ىٕ، ؤ (hamza – همزة)
A	a	ـَ (fatḥa – فتحة)
U	u	ـُ (ḍamma – ضمّة)
I	i	ـِ (kasra – كسرة)

Acknowledgements

I would like to express my deep gratitude to the Routledge team who have shepherded this book through the whole process from the acquisition stage to the time of its formal publication. In particular, I would like to thank Andrea Hartill, Senior Commissioning Editor for Language Learning; Isabelle Cheng, Editorial Assistant for English Language and Linguistics; and Geraldine Martin, Senior Production Editor. My sincere thanks also to Thérèse Wassily Saba for a superb copy-editing job. All four were instrumental in turning a collection of notes for limited class use into the final shape the book has taken.

I am also grateful to the anonymous readers who read earlier drafts of the book and offered many valuable comments and suggestions, particularly in the area of grammar presentation.

The two other voices in the audio recordings, in addition to the author's, are those of Rahaf Al-Masri and Jamal Meri. I am grateful to both for helping with the recording and, additionally, for Ms Al-Masri's role in arranging for the recording sessions in Jordan.

Finally, I am indebted to my students in the Introduction to Qur'anic Arabic class at Cornell University, who inspired me to write the book in the first place and who, through their intelligent questions, comments, and suggestions, have contributed to its effectiveness as an instructional tool.

Acknowledgements

I would like to express my deep gratitude to the Routledge team who have shepherded this book through the whole process from the acquisition stage to the time of its formal publication. In particular, I would like to thank Andrea Hartill, Senior Commissioning Editor for Language Learning; Isabelle Cheng, Editorial Assistant for English Language and Linguistics; and Geraldine Martin, Senior Production Editor. My sincere thanks also to Thérèse Wassily Saba for a superb copy-editing job. All four were instrumental in turning a collection of notes for limited class use into the final shape the book has taken.

I am also grateful to the anonymous readers who read earlier drafts of the book and offered many valuable comments and suggestions, particularly in the area of grammar presentation.

The two other voices in the audio recordings, in addition to the author's, are those of Rahaf Al-Masri and Jamal Meri. I am grateful to both for helping with the recording and, additionally, for Ms Al-Masri's role in arranging for the recording sessions in Jordan.

Finally, I am indebted to my students in the Introduction to Qur'anic Arabic class at Cornell University, who inspired me to write the book in the first place and who, through their intelligent questions, comments, and suggestions, have contributed to its effectiveness as an instructional tool.

Lesson One	الدرس رقم ١
	١. سورة الفاتحة، مكّيّة

بِسمِ اللهِ الرحمنِ الرحيمِ {١} الحَمدُ للهِ رَبِّ العالَمِينَ {٢} الرَّحمنِ الرَّحيمِ {٣} مالِكِ يَومِ الدين {٤} إِيّاكَ نَعبُدُ وإِيّاكَ نَستَعِين {٥} اهدِنا الصِراطَ المُستَقيمَ {٦} صِراطَ الّذينَ أَنعَمتَ عَلَيهِم غَيرِ المَغضوبِ عَلَيهِم وَلا الضالّين {٧}

■ New words

Nouns

beneficent, compassionate	رَحمن²	name	اسم¹
praise	حَمْد	merciful	رَحيم
world	عالَم	lord	رَبّ
day	يَوم	master	مالِك
path	صِراط	judgement	دين
subject to wrath	مَغضوب	straight	مُستَقيم
		those who go astray one who goes astray + ين) masculine plural (m. pl.) suffix	ضالّين

Verbs

we seek help	نَستَعين	we worship	نَعبُد
you favored	أنعَمتَ	show us, guide us	إهدِنا

Particles

the	ال	in	بِ
you	إيّاك	to	لِ
those who	الّذين	and	وَ
not, other than	غير	on whom, on them (them هم on, ³على)	عَلَيهِم
		not, nor	لا

■ Words to remember

Write down the meanings of the following words from memory.

رَحمن	....	سم (اسم)	....
رَبّ	....	رَحيم	....
دين	....	يَوم	....
عَلَيهِم	....	نَعبُد	....
		غير	....

---

³ Note that when a suffix is attached to the preposition على the final ى (ألف مقصورة) is turned into ي.

١١٤. سورة الناس، مكّيّة

قُل أَعوذُ بِرَبِّ الناسِ {١} مَلِكِ الناسِ {٢} إِلَهِ الناسِ {٣} مِن شَرِّ الوَسواسِ الخَنّاسِ {٤} الَّذي يُوَسوِسُ في صُدورِ الناسِ {٥} مِنَ الجِنّةِ وَالناسِ {٦}

■ New words

Nouns

king	مَلِك	mankind	ناس
evil	شَرّ	God	إله
sneaking	خَنّاس	whisperer	وَسواس
jinn	جِنّة	chests, hearts	صُدور

Verbs

I seek refuge	أعوذ	Say! (Imperative)	قُل!
		He whispers	يُوَسوِس

Particles

(that) who	الَّذي	from	مِن
		in	في

■ **Grammar: The definite article and the sun and moon letters**

Definiteness in Arabic is expressed by attaching the prefix ال [al] "the" to nouns and adjectives:

وسواس   whisperer

الوسواس   the whisperer

If ال is followed by a *sun* letter, it is assimilated to (becomes the same as) that letter, which results in a doubled consonant in pronunciation but not in writing, as in الناس, which is pronounced *an-nās*. ل remains unchanged before *moon* letters, as in المستقيم "the straight", which is pronounced *al-mustaqīm*.

In the following, the words on the first line all begin with a sun letter following the definite article, and those on the second all begin with a moon letter.

الرحمن، الرحيم، الدين، السراط، الضالين

الفاتحة، الحمد، العالمين، المغضوب، الوسواس، الخنّاس، الجنّة

■ **Words to remember**

Write down the meanings of the following words from memory.

	ناس		قُل
....		....	
	إله		مَلِك
....		....	
	شَرّ		مِن
....		....	
	في		الّذي
....		....	

١١٣. سورة الفلق، مكّيّة

قُل أَعوذُ بِرَبِّ الفَلَق {١} مِن شَرِّ ما خَلَق {٢} وَمِن شَرِّ غاسِقٍ إذا وَقَب {٣} وَمِن شَرِّ النَفّاثاتِ في العُقَد {٤} وَمِن شَرِّ حاسِدٍ إذا حَسَد {٥}

■ New words

Nouns

darkness	غاسِق	daybreak	فَلَق
knots	عُقَد	blowers [نفّاثة blower + ات feminine plural (f. pl.) suffix]	نَفّاثات
		envier	حاسِد

Verbs

it became intense	وَقَب	(he) created	خَلَق
		(he) envied	حَسَد

Particles

if, when	اذا	that which	ما

■ Words to remember

Write down the meanings of the following words from memory.

خَلَق ....   ما ....

حاسِد ....   اذا ....

حَسَد ....

١١٢. سورة التوحيد، مكّيّة

قُلْ هُوَ اللهُ أَحَد {١} اللهُ الصَّمَد {٢} لَم يَلِد وَلَم يولَد {٣} وَلَم يَكُن لَهُ كُفُوًا
أَحَد {٤}

■ New words

Nouns

eternal	صَمَد	one	أَحَد
		one who is comparable	كُفُوًا

Verbs

he is begotten	يولَد	he begets	يَلِد
		is	يَكُن

Particles

did not	لَم	he	هُو
		for him, unto him (ل "to, for", ﻪ "him")	لَه

■ Words to remember

Write down the meanings of the following words from memory.

....	أَحَد	....	هُو
....	يَلِد	....	لَم
....	يَكُن	....	يولَد
		....	لَه

بسم الله الرحمن الرحيم

تَبَّت يَدا أَبي لَهَبٍ وَتَبّ {١} ما أَغنى عَنهُ مالُهُ وَما كَسَبَ {٢} سَيَصلى نارًا
ذاتَ لَهَبٍ {٣} وامرَأَتُهُ حَمّالَةَ الحَطَب {٤} في جيدِها حَبلٌ مِن مَسَد {٥}

■ New words

Nouns

Abī Lahab (also spelled *Abū Lahab* in the nominative case, is Prophet Muhammad's uncle known for his hostility to him)	أَبي لَهَب	(the two) hands (of)	يَدا
fire (ًا at the end of the word is a case marker. Cases are introduced in Lesson 5 and summarized in the Grammar appendix)	نارًا	his wealth (مال wealth + ـه his)	مالُه
his wife (امرأة wife + ـه his)	امرأته	flame	لَهَب
wood	حَطَب	carrier	حمّالة
rope	حَبل	her neck (جيد neck + ها her)	جيدِها
		palm-fiber	مَسَد

Verbs

(he) perished, may he perish!	تَبّ	(they) perished, may they perish!	تبّت
he gained	كَسَب	(it) exempted, made self-sufficient	أغنى
		he will be burned	سَيصلى

Particles

for him (عن for, about + ـه him)	عنه	(did) not	ما
		of, with, that has	ذات

■ Words to remember

Write down the meanings of the following words from memory.

	ما		يدا
....	عنه	....	أغنى
....	كَسَب	....	مالُه
....	ذات	....	نار
		....	امرأته

١١٠. سورة النصر، مدنيّة

بسم الله الرحمن الرحيم

إذا جاء نَصرُ اللهِ والفَتح {١} وَرَأيتَ الناسَ يَدخُلونَ في دينِ اللهِ أفواجا {٢}

فَسَبِّح بِحَمدِ رَبِّكَ واستَغفِرهُ إنّهُ كانَ تَوّابا {٣}

■ New words

Nouns

conquest	فَتْح	succor, triumph	نَصْر
troops, groups (ا + أفواج case marker)	أفواجاً	religion	دين
		ready to show mercy (ا + توّاب)	تَوّابا

Verbs

you (m. sg.) saw	رأيتَ	(it) came	جاء
glorify!	سَبِّح!	they enter	يدخُلون
He was	كان	seek forgiveness!	استَغفِر!

Particles

lo, that, verily	إنّ	then, and	فَ

◾ Word study

The word الله is pronounced in two slightly different ways, depending on the vowel preceding it. The two pronunciations are represented by the following two sets of examples:

١.   بسمِ الله الرحيم، الحمدُ لله ربّ العالمين، في دينِ اللهِ أفواجاً

٢.   قُل هُو اللهُ أَحَد، اللهُ الصمَد، نصرُ الله والفَتح

Questions

1.   Describe the difference between the two pronunciations.
2.   How do you explain the difference?

◾ Words to remember

Write down the meanings of the following words from memory.

....	نَصر	....	جاء
....	يبخُلون	....	رأيتَ
....	فَ	....	دين
....	إنّ	....	لستَغفِر
		....	كان

١٠٩. سورة الكافرون، مكِّية

بسم الله الرحمن الرحيم

قُل يا أَيُّها الكافِرونَ {١} لا أَعبُدُ ما تَعبُدونَ {٢} وَلا أَنتُم عابِدونَ ما أَعبُدُ {٣} وَلا أَنا عابِدٌ ما عَبَدتُّم {٤} وَلا أَنتُم عابِدونَ ما أَعبُدُ {٥} لَكُم دينُكُم وَلِيَ دين {٦}

■ New words

Nouns

worshipers, worshiping	عابِدون	unbelievers	كافِرون
		worshiper	عابِد

Verbs

you (m. pl.) worship	تَعبُدون	I worship	أَعبُدُ
		you (m. pl.) worshiped	عَبَدتُّم

Particles

O, you (followed by definite nouns)	أَيّها	O, you (followed by indefinite nouns)	يا
you (pl.)	أَنتُم	(do) not	لا
for you, unto you, to you	لَكُم	I	أَنا
		for me, unto me, to me	لِي

◼ Grammar: The plural of nouns and adjectives

Nouns and adjectives in Arabic can be pluralized in one of two principal ways: by adding a suffix to the word or by changing its internal structure. Plurals formed by the addition of a suffix are called *sound plurals*; those formed by an internal vowel change are called *broken plurals*.

Sound plurals

Sound plurals are of two types: *masculine* and *feminine*. Masculine sound plurals are formed by adding the suffix ون (nominative), or ين (accusative and genitive)[1] to the singular noun.

disbeliever – disbelievers	كافِر – كافِرون/كافِرين
worshiper – worshipers	عابِد – عابِدون/عابِدين

Feminine sound plurals are formed by adding the suffix ات to the noun. If the noun ends in التاء المربوطة, it is dropped:

blower – blowers (on knots)	نَفّاثة – نفّاثات

Broken plurals

These plurals are formed by changing the vowels of the word; the consonants are usually not affected. Think of English words like *goose – geese* and *foot – feet*. Examples of broken plurals you have seen so far are:

صُدور "chests, hearts", plural of صَدر

أفواج "groups", plural of فَوج

عُقَد "knots", plural of عُقدة

From now on, nouns with the plural suffixes ون/ين and ات will be listed in their singular forms. Broken plurals will be listed in the form they are found in the *sūras*.

---

[1] See Cases in Lesson 5.

■ Words to remember

Write down the meanings of the following words from memory.

....	أيّها	....	يا
....	لا	....	كافِر
....	تَعبُدون	....	أعبُد
....	عابِد	....	أنتُم
....	عَبَدتُم	....	أنا
....	لي	....	لكُم

١٠٨. سورة الكوثر، مكّيّة

بسم الله الرحمن الرحيم

إنّا أعطَيناكَ الكَوثَر {١} فَصَلِّ لِرَبِّكَ وانحَر {٢} إنَّ شانِئَكَ هُوَ الأبتَر {٣}

▨ New words

Nouns

your (m. sg.) insulter (شانِئ insulter + ك your)	شانِئَك	abundance	كَوثَر
		one without posterity	أبتَر

Verbs

you (m. sg.) pray!	صَلِّ!	we gave you (m. sg.) (أعطى gave + نا we + ك you)	أعطيناك
		you (m. sg.) sacrifice!	انحَر!

Particles

that we; truly we (إنّ that, truly + نا we)	إنّا

▨ Words to remember

Write down the meanings of the following words from memory.

	أعطيناك	....		إنّا	....
				صَلِّ	....

١٠٧. سورة الماعون، مكّية

بسم الله الرحمن الرحيم

أَرَأَيتَ الَّذي يُكَذِّبُ بِالدّين {١} فَذَلِكَ الَّذي يَدُعُّ اليَتيم {٢} وَلا يَحُضُّ عَلى طَعامِ المِسكين {٣} فَوَيلٌ لِلمُصَلّين {٤} الَّذينَ هُم عَن صَلاتِهِم ساهون {٥} الَّذينَ هُم يُراؤُون {٦} وَيَمنَعونَ الماعون {٧}

■ New words

Nouns

feeding	طَعام	orphan	يَتيم
woe	وَيلٌ	needy person	مِسكين
prayer	صَلاة	worshiper, one who prays	مُصَلّي
small kindness	ماعون	heedless	ساهي (ساهون)

Verbs

(he) denies, thinks something is a lie	يُكَذِّب	Did you see? (أ yes/no question particle + the verb رَأَيتَ you, m. sg., saw)	أَرَأَيتَ
(he) urges	يَحُضُّ	(he) repels	يَدُعُّ
they refuse	يَمنَعون	they show off	يُراءون

Particles

they (m.)	هُم	that is he, that is the one	ذلك
		of, about, from	عَن

■ Notes

When the preposition ل is prefixed to a word starting with the definite article ال, the ا is dropped and the preposition is joined directly with the ل of the definite article.

$$ل + المصلّين = للمصلّين$$

The same thing happens when ل is prefixed to the word الله:

$$ل + الله = لله$$

Note also that the word مُصلّين consists of the word مُصلّي "one who prays" + the plural suffix ين. The final ي of مصلّي is dropped when the plural suffix is attached.

The word ساهون consists of the singular noun ساهي + the plural suffix ون. The final ي is deleted before the plural suffix.

■ Grammar: Subject-person markers on the perfect verb

Arabic verbs have two tenses: the *perfect* (الماضي) and the *imperfect* (المضارع). The perfect corresponds roughly to the past tense in English, and generally indicates completed action, and the imperfect corresponds to the present tense and indicates actions that have not been completed.

Different persons are expressed on the perfect verb by attaching different suffixes to it, except in the case of the third person masculine singular (the one corresponding to *he wrote*, *he was*, etc.), where no suffix is attached.

You have seen three of these markers so far. They are shown in the following table, along with the third person masculine singular conjugation.

he worshiped	عبد	–
you (m. sg.) worshiped	عبدتَ	ـتَ
you (m. pl.) worshiped	عبدتُم	ـتُم –
we worshiped	عبدنا	نا –

Please note that from now on verbs in the perfect tense will be listed in the word lists without their subject markers.

■ Exercise

Given the meanings of the verbs in Column A and using the above table, give a full translation of the words in Column B. The first word is given as an example.

A		B	
Word without suffix		**Word with suffix**	**Full translation**
أنعم	he favored	أنعمتَ	you (m. sg.) favored
ورأى	and he saw	ورأيتَ	
عبد	he worshiped	عبدتُم	
أرأى	did he see	أرأيتَ	

Note the change from رأى to رأي when the suffix is added, which is similar to the change you saw before with على and عليهم.

■ **Words to remember**

Write down the meanings of the following words from memory.

رأيتَ	....	أ	....
ذلك	....	يُكذّب	....
طَعام	....	يَتيم	....
وَيل	....	مِسكين	....
هُم	....	مُصَلّين	....
صَلاة	....	عَن	....

Lesson Three	الدرس رقم ٣
	١٠٦. سورة قُرَيش، مكّية

بسم الله الرحمن الرحيم

لِإيلافِ قُرَيش {١} إيلافِهِم رِحلَةَ الشِتاءِ والصَّيف {٢} فَلْيَعبُدوا رَبَّ هَذا البَيت {٣} الَّذي أَطعَمَهُم مِّن جوعٍ وَآمَنَهُم مِّن خَوف {٤}

New words

Nouns

Quraysh (the name of the Prophet's tribe)	قُرَيش	for the taming (ل for + إيلاف taming)	لايلاف
trip, journey	رحلة	their taming (هم + إيلاف their)	إيلافهم
summer	صَيف	winter	شِتاء
(he) fed	أطعَم	house	بَيت
fear	خَوف	hunger	جوع

Verbs

| he fed them (أطعَم he fed, هُم them) | أطعمهم | so let them worship (ف so, ل let, have, used to give a command to a subject in the third person, يعبدوا they worship) | فليعبدوا |
| | | he made them safe (آمَن he made safe, هُم them) | آمَنهم |

■ Words to remember

Write down the meanings of the following words from memory.

صَيف	....	شِتاء	....
أطعَم	....	بَيت	....
آمَن	....	جوع	....
		خَوف	....

١٠٥. سورة الفيل، مكّيّة

بسم الله الرحمن الرحيم

أَلَم تَرَ كَيفَ فَعَلَ رَبُّكَ بِأَصحابِ الفيل {١} أَلَم يَجعَل كَيدَهُم في تَضليل {٢} وَأَرسَلَ عَلَيهِم طَيرًا أَبابيل {٣} تَرميهِم بِحِجارَةٍ مِّن سِجّيل {٤} فَجَعَلَهُم كَعَصفٍ مَأكول {٥}

■ New words

Nouns

elephant	فيل	owners, people of	أصحاب
nothing	تضليل	evil planning	كَيد
swarms	أبابيل	birds, flying things	طيراً
baked clay	سِجّيل	stones	حِجارة
eaten, devoured	مأكول	green crops	عَصف

Verbs

did	فَعَل	you (m. sg.) saw (See Moods in Lesson 5 and the Grammar appendix)	تَرَ
he sent	أرسَل	he makes	يجعَل
So he made them (ف + جعل + هم)	فجعلهم	they pelt, throw (at) them they, i.e., the flying things, throw; هِم them) (ترمي	ترميهِم

Particles

how	كَيفَ	(did) not? (أ yes /no question particle + لم did not)	أَلَم
		like	كَ

■ Grammar: Subject-person markers on the imperfect verb

As was mentioned above, Arabic verbs have two tenses: the *perfect* and the *imperfect*. We have already seen some of the perfect subject markers. The imperfect subject markers are attached to the verb as prefixes or, in some cases, both prefixes and suffixes. The following table shows the most commonly used imperfect subject markers:

he worships	هو	يَعْبُد	يَ
she worships	هـي	تعبُد	تَ
they (m.) worship	هـم	يعبُدون	يـ – ون
you (m. pl.) worship	انتُم	تعبُّدون	تَـ – ون
I worship	أنا	أعبُد	أ –
we worship	نحن	نعبُد	نَ

■ Note

Non-human plural nouns are treated as singular feminine nouns for purposes of agreement. "Birds or flying things" would be referred to by the pronoun "she", not "they".

Note also that from now on verbs will be listed in the word lists in their simplest forms, without subject markers. Verbs found in the perfect tense *sūras*, will be shown in their basic third person singular perfect form only, and verbs that occur in the imperfect will be shown in both their third person singular perfect and imperfect forms, as in: عبد – يعبد (which literally translates as "he worshiped – he worships").

■ Exercise

Given the meanings of the verbs in Column A and using the above table, give a full translation of the words in Column B. The first verb is given as an example.

A		B	
Word without suffix		**Word with suffix**	**Full translation**
عبد	he worshiped	نعبد	we worship
دخل	he entered	يدخلون	
كذّب	he denied	يُكذّب	
منع	he held back	يمنعون	

■ Words to remember

Write down the meanings of the following words from memory.

....	تَرَ	....	لَم
....	فَعَل	....	كَيفَ
....	جَعَل – يجعَل	....	أصحاب
....	طير	....	أرسَل
....	كَ	....	حِجارة
		....	مأكول

٤ ٠ ١. سورة الهُمَزة، مكّية

بسم الله الرحمن الرحيم

وَيْلٌ لِكُلِّ هُمَزَةٍ لُمَزَة {١} الّذي جَمَعَ مالاً وَعَدَّدَه {٢} يَحسَبُ أَنَّ مالَهُ أَخلَدَه {٣} كَلاّ لَيُنبَذَنَّ في الحُطَمَة {٤} وَما أَدراكَ ما الحُطَمَة {٥} نارُ اللهِ الموقَدَة {٦} الّتي تَطَّلِعُ عَلى الأَفئِدَة {٧} إِنَّها عَلَيهِم مُؤصَدَة {٨} في عَمَدٍ مُمَدَّدَة {٩}

■ New words

Nouns

fault-finder, back-biter	لُمَزَة	slanderer	هُمَزَة
consuming one	حُطَمَة	wealth	مال
hearts	أَفئِدَة	kindled, lit	موقَد
columns	عَمَد	closed	مُؤصَد
		outstretched, extended	مُمَدَّد

Verbs

he counted (عدّد he counted + ه him, it)	عدّده	he collected	جَمَع
he rendered immortal (أَخلد he made immortal + ه him, it)	أخلده	to think	حسِب – يحسَب
he made you aware (أدرى he made aware + كَ you, m. sg.)	أدراكَ	he will be flung	يُنبَذَنَّ
		to leap	اطّلَع – يطّلِع

Particles

that	أَنَّ	every	كُلّ
verily	لَ	no, not at all	كَلَّا
on, over them (على on, هِم them)	عليهم	which (f. sg.)	الّتي

◼ Grammar: Emphasizing meaning

Different tools are used to emphasize meaning in the Qur'ān. For example, in الفاتحة, word order is used to emphasize the pronoun "you" in the verse: إيّاك نعبد. The normal order would be: نعبد إيّاك ونستعين إيّاك (or نعبدك ونستعينك), وإيّاك نستعين, which would be translated as "we worship you and we seek help from you". The order used in the *sūra* gives the meaning added weight: "You [and no other] we worship, and you [and no other] we seek help from".

Other commonly used tools are the following: إنّ "verily, truly", كَلَّا "nay, definitely not", لَ prefixed to verbs, and نّ suffixed to verbs. The last two are often untranslatable; they simply add emphasis to the meaning. The use of إنّ is demonstrated in the following verse:

Verily we gave you [the] abundance.	إنّا أعطيناك الكوثر.

The other three are used in the verse:

Nay, [verily, truly] he will be thrown into the consuming one (fire).	كلّا لينبذنّ في الحطمة.

◼ Words to remember

Write down the meanings of the following words from memory.

....	جَمَع	....	كُلّ
....	حسِب – يحسَب	....	مال
....	كَلَّا	....	أنَّ
....	أدرى	....	لَ
....	الّتي	....	موقَد
		....	على

١٠٣. سورة العصر، مكّية

بسم الله الرحمن الرحيم

وَالعَصر {١} إنَّ الإنسانَ لَفي خُسر {٢} إلاّ الَّذينَ آمَنوا وَعَمِلوا الصالِحاتِ
وَتَواصَوا بِالحَقِّ وَتَواصَوا بِالصَبر {٣}

■ New words

Nouns

		by the declining day, mid-afternoon (و and, used here in the sense of "by" to initiate an oath (عصر + ال + و)	والعَصر
mankind	إنسان	state of loss	خُسر
to do	عمل – يعمل	to believe	آمَن – يؤمِن
to exhort one another	تواصى – يتواصى	good deed	صالحة
endurance, patience	صَبر	truth	حَقٌّ

Particle

except	الّا

■ Words to remember

Write down the meanings of the following words from memory.

إنسان	....	عَصر	....
آمَنوا	....	الّا	....
صالحات	....	عمِلوا	....
صَبر	....	حَقّ	....

١٠٢. سورة التكاثر، مكّية

بسم الله الرحمن الرحيم

أَلهاكُمُ التَكاثُر {١} حَتّى زُرتُمُ المَقابِر {٢} كَلّا سَوفَ تَعلَمون {٣} ثُمَّ كَلّا سَوفَ تَعلَمون {٤} كَلّا لَو تَعلَمونَ عِلمَ اليَقين {٥} لَتَرَوُنَّ الجَحيم {٦} ثُمَّ لَتَرَوُنَّها عَينَ اليَقين {٧} ثُمَّ لَتُسأَلُنَّ يَومَئِذٍ عَنِ النَعيم {٨}

■ New words

Nouns

increase	تَكاثُر	it distracted you (m. pl.)	أَلهاكُم
knowledge	عِلم	graves	مَقابِر
hell-fire	جَحيم	certainty	يَقين
that day	يَومَئِذٍ	vision	عَين
		pleasure	نَعيم

Verbs

to know	عَلِمَ – يَعلَم	you (m. pl.) visited	زُرتُم
you (m. pl.) will be asked	تُسأَلُنَّ	you (m. pl.) will behold, see	تَرَوُنَّ

زرتم is made up of the verb زار "(he) visited" and the person marker تُم "you (m. pl.)". The ا of زار is deleted when certain subject markers are attached. For more on this refer to the discussion of hollow roots under Root types in Lesson 10 and under Root types and verb conjugations in the Grammar appendix.

Particles

will	سَوفَ	until	حَتّى
if	لَو	and then	ثُمَّ

▨ Grammar: Pronominal suffixes attached to verbs, nouns, and particles

A set of pronoun suffixes are attached to nouns, verbs, prepositions, and particles like إنّ "truly, verily". When attached to nouns, these suffixes indicate possession; when attached to verbs or prepositions, they function as objects of these verbs and prepositions; and when attached to إنّ, they function as the subject of the clause beginning with this particle. The following are the pronouns you have seen so far attached to a noun, a verb, a preposition, and the particle إنّ:

		money, wealth مال	he sent أرسل	on على	verily, truly إنّ
		possessive	object of verb	object of preposition	subject of إنّ clause
his/him/he	ـه	مالُه	أرسله	عليه	إنّه
her/she	ها	مالها	أرسلها	عليها	إنّها
their/them/they	هُم	مالهم	أرسلهم	عليهم	إنّهم
your/you (m. sg.)	كَ	مالكَ	أرسلكَ	عليكَ	إنّكَ
your/you (pl.)	كُم	مالكم	أرسلكم	عليكم	إنّكم
our/us/we	نا	مالنا	أرسلنا	علينا	إنّا or إنّنا

From now on nouns, verbs, and particles will be listed in the word lists in their simplest forms, i.e., without any affixes.

▨ Exercise

Given the meaning of the words in Column A and using the above table, give a full translation of the words in Column B. The first word is given as an example.

A		B	
Word without suffix		Word with suffix	Full translation
على	on	عليهم	on them
إهدِ	guide!	إهدِنا	
مال	wealth	ماله	
جيد	neck	جيدها	
واستغفر	and ask forgiveness	واستغفره	
إنَّ	verily	إنَّه	
دين	religion	دينكم	
أعطينا	we gave	أعطيناكَ	
لربّ	to [a] Lord	لربّك	
شانئ	insulter	شانئك	
صلاة	prayer	صلاتهم	
إيلاف	taming	ايلافهم	
أطعم	he fed	أطعمهم	
أَمَن	he made safe	آمنهم	
فجعل	and he made	فجعلهم	
أدرى	he made aware	أدراكَ	
ترون	you (pl.) see	ترونها	

◼ Grammar: Expressing future time

....

سوف in سوف تَعلمون and the prefix س in سَيصلى, followed by the imperfect, indicate the future time. Both are translated as "will". س, being a one-letter particle, is attached to the following verb.

◼ Grammar: ألف مقصورة

....

The ألف مقصورة, which is only found at the end of a word, is changed to either ي or ا, mostly ا, when a suffix follows. The words أدراك and ألهاكم are derived from أدرى and ألهى, respectively.

■ Words to remember

Write down the meanings of the following words from memory.

زُرْتُم	....	حَتَّى	....
سَوفَ	....	مَقابِر	....
ثُمَّ	....	عَلِم – يَعلَم	....
عِلم	....	لَو	....
جَحيم	....	تَرَوُنَّ	....
تُسأَلُنَّ	....	عَين	....
نَعيم	....	يَومَئِذٍ	....

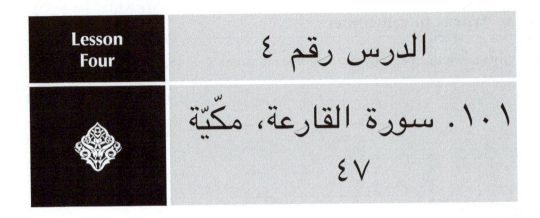

بسم الله الرحمن الرحيم

القارِعَة {١} ما القارِعَة {٢} وَما أَدراكَ ما القارِعَة {٣} يَومَ يَكونُ الناسُ كالفَراشِ المَبثوث {٤} وَتَكونُ الجِبالُ كالعِهنِ المَنفوش {٥} فَأَما مَن ثَقُلَت مَوازينُه {٦} فَهُوَ في عيشَةٍ راضِيَة {٧} وَأَما مَن خَفَّت مَوازينُه {٨} فَأُمُّهُ هاوِيَة {٩} وَما أَدراكَ ما هِيَ {١٠} نارٌ حامِيَة {١١}

New words

Nouns

moths	فَراش	calamity	قارعة
mountains	جِبال	scattered	مَبثوث
carded	مَنفوش	wool	عِهن
life	عيشة	scales	مَوازين
mother	أُمّ	pleasant	راضي
hot	حامي	bereft and hungry	هاوي

Verbs

to be heavy	ثَقُل – يثقُل	to be	كان – يكون
		to be light	خَفَّ – يخِفّ

Particles

who	مَن	as for	أمّا
		she	هِيَ

◼ Grammar: The different functions of ما

The particle ما has at least three different meanings/grammatical functions, as shown in the following verses. Translate all occurrences of ما in the verses into English.

a	ما أغنى عنه ماله وما كسب	
b	لا أعبد ما تعبدون	
c	وما أدراك ما الحطمة (two occurrences)	

◼ Exercise: Word analysis

Analyze the following verbs into a stem and affixes, as shown in the example. Remember that the stem of a verb corresponds to the third person masculine singular perfect conjugation. The first one is given as an example.

Affixes	Stem		
you (m. sg.) كَ، we نا	he gave أعطى	we gave you (m. sg.)	أعطيناك
		she throws [at] them	ترميهم
		and he made them	فجعلهم
		and he counted it [him]	وعدّده
		it [he] distracted you (pl.)	ألهاكم
		it [he] made you aware	أدراكَ
		they enter	يدخلون
		you (pl.) know	تعلمون

◾ Grammar: The pronunciation of the object/possessive pronouns ـه and هم

It was shown above that the long *a* of the word الله is pronounced like the *a* of *father* in some cases and the *a* of *can* in others, depending on the vowel preceding the word. A similar phenomenon is observed in the pronunciation of the vowels in the pronoun هم "them, their" and following the pronoun ـه "him, his". In a certain environment, the vowel is realized as ِ (كسرة), and in another as ُ (ضمّة). This is illustrated in the following examples.

◾ Exercise

Study the examples and write the rule for the pronunciation of the vowel. Your rule should say that the vowel is pronounced as a كسرة if it follows or precedes a certain consonant or vowel, and is pronounced ضمّة if it follows or precedes another consonant or vowel.

كسرة: بِهِ، لِرَبِّهِ، صَلاتِهِم، عَلَيهِم، ترميهِم

ضمّة: مالُهُ، امرأَتُهُ، لَهُ، إنَّهُ، واستغفِرْهُ، عَنْهُ، فأُمُّهُ، أَطعمَهُم، آمَنَهُم، كيدَهُم، فجعلَهُم

◾ Words to remember

Write down the meanings of the following words from memory.

	جِبال		كان – يكون
....	مَن	....	أمّا
....	مَوازين	....	ثَقُل
....	راضي	....	عيشة
....	أمّ	....	خَفّ
....	حامي	....	هي

١٠٠. سورة العاديات، مكّية

بسم الله الرحمن الرحيم

وَالعادِياتِ ضَبْحا {١} فَالمورِياتِ قَدْحا {٢} فَالمُغيراتِ صُبْحا {٣} فَأَثَرْنَ بِهِ نَقْعا {٤} فَوَسَطْنَ بِهِ جَمْعا {٥} إِنَّ الإنسانَ لِرَبِّهِ لَكَنود {٦} وَإِنَّهُ عَلى ذَلِكَ لَشَهيد {٧} وَإِنَّهُ لِحُبِّ الخَيرِ لَشَديد {٨} أَفَلا يَعْلَمُ إِذا بُعْثِرَ ما في القُبور {٩} وَحُصِّلَ ما في الصُدور {١٠} إِنَّ رَبَّهُم بِهِم يَومَئِذٍ لَخَبير {١١}

■ New words

Nouns

snorting	ضَبْحاً	runners	عادِيات
sparks	قَدْحاً	striking (fire)	مورِيات
in the morning	صُبْحاً	raiding	مُغيرات
gathering	جَمْعاً	dust	نَقعاً
witness	شَهيد	ingrate	كَنود
wealth, goods	خَيْر	love	حُبّ
graves	قُبور	intense	شَديد
knowing, perfectly informed	خَبير	chests, breasts	صُدور

Verbs

they (f.) went into the middle	وَسَطْنَ	they (f.) stirred up	أَثَرْنَ
(it) was brought out, made known	حُصِّل	(it) was scattered	بُعثِر

Particles

that	ذلِك

■ Grammar: The passive voice

A verb in the perfect is changed from the active voice to the passive voice by an internal vowel change, as follows (فتحة-فتحة is changed to ضمّة-كسرة – *fatḥa-fatḥa* is changed to *ḍamma-kasra*):

Active	Passive
بَعثَر	بُعثِر
حَصَّل	حُصِّل

■ Exercise: Word analysis

Analyze the following nouns into a stem and affixes, giving the English translation of each element. The stem of a noun is the form without affixes. For example, in the word لربّك "to your Lord", the stem is ربّ "Lord". Note that ات at the end of a word typically stands for the feminine plural suffix. The singular form usually ends in تاء مربوطة, as in الصالحات "good deeds", for which the singular is صالحة "a good deed". The first word is given as an example.

Stem and affixes	English translation	Noun
plural marker ات، and, by و، runner عادية	and (by) the runners	والعاديات
		فالموريات
		فَالْمُغيرات
		لربّه
		ربّهم

■ Words to remember

Write down the meanings of the following words from memory.

....	جَمْعاً	....	صُبحاً
....	شَهيد	....	ذلك
....	خَيْر	....	حُبّ
....	بُعثِر	....	شَديد
....	صُدور	....	قُبور

٩٩. سورة الزلزلة، مكّيّة

بسم الله الرحمن الرحيم

إذا زُلزِلَتِ الأرضُ زِلزالَها {١} وَأَخرَجَتِ الأرضُ أثقالَها{٢} وَقالَ الإنسانُ ما لَها {٣} يَومَئِذٍ تُحَدِّثُ أخبارَها {٤} بِأنَّ رَبَّكَ أوحى لَها {٥} يَومَئِذٍ يَصدُرُ النّاسُ أشتاتًا لِيُرَوا أعمالَهُم {٦} فَمَن يَعمَل مِثقالَ ذَرَّةٍ خَيرًا يَرَه {٧} وَمَن يَعمَل مِثقالَ ذَرَّةٍ شَرًّا يَرَه {٨}

■ New words

Nouns

shaking, earthquake	زِلزال	earth	أرْض
news, chronicles	أخبار	burdens	أثقال
deeds	أعمال	scattered groups	أشتات
atom	ذَرّة	weight	مِثقال

Verbs

to bring out	أخرج – يُخرِج	to be shaken	زُلزِل
to tell, relate	حَدّث – يُحَدِّث	to say	قال – يقول
to issue forth	صَدَر – يصدُر	he inspired	أوحى
to do	عَمِل – يَعمَل	they (m.) will be shown	يُرَوا
		to see	رأى – يرى (يَرَ)

يَرَ is the jussive form of يرى, the imperfect of رأى. The deletion of the final vowel is discussed under Moods of the imperfect verb in the Grammar appendix.

Particle

in order to	لِ

Grammar: More on subject markers on the perfect verb

So far, you have been introduced to three subject markers on the verb in the perfect. In العاديات a fourth marker is found, namely the third person feminine plural نَ, found in the two words فأثرن and فوسطن, and in الزلزلة another marker is found, ـت "she". The two are shown in the following table together with the ones you have already seen.

he worshiped	عبد	–
she worshiped	عبدَت	ت –
they (f.) worshiped	عبدنَ	نَ –
you (m. sg.) worshiped	عبدتَ	تَ –
you (m. pl.) worshiped	عبدتُم	تُم –
we worshiped	عبدنا	نا –

Exercise: Word analysis

Analyze the following words into a stem and affixes, giving the English translation of each element. Follow the examples.

Verbs

Stem and affixes	English translation	Verb
she ت and، و ،he brought out أخرج	And she brought out	وأخرجت
		وأرسَل
		فَجَعلَهُم
		وقال
		تُحَدِّث

Nouns

Stem and affixes	English translation	Noun
her ها، weights أثقال	her weights	أثقالها
		الإنسان
		أخبارها
		ربّك
		أعمالهم

■ Words to remember

Write down the meanings of the following words from memory.

....	أخرج	....	أرْض
....	قال	....	أثقال
....	أخبار	....	حَدَّث – يُحَدِّث
....	صَدَر – يصدُر	....	أوحى
....	يُرَوا	....	لِ
....	عَمِل – يَعمَل	....	أعمال
....	رأى – يرى (يَرَ)	....	مِثقال

٩٨. سورة البيّنة، مدنيّة

بسم الله الرحمن الرحيم

لَمْ يَكُنِ الَّذِينَ كَفَرُوا مِنْ أَهْلِ الكِتَابِ والمُشرِكِينَ مُنفَكِّينَ حَتَّى تَأْتِيَهُمُ البَيِّنَة {١} رَسُولٌ مِّنَ اللَّهِ يَتلُو صُحُفًا مُطَهَّرَة {٢} فِيهَا كُتُبٌ قَيِّمَة {٣} وَمَا تَفَرَّقَ الَّذِينَ أُوتُوا الكِتَابَ إِلَّا مِن بَعدِ مَا جَاءتهُمُ البَيِّنَة {٤} وَمَا أُمِرُوا إِلَّا لِيَعبُدُوا اللَّهَ مُخلِصِينَ لَهُ الدِّينَ حُنَفَاء وَيُقِيمُوا الصَّلَاةَ وَيُؤتُوا الزَّكَاةَ وَذَلِكَ دِينُ القَيِّمَة {٥} إِنَّ الَّذِينَ كَفَرُوا مِنْ أَهْلِ الكِتَابِ والمُشرِكِينَ فِي نَارِ جَهَنَّمَ خَالِدِينَ فِيهَا أُولَئِكَ هُمْ شَرُّ البَرِيَّة {٦} إِنَّ الَّذِينَ آمَنُوا وَعَمِلُوا الصَّالِحَاتِ أُولَئِكَ هُمْ خَيرُ البَرِيَّة {٧} جَزَاؤُهُمْ عِندَ رَبِّهِمْ جَنَّاتُ عَدنٍ تَجرِي مِن تَحتِهَا الأَنهَارُ خَالِدِينَ فِيهَا أَبَدًا رَضِيَ اللَّهُ عَنهُمْ وَرَضُوا عَنهُ ذَلِكَ لِمَن خَشِيَ رَبَّه {٨}

New words

Nouns

book	كِتاب (ج. كُتُب)	people	أهل
one who ceases	مُنفَكّ	idolater, polytheist	مُشرِك
messenger	رسول	proof	بَيِّنة
purified	مُطَهَر	pages	صُحُف
pure, faithful	مُخلِص	correct	قَيِّم
upright (pl.)	حُنَفَاء	religion	دين
alms	زَكاة	prayer	صَلاة

everlasting	خالِد	hell	جَهَنَّم
reward	جزاء	created beings	بَرِيّة
rivers	أنهار	the Garden of Eden	جنّة (ج. جَنّات) عَدْن
		for ever	أَبَداً

Note that .ج stands for جمع "plural".

Verbs

to come	أتى – يأتي	to disbelieve	كَفَر
to be divided	تَفَرَّق – يتفرّق	to recite	تَلا – يتلو
to come	جاء – يجيء	they were given	أوتوا
to worship	عَبَد – يعبُد	to be ordered	أُمِر
to give	آتى – يؤتي	to establish	أقام – يُقيم
to be content	رَضِي – يرضى	to flow	جَرى – يَجري
		to fear	خَشِي – يخشى

Particles

| those | أولئك | after | بَعْد |
| under | تَحْت | at, with | عِند |

▪ Grammar: More on subject markers

The word كفروا, translated as "they disbelieved", includes a subject marker you have not seen thus far, وا "they". The suffix is actually pronounced as if it has no ا in it. The ا is called واو الجماعة "wāw of plurality". It is found at the ends of verbs referring to plural persons, in which the presence of ا is an orthographic convention, with no phonetic value of its own, like the e in the English word *favorite*. The following table includes all the subject markers on the perfect verb you have been introduced to so far:

Translation	Example	Subject marker
he worshiped	عبد	—
she worshiped	عبدَت	ت –
they (m.) worshiped	عبدوا	وا –
they (f.) worshiped	عبدنَ	نَ –
you (m. sg.) worshiped	عبدتَ	تَ –
you (m. pl.) worshiped	عبدتُم	تُم –
we worshiped	عبدنا	نا –

■ Grammar: Passive voice

We have seen three examples of verbs in the passive voice, حُصِّل, بُعثر, and زُلزِلَت. Two more passive verbs are found in this *sura*: أوتوا "they were given" and أُمِروا "they were ordered". Their active counterparts are: آتوا "they gave" and أمَروا "they ordered".

■ Grammar: Negation

Several particles are used to negate words, phrases, and sentences in Arabic. You have already seen the word غير, translated as "not, un-, or other than", used in المغضوب عليهم "not those who are the subject of anger".

In general, negation rules can be divided into two main types, verbal and non-verbal: the particles لم, ما, لا, and لن are used in verbal negation, while ليس and غير are used in non-verbal negation. However, ما is sometimes used to negate non-verbal elements, and ليس is used to negate verbal elements. In this *sura*, the standard rules are followed, لم and ما are used to negate verbal elements in the past tense. The difference between لم and ما is that the former is followed by the imperfect form of the verb, while the latter is followed by the perfect. Both forms of negation are common, acceptable, and similar in meaning. This is illustrated by the verb كفر as follows:

They did not disbelieve		They disbelieved
لم يكفروا	ما كفروا	كفروا

Note the structural similarity between لم followed by the imperfect form of the verb and English *did* followed by the infinitive: *disbelieved*, but *did not disbelieve*.

■ Grammar: Number

Arabic nouns and adjectives can be *singular*, *dual*, or *plural*. We haven't seen examples of the dual yet, so it will not be introduced at this point.

One of the main ways to mark plurality is by adding a suffix to the singular noun or adjective. For masculine nouns, the suffix is ون or ين as in خالدين, الكافرون, المشركين, منفكّين, مخلصين, depending on the case of the noun or adjective (see Cases below.) For feminine nouns and adjectives, the suffix ات is used, as in جنّات, الصالحات.

■ Grammar: Cases

Arabic nouns and adjectives may have different endings, depending on their function in the sentence, i.e., whether the word is the subject of the sentence, the object of a verb or a preposition, which case the word it modifies is in, etc. The rules of this system, which is called the case system, are quite complicated, but have no bearing on the meaning. They are presented in detail in the Grammar appendix. For now, what you need to know is that pairs of words like كافرون and كافرين and triplets like الكتابُ/الكتابَ/الكتابِ and ربُّك/ربَّك/ربِّك are forms of the same word with the same meaning.

■ Grammar: Moods

While Arabic nouns and adjectives have a case system, Arabic verbs have a mood system. The case and mood systems are referred to collectively in Arabic grammar as *I'rāb*. The mood system affects only the verbs in the imperfect. Like the case system, it is quite complicated, and just as differences in case assignment do not result in differences in meaning, different moods do not result in differences in meaning. The rules of mood assignment are presented in detail in the Grammar appendix. For now, all you need to know is that pairs of verbs like يعبدون and يعبدوا, and يُقيمون and يُقيموا are variants of the same verb and are identical in meaning.

■ Grammar: Verb-subject disagreement

Arabic sentences may begin with the verb or the subject. If the verb precedes the subject, then it remains in the singular even when the subject is in the plural.

لم يكن الذين كفروا (instead of يكونوا)

وما تفرّق الذين أوتوا الكتاب (instead of تفرّقوا)

If the subject precedes the verb or if the verb with a plural subject is used only with the subject marker and not a subject word, then the plural form is used, as in إنّ الذين آمنوا وعملوا الصالحات إنّ الذين كفروا.

■ Exercise: Stems and affixes

For each of the following verbs and nouns, first give an English translation of the word, then identify the stem and affixes, giving the meaning of each. Follow the examples. Remember that the stem of a verb is the form corresponding to English *he + past tense* and for nouns it is the form without the definite article, prepositions, conjunctions, possessive pronouns, and plural and case markers.

Verbs

Stem and affixes	Translation	Verb
كفر he disbelieved, وا they	they disbelieved	كفروا
		جاءتهم
		أُمروا
	so that they worship	ليعبدوا
		آمنوا
	.	وعملوا

Nouns

Stem and affixes	Translation	Noun or adjective
مشرك polytheist، و and، ال the، ين plural marker	and the polytheists	والمشركين
		مخلصين
		خالدين
		الصالحات
		جزاؤهم
		جنّات

Write down the meanings of the following from memory.

....	أهل	....	كَفَر
....	مُشْرك	....	كُتُب
....	أتى - يأتي	....	تَفَرَّق
....	رسول	....	بَعْد
....	عَبَد - يعبُد	....	مُخلص
....	دين	....	صَلاة
....	جَهَنَّم	....	أنهار
....	جَنّات عَدْن	....	رَضِي
....	خَشِي	....	تَحْت

٩٧. سورة القدر، مكّية

بسم الله الرحمن الرحيم

إِنّا أَنزَلناهُ في لَيلَةِ القَدرِ {١} وَما أَدراكَ ما لَيلَةُ القَدرِ {٢} لَيلَةُ القَدرِ خَيرٌ مِن أَلفِ شَهرٍ {٣} تَنَزَّلُ المَلائِكَةُ والروحُ فيها بِإذنِ رَبِّهِم مِن كُلِّ أَمرٍ {٤} سَلامٌ هِيَ حَتّى مَطلَعِ الفَجرِ{٥}

▪ New words

Nouns

thousand	أَلْف	the Night of Predestination, Power	لَيلَة القَدْر
angels	ملائكة	month	شَهْر
permission	إِذْن	spirit	روح
peace	سَلام	decree, order	أَمْر
dawn	فَجْر	the time of rising	مَطلَع

Verbs

to descend	تَنَزَّل – يتنزَّل	to reveal, bring down	أنزَل – يُنزِل

▪ Grammar

The verb تنزّل "she descends" is originally تتنزّل. One ت is deleted, probably to simplify pronunciation. (Remember that non-human plurals, in this case الملائكة, are treated as feminine singular nouns, hence "she".)

■ Exercise: Word analysis

Translate fully and then analyze the two verbs أنزلناه and أدراك into a stem and affixes, giving the English translation of each element.

Stem and affixes	Translation	Verb
		أنزلناه
		أدراك

■ Words to remember

Write down the meanings of the following from memory.

....	ليلة القَدْر	....	أنزَل
....	شَهْر	....	أَلْف
....	ملائكة	....	تَنَزَّل
....	سَلام	....	أَمْر
		....	فَجْر

٩٦. سورة العَلَق (مَكِّيّة، وهي أوّل ما نزل من القرآن)

بسم الله الرحمن الرحيم

اقرأ باسم رَبِّكَ الَّذي خَلَقَ {١} خَلَقَ الإنسانَ مِن عَلَق {٢} اقرأ وَرَبُّكَ الأكرَم {٣} الَّذي عَلَّمَ بالقَلَم {٤} عَلَّمَ الإنسانَ ما لَم يَعلَم {٥} كَلا إنَّ الإنسانَ لَيَطغى {٦} أن رَّآهُ استغنى {٧} إنَّ إلى رَبِّكَ الرُّجعى {٨} أَرَأَيتَ الَّذي يَنهى {٩} عَبدًا إذا صَلَّى {١٠} أَرَأَيتَ إن كانَ عَلى الهُدى {١١} أو أَمَرَ بالتَّقوى {١٢} أَرَأَيتَ إن كَذَّبَ وَتَوَلَّى {١٣} أَلَم يَعلَم بِأنَّ اللَّهَ يَرى {١٤} كَلا لَئِن لَّم يَنتَهِ لَنَسفَعًا بالنَّاصِية {١٥} ناصِيةٍ كاذِبَةٍ خاطِئَة {١٦} فَليَدعُ نادِيَه {١٧} سَندعُ الزَّبانِية {١٨} كَلا لا تُطِعهُ واسجُد واقتَرِب {١٩}

◼ New words

Nouns

most bounteous, generous	أَكرَم	clot	عَلَق
return	رُجعى	pen	قَلَم
guidance	هُدى	slave	عَبْد
piety	تَقْوى	to order, enjoin	أَمَر
lying	كاذِب	forelock	ناصِية
henchmen	زَّبانِية	sinful	خاطِئ

Verbs

to create	خَلَق	read (imperative)	إقرأ
is rebellious	يَطغى	(he) taught	عَلَّم
to dissuade	نَهى – يَنهْى	to be independent	استَغنْى
to deny	كَذَّب	to pray	صَلَّى
to cease, put an end	انتَهى – يَنتْهَي	to go away, not to heed	تَوَلَّى
to call upon	دعا – يدعو	we seize	نَسْفَعاً
to prostrate, kneel	سَجَد – يَسجُد	to obey	أطاع – يُطيع
		to draw near	اقتَرَب – يقْتَرب

Particles

if	إن	that (when)	أَنْ

Note that فليدع and سندع are shortened forms of the two verbs يدعو "he calls" and ندعو "we call".

▇ Grammar: The imperative

The imperative or command form in Arabic is often formed by prefixing the letter ا (*alif*) to the verb:

Imperative		Imperfect declarative	
and ask forgiveness of Him!	واستغفره	You ask forgiveness of Him.	تستغفره
Read!	اقرأ	You read.	تقرأ
Prostrate!	اسجُد	You prostrate yourself.	تسجُد
Get closer!	اقترب	You read.	تقترب

In other cases, no ا is prefixed to the verb, as in قُل "Say!", فسبِّح "So glorify!". The presence or absence of the imperative ا is a function of verb type, which we will discuss later in the book. For now, try to recognize this ا and develop the ability to isolate it when analyzing words into stems and affixes.

■ Exercise: Word analysis

Translate fully and then analyze the following words into a stem and affixes, giving the English translation of each element.

Stem and affixes	Translation	Word
human being إنسان، the ال	the human being	الإنسان
		وربّك
		بالقلم
		بالناصية
		يعلم

■ Words to remember

Write down the meanings of the following from memory.

....	خَلَق	....	إقرأ
....	عَلَّم	....	أكرَم
....	استَغْنى	....	طغى
....	عَبْد	....	رُجعى
....	هُدى	....	صَلّى
....	تَقْوى	....	أمَر
....	كَذَّب	....	إنْ
....	كاذِب	....	تَوَلّى
....	دعا	....	خاطِئ
....	سَجَد	....	أطاع
		....	اقتَرَب

٩٥. سورة التين، مكّيّة

بسم الله الرحمن الرحيم

والتينِ والزَيتونِ {١} وطورِ سينينَ {٢} وهَذا البَلَدِ الأمينِ {٣} لَقَد خَلَقنا الإنسانَ في أحسَنِ تَقويم {٤} ثُمَّ رَدَدناهُ أسفَلَ سافلينَ {٥} إلّا الَّذينَ آمَنوا وَعَمِلوا الصّالِحاتِ فَلَهُم أجرٌ غَيرُ مَمنون {٦} فَما يُكَذِّبُكَ بَعدُ بِالدّينِ {٧} أَلَيسَ اللَّهُ بِأحكَمِ الحاكِمينَ {٨}

■ New words

Nouns

olive	زَيْتون	fig	تين
land, country	بَلَد	Mount Sinai	طور سينين
stature	تقويم	best	أحسَن
low	سافِل	lowest	أسفَل
failing	مَمنون	reward	أجْر
judge	حاكِم	most conclusive	أحْكَم

Verbs

to return	ردّ	to create	خَلَق – يخلِق

Particles

henceforth, still	بَعْد	surely (affirming the completion of an act)	لَقَد
		not	غَيْر

∎ Grammar

و

The general meaning of the conjunction و is "and". In the Qur'ān, it is often used to initiate an oath with the meaning "by". So والعاديات is translated as "by the runners", and والتين والزيتون as "by the fig and the olive".

ب

The general meaning of the preposition ب is "in", "by", or "with". In some cases, it is used simply for emphasis with no prepositional function, as in أليس الله بأحكم الحاكمين؟ "Isn't Allah the most conclusive of judges?"

∎ Exercise: Word analysis

Translate fully and then analyze the following words into a stem and affixes, giving the English translation of each element.

Stem and affixes	Translation	Word
plural marker ات، good deed صالحة، the ال	the good deeds	الصالحات
he returned ردّ		رددناه
		بالدين
		خلقنا
		وعملوا
		الحاكمين
		يكذّبك

∎ Words to remember

Write down the meanings of the following from memory.

	زَيْتون		تين
....	لَقَد	....	بَلَد
....	أحسَن	....	خَلَق
....	سافِل	....	أسفَل
....	غَيْر	....	أجْر
....	حاكِم	....	أحْكَم

٩٤. سورة الشرح، مكّية

بسم الله الرحمن الرحيم

أَلَم نَشرَح لكَ صَدرَك {١} وَوَضَعنا عنكَ وِزرَك {٢} الّذي أَنقَضَ ظَهرَك {٣} وَرَفَعنا لَكَ ذِكرَك {٤} فَإِنَّ مع العُسرِ يُسرا {٥} إِنَّ مع العُسرِ يُسرا {٦} فَإِذا فَرَغتَ فانصَب {٧} وإلى ربِّكَ فارغَب {٨}

■ New words

Nouns

burden	وِزر	bosom, chest	صَدْر
fame	ذِكْر	back	ظَهْر
ease	يُسْر	hardship	عُسْر

Verbs

to put down, ease	وَضَع	to dilate, open up	شَرَح – يشرَح
to raise, exalt	رَفَع – يرفَع	to weigh down	أنقَض – يُنقِض
Toil, work hard! (imperative)	انْصَب!	to be relieved	فَرَغ – يفرَغ
		Please! (Imperative of رغب – يرغب to please)	ارغَب!

■ Exercise: Word analysis

Translate fully and then analyze the following words into a stem and affixes, giving the English translation of each element.

Stem and affixes	Translation	Word
		نشرَح
		صدرك
		ووضعنا
		ظَهْرَك
		ورفعنا
	you have been relieved	فَرَغْتَ
		فارغب

■ Words to remember

Write down the meanings of the following from memory.

وَضَع	....	صَدْر	....
رَفَع	....	ظَهْر	....
عُسْر	....	ذِكْر	....
		يُسْر	....

بسم الله الرحمن الرحيم

والضُّحى {١} واللَّيلِ إذا سَجى {٢} ما وَدَّعَكَ رَبُّكَ وما قَلى {٣} وَلَلآخِرَةُ خَيرٌ لَكَ مِنَ الأُولى {٤} وَلَسَوفَ يُعطيكَ رَبُّكَ فَتَرضى {٥} أَلَم يَجِدكَ يَتيمًا فَأَوى {٦} وَوَجَدَكَ ضالاً فَهَدى {٧} وَوَجَدَكَ عائِلاً فَأَغنى {٨} فَأَمَّا اليَتيمَ فلا تَقهَر {٩} وَأَمَّا السّائِلَ فَلا تَنهَر {١٠} وَأَمَّا بِنِعمَةِ رَبِّكَ فَحَدِّث {١١}

■ New words

Nouns

night	لَيْل	morning hours	ضُحى
good, better	خَيْر	Afterlife	أخِرة
one who has lost his way	ضالّ	first, this Life	أولى
beggar, one asking for help	سائِل	destitute	عائِل
		bounty, blessing	نِعمة

Verbs

to forsake	ودّع	to be still	سَجى
to give	أعطى - يُعطي	to hate	قَلى
to find	وَجَد - يَجِد	to be content	رَضِي - يَرْضى
to lead in the right direction	هَدى	to offer shelter	أوى
to oppress	قَهَر - يقهَر	to make rich	أغنى
		to repulse	نَهَر - ينهَر

Particles

Will (both سوف and the prefix سَ can be used before the imperfect verb to indicate future time)	سَوفَ = سَ

◼ Grammar

وجدك – يجدك

You may have noticed that the two forms وجدك and يجدك are related. Verbs like وجد, whose first consonant is a و lose this و in imperfect conjugations, as shown in the following table:

		Perfect	Imperfect
he		وجد	يجد
she		وجدَت	تَجِد
they (m.)		وجدوا	يجدون
they (f.)		وجدنَ	يجدنَ
you (m. sg.)		وجدتَ	تجِد
you (m. pl.)		وجدتُم	تجدون
I		وجدتُ	أجِد
we		وجدنا	نجِد

◼ Exercise 1: Word analysis

Translate fully and then analyze the following words into a stem and affixes, giving the English translation of each element.

Stem and affixes	Translation	Word
وجد he found، ي . . . .، ك . . .		يجدَك
		ووجدك
		يُعْطيك
رضِي he was content، ف . . . .، ت . . .		فترضى
		ودَّعَك
		فأغنى

Exercise 2: Opposites

Write each word in row ب under its opposite in row أ, as in the example:

أ	ثَقُل	رفع	شِتاء	خرج	عُسْر	آخِرة	شَرّ
	خَفّ						
ب	أولى	دخل	يُسْر	أنزل	خَيْر	خَفّ	صَيْف

Words to remember

Write down the meanings of the following from memory.

لَيْل	....	ضُحى	....
خَيْر	....	آخِرة	....
سَوْفَ	....	أولى	....
رَضِي – يَرْضى	....	أعطى – يُعطي	....
ضالّ	....	وَجَد – يَجد	....
أغنى	....	هَدى	....
نِعمة	....	سائِل	....

■ Exercise 2: Opposites

Write each word in row ب under its opposite in row أ, as in the example:

أ	ثَقُل	رفع	شِتاء	خرج	عُسْر	آخِرة	شَرّ
	خَفّ						
ب	أولى	دخل	يُسْر	أنزل	خَيْر	خَفّ	صَيْف

■ Words to remember

Write down the meanings of the following from memory.

ضُحى	....	لَيْل	....
آخِرة	....	خَيْر	....
أولى	....	سَوْفَ	....
أعطى – يُعطي	....	رَضِي – يَرْضى	....
وَجَد – يَجد	....	ضالّ	....
هَدى	....	أغنى	....
سائِل	....	نِعمة	....

Particles

Will (both سوف and the prefix س can be used before the imperfect verb to indicate future time)	سَوفَ = سَ

■ Grammar

وجدك – يجدك

You may have noticed that the two forms وجدك and يجدك are related. Verbs like وجد, whose first consonant is a و lose this و in imperfect conjugations, as shown in the following table:

		Perfect	Imperfect
he		وجد	يجد
she		وجدَت	تَجد
they (m.)		وجدوا	يجدون
they (f.)		وجدنَ	يجدنَ
you (m. sg.)		وجدتَ	تجد
you (m. pl.)		وجدتُم	تجدون
I		وجدتُ	أجد
we		وجدنا	نجد

■ Exercise 1: Word analysis

Translate fully and then analyze the following words into a stem and affixes, giving the English translation of each element.

Stem and affixes	Translation	Word
وجد he found، ي . . . ،ك . . .		يجدَك
		ووجدك
		يُعْطيك
رضي he was content، ف . . . ،ت . . .		فترضى
		ودَّعَك
		فأغنى

٩٢. سورة الليل، مكّية

بسم الله الرحمن الرحيم

وَاللَّيلِ إِذا يَغشى {١} وَالنَّهارِ إِذا تَجَلّى {٢} وَما خَلَقَ الذَّكَرَ وَالأُنثى {٣} إِنَّ سَعيَكُم لَشَتّى {٤} فَأَمّا مَن أَعطى وَاتَّقى {٥} وَصَدَّقَ بِالحُسنى {٦} فَسَنُيَسِّرُهُ لِليُسرى {٧} وَأَمّا مَن بَخِلَ وَاستَغنى {٨} وَكَذَّبَ بِالحُسنى {٩} فَسَنُيَسِّرُهُ لِلعُسرى {١٠} وَما يُغني عَنهُ مالُهُ إِذا تَرَدّى {١١} إِنَّ عَلَينا لَلهُدى {١٢} وَإِنَّ لَنا لَلآخِرَةَ وَالأولى {١٣} فَأَنذَرتُكُم نارًا تَلَظّى {١٤} لا يَصلاها إِلّا الأَشقى {١٥} الَّذي كَذَّبَ وَتَوَلّى {١٦} وَسَيُجَنَّبُها الأَتقى {١٧} الَّذي يُؤتي مالَهُ يَتَزَكّى {١٨} وَما لِأَحَدٍ عِندَهُ مِن نِعمَةٍ تُجزى {١٩} إِلّا ابتِغاءَ وَجهِ رَبِّهِ الأَعلى {٢٠} وَلَسَوفَ يَرضى {٢١}

New words

Nouns

male	ذَكَر	day	نَهار
effort	سَعْي	female	أُنثى
goodness	حُسنى	dispersed, scattered	شَتّى
adversity	عُسرى	state of ease	يُسرى
most wretched	أَشقى	guidance	هُدى
seeking, in search of	ابتِغاء	righteous	أَتْقى
most high	أَعْلى	face	وَجه

Verbs

to be resplendent	تَجَلّى	to enshroud	غَشِي – يَغشى
to believe	صَدّق	to be dutiful (towards Allah)	اتّقى
to be miserly	بَخِل	to ease, make easy	يَسَّر – يُيَسِّر
to make independent	أغنى – يُغني	to deem oneself independent	استَغنى
to flame	تلَظّى – يتَلَظّى	to perish	تَرَدّى
to be exposed to heat	صلِي – يَصلى	to warn	أنذَر
to be made to avoid	جُنِّب – يُجَنَّب	to turn away	تَوَلّى
to grow in goodness	تَزَكّى – يتزكّى	to give	آتى – يُؤتي
		to be rewarded	جُزِي – يُجزى

■ Grammar: Subject markers revisited

So far, the conjugation of perfect verbs has been in six persons, those corresponding to *he, she, they (f.), you (m. sg.), you (m. pl.),* and *we.* In addition to examples of these conjugations, you have seen examples of conjugations in the third person masculine plural (وعملوا "and they did") and the first person singular (فأنذرتُكم "so I warned you"). All these persons are shown on the verb عبد in the following table:

he worshiped	عبد	–
she worshiped	عبدَت	ت –
they (m.) worshiped	عبَدوا	وا –
they (f.) worshiped	عبدنَ	نَ –
you (m. sg.) worshiped	عبدتَ	تَ –
you (m. pl.) worshiped	عبدتُم	تُم –
I worshiped	عبدتُ	تُ –
we worshiped	عبدنا	نا –

The following table shows the conjugation of the verb عبد in the perfect and imperfect in the persons you have seen so far. The Arabic "separate" pronouns are used in addition to the corresponding English pronouns used in the translations, such as *he, she,* etc.

Imperfect	Perfect		
يعبُد	عبد	he	هو
تعبُد	عبدَت	she	هـي
يعبدون	عبدوا	they (m.)	هُم
–	عبدْنَ	they (f.)	هُنّ
–	عبدتَ	you (m. sg.)	انتَ
تعبُدون	عبدتُم	you (m. pl.)	انتُم
أعبد	عبدتُ	I	أنا
نعبُد	عبدنا	we	نحنُ

Grammar: Possessive/object pronouns

In addition to the perfect and imperfect subject markers, you have seen another set of suffixes attached to nouns, verbs, prepositions, and other particles to indicate possession, to refer to the object of a verb or a preposition, etc. The table in which they appeared before is reproduced below.

his/him/he	ـه	مالُه	أرسله	عليه	إنّه
her/she	ها	مالها	أرسلها	عليها	إنّها
their/them/they	هُم	مالهم	أرسلهم	عليهم	إنّهم
your/you (m. sg.)	كَ	مالكَ	أرسلكَ	عليكَ	إنّكَ
your/you (pl.)	كُم	مالكم	أرسلكم	عليكم	إنّكم
our/us/we	نا	مالنا	أرسلنا	علينا	إنّا or إنّنا

Exercise

1. The particle ما is used three times in this *sūra* with two different meanings. Identify its three occurrences and show what each one means.
2. Given the meanings of the stems in column أ, translate the words in column ب. The first one is given as an example.

ب		أ	
and ask forgiveness (from) him!	واستَغْفِرْه	he asked forgiveness	استَغْفَر
	أعطِيناكَ	he gave	أعطى
	تَرْمِيهِم	he threw	رَمى
	وأَخْرَجَت	he took out, brought out	أخْرَج
	جاءَتْهُم	he came	جاء
	أنزلناه	he brought down	أنزَل
	وَرَبُّكَ	Lord	رَبّ
	أَرَأَيْتَ	he saw	رأى
	رَدَدْناه	he returned	رَدّ
	سعيَكُم	effort	سَعي
	علينا	on	على
	فَسَنُيَسِّرُه	he made easy	يَسَّر
	فأَنذَرْتُكُم	he warned	أنذَر

■ Words to remember

Write down the meanings of the following words from memory.

	نَهار		غَشِي
....	ذَكَر	....	خَلَق
....	اتَّقى	....	أُنثى
....	حُسْنى	....	صَدّق
....	يُسْرى	....	يَسَّر
....	استَغْنى	....	بَخِل
....	يُغْني	....	عُسْرى
....	أنذَر	....	هُدى
....	أشْقى	....	صلّى - يَصْلى
....	يُجَنَّب	....	تَوَلّى
....	آتى - يُؤتي	....	أتْقى
....	تَجزى	....	تَزَكّى
....	أعْلى	....	وَجه

بسم الله الرحمن الرحيم

وَالشَّمسِ وَضُحاها {١} وَالقَمَرِ إِذا تَلاها {٢} وَالنَّهارِ إِذا جَلّاها {٣} وَاللَّيلِ إِذا يَغشاها {٤} وَالسَّماءِ وَما بَناها {٥} وَالأَرضِ وَما طَحاها {٦} وَنَفسٍ وَما سَوّاها {٧} فَأَلهَمَها فُجورَها وَتَقواها {٨} قَد أَفلَحَ مَن زَكّاها {٩} وَقَد خابَ مَن دَسّاها {١٠} كَذَّبَت ثَمودُ بِطَغواها {١١} إِذِ انبَعَثَ أَشقاها {١٢} فَقالَ لَهُم رَسولُ اللَّهِ ناقَةَ اللَّهِ وَسُقياها {١٣} فَكَذَّبوهُ فَعَقَروها فَدَمدَمَ عَلَيهِم رَبُّهُم بِذَنبِهِم فَسَوّاها {١٤} وَلا يَخافُ عُقباها {١٥}

New words

Nouns

brightness, morning hours	ضُحى	sun	شَمْس
heaven	سَماء	moon	قَمَر
immorality, wickedness	فُجور	soul	نَفْس
Thamūd (name of a tribe)	ثَمود	piety	تَقْوى
the basest	أشقى	rebellious pride	طَغوى
drinking, watering	سُقيا	she-camel	ناقة
sequel, what comes after	عُقْبى	sin	ذَنْب

Verbs

to reveal	جَلَّى	to follow	تَلَى
to spread	طَحى	to build	بَنَى
to inspire	أَلهَم	to perfect	سَوّى
to cause to grow	زَكّى	to be successful	أَفْلَح
to stunt	دَسّى	to be a failure	خاب
to hamstring	عَقَر	to break forth	انبَعَث
to dread, fear	خاف – يَخاف	to doom	دَمْدَم

Particle

قد

When this particle is followed by a verb in the perfect tense, it simply indicates the completion of the action of that verb. It does not have a meaning of its own.

■ Exercise 1: The definite article and the sun and moon letters revisited

It was pointed out above that the ل of the definite article is assimilated with the first consonant in the noun or adjective to which it is attached in certain cases but not in others. The difference between the two groups of consonants is shown in the following forms. Study the forms and answer the questions below.

the eternally besought	aṣ-ṣamad	الصَمَد
and the triumph	w-al-fatḥ	والفَتْح
the disbelievers	al-kāfirūn	الكافرون
the one without posterity	al-'abtar	الأبْتَر
the orphan	al-yatīm	اليتيم
the needy	al-miskīn	المسكين
the winter	aš-šitā'	الشتاء
and the summer	w-aṣ-ṣayf	والصيف
the house	al-bayt	البيت

the elephant	al-fīl	الفيل
the consuming one	al-ḥuṭama	الحُطَمة
the kindled	al-mūqada	الموقَدة
the declining day	w-al-ʿaṣr	والعَصر
pleasure	an-naʿīm	النعيم
the mountains	al-jibāl	الجِبال
(the) mankind	al-ʾinsān	الإنسان
and the fig	w-at-tīn	والتين
and the olive	w-az-zaytūn	والزيتون
the beggar	as-sāʾil	السائل
and the morning hours	w-aḍ-ḍuḥā	والضُحى
and the night	w-al-layl	والليل
and the sun	w-aš-šams	والشمس
and the moon	w-al-qamar	والقَمَر

Questions

a. Identify the two sets of consonants with the two distinct types of behavior in the assimilation process. What is common to each set?

b. One group of consonants is referred to in Arabic grammar as the sun letters and the other as the moon letters. Can you explain the reason behind this terminology?

■ Exercise 2: Word analysis

For the following words, give a full English translation, then identify the stem. Three are given as examples. Some stems end in *alif maqsūra* (ى), and others with regular *alif*. The correct variant is given in the Stem column.

Stem	Translation	Word
ضُحى	and her morning hours	وَضُحاها
تلا	he followed her	تَلاها
ى		جَلّاها
غشي		يَغشاها
ى		بَناها
ا		طَحاها
ى		سَوّاها
		فَأَلهَمَها
		فُجورَها
ى		وَتَقواها
ى		زَكّاها
ى		بِطَغواها
ى		أَشقاها
ا		وَسُقياها
		فَعَقَروها
ى		عُقباها

▣ Words to remember

Write down the meanings of the following from memory.

....	ضُحى	....	شَمْس
....	سَماء	....	قَمَر
....	نَفْس	....	بَنى
....	فُجور	....	سَوّى
....	أَفْلَح	....	تَقْوى
....	خاب	....	زَكّى
....	طَغوى	....	ثَمود
....	أَشقى	....	انبَعَث
....	خاف	....	ذَنْب

٩٠. سورة البلد، مكّية

بسم الله الرحمن الرحيم

لا أُقسِمُ بِهَذا البَلَدِ ﴿١﴾ وَأَنتَ حِلٌّ بِهَذا البَلَدِ ﴿٢﴾ وَوالِدٍ وَما وَلَدَ ﴿٣﴾ لَقَد خَلَقنا الإِنسانَ في كَبَدٍ ﴿٤﴾ أَيَحسَبُ أَن لَن يَقدِرَ عَلَيهِ أَحَدٌ ﴿٥﴾ يَقولُ أَهلَكتُ مالاً لُبَدا ﴿٦﴾ أَيَحسَبُ أَن لَم يَرَهُ أَحَدٌ ﴿٧﴾ أَلَم نَجعَل لَهُ عَينَينِ ﴿٨﴾ وَلِسانًا وَشَفَتَينِ ﴿٩﴾ وَهَدَيناهُ النَجدَينِ ﴿١٠﴾ فَلا اقتَحَمَ العَقَبَةَ ﴿١١﴾ وَما أَدراكَ ما العَقَبَةُ ﴿١٢﴾ فَكُّ رَقَبَةٍ ﴿١٣﴾ أَو إِطعامٌ في يَومٍ ذي مَسغَبَةٍ ﴿١٤﴾ يَتيمًا ذا مَقرَبَةٍ ﴿١٥﴾ أَو مِسكينًا ذا مَترَبَةٍ ﴿١٦﴾ ثُمَّ كانَ مِنَ الَّذينَ آمَنوا وَتَواصَوا بِالصَبرِ وَتَواصَوا بِالمَرحَمَةِ ﴿١٧﴾ أُولَئِكَ أَصحابُ المَيمَنَةِ ﴿١٨﴾ والَّذينَ كَفَروا بِآياتِنا هُم أَصحابُ المَشأَمَةِ ﴿١٩﴾ عَلَيهِم نارٌ مُؤصَدَة ﴿٢٠﴾

◾ New words

Nouns

begetter, father	والِد	indweller	حِلّ
vast	لُبَد	in affliction, suffering	كَبَد
tongue	لِسان	two eyes	عَينَين
two elevations, two ways	نجدين	two lips	شَفَتَين
freeing	فَكّ	the ascent	العَقَبة
feeding	إطعام	slave (literally, neck)	رَقَبة
near of kin	مَقرَبة	hunger	مَسغَبة
mercy, compassion	مَرحَمة	misery	مَترَبة
Qur'ānic verse, revelation	آية (ج. آيات)	right hand	مَيمَنة
		left hand	مَشأَمة

Verbs

to beget	وَلَد	to swear	أَقسَم – يُقسِم
to destroy	أهلَك	to be able to	قدِر – يقدِر
to guide	هَدى	to make	جَعَل – يَجعَل
		to take on	اقتحَم

Particle

of, with, characterized by	ذ

■ Grammar

رأى – يرى

The verb رأى "he saw", with the imperfect form يرى "he sees" is exceptional in a number of ways. The following table shows its conjugation in the persons you have learned so far:

	Perfect	Imperfect
he	رأى	يرى
she	رأت	ترى
they (m.)	رأوا	يرون
they (f.)	رأينَ	يرين
you (m. sg.)	رأيتَ	ترى
you (m. pl.)	رأيتُم	ترون
I	رأيتُ	أرى
we	رأينا	نرى

A common form of the verb that you will see, particularly following the negation particle لم, is one that simply has the person marker and the letter رـ, as in لم يرَ "he did not see", لم ترَ "she did not see".

Exercise 1: Word analysis

Translate fully and then analyze the following words into a stem and affixes, giving the English translation of each element.

Stem + affixes	Translation	Word
حسب he thought، أ question particle، ي he + imperfect	Does he think?	أيحسَب
		خلقنا
	I wasted	أهلكتُ
		وهديناه
أدرى he made aware، ك . . .		أدراك
تواصى he exhorted، و . . .، وا . . .	they exhorted one another	وتواصوا
		بالصبر
		بالمرحمة
أية verse, sign، ب . . .، ات . . .، نا . . .		بآياتنا
		كفروا

Exercise 2: Opposites

Write each word in row ب under its opposite in row أ, as in the examples:

أ	أعطى	صَدَّق	يُسرى	ذكَر	أشقى	أسفل	نَهار	سماء	زكّى	فُجور	والِد	أفلَح	مَيمَنة
	بخِل				أتقى				دَسّى				
ب	خاب	أتقى	أعلى	تقوى	بخِل	عُسرى	مشأمة	أنثى	وَلَد	ليل	دَسّى	كذّب	أرض

■ Words to remember

Write down the meanings of the following from memory.

والِد	....	أَقسَم	....
خَلَق	....	وَلَد	....
أهلَك	....	قدِر	....
عَينَين	....	جَعَل	....
هَدى	....	لِسان	....
إطعام	....	رَقَبة	....
مَرحَمة	....	مَقرَبة	....
آية	....	مَيمَنة	....
		مشأَمة	....

بسم الله الرحمن الرحيم

وَالفَجْرِ {١} وَلَيَالٍ عَشْرٍ {٢} وَالشَّفْعِ وَالوَتْرِ {٣} وَاللَّيْلِ إِذَا يَسْرِ {٤} هَلْ فِي ذَلِكَ قَسَمٌ لِّذِي حِجْرٍ {٥} أَلَمْ تَرَ كَيْفَ فَعَلَ رَبُّكَ بِعَادٍ {٦} إِرَمَ ذَاتِ العِمَادِ {٧} الَّتِي لَمْ يُخْلَقْ مِثْلُها فِي البِلادِ {٨} وَثَمُودَ الَّذِينَ جَابُوا الصَّخْرَ بِالوَادِ {٩} وَفِرعَوْنَ ذِي الأَوْتَادِ {١٠} الَّذِينَ طَغَوْا فِي البِلادِ {١١} فَأَكْثَرُوا فِيهَا الفَسَادَ {١٢} فَصَبَّ عَلَيْهِم رَبُّكَ سَوْطَ عَذَابٍ {١٣} إِنَّ رَبَّكَ لَبِالمِرصَادِ {١٤} فَأَمَّا الإِنسَانُ إِذَا مَا ابْتَلاهُ رَبُّهُ فَأَكْرَمَهُ وَنَعَّمَهُ فَيَقُولُ رَبِّي أَكْرَمَنِي {١٥} وَأَمَّا إِذَا مَا ابْتَلاهُ فَقَدَرَ عَلَيْهِ رِزْقَهُ فَيَقُولُ رَبِّي أَهَانَنِي {١٦} كَلاَّ بَل لا تُكْرِمُونَ اليَتِيمَ {١٧} وَلا تَحَاضُّونَ عَلَى طَعَامِ المِسكِينِ {١٨} وَتَأْكُلُونَ التُّرَاثَ أَكْلاً لَّمًا {١٩} وَتُحِبُّونَ المَالَ حُبًّا جَمًّا {٢٠} كَلاَّ إِذَا دُكَّتِ الأَرْضُ دَكًّا دَكًّا {٢١} وَجَاءَ رَبُّكَ وَالمَلَكُ صَفًّا صَفًّا {٢٢} وَجِيءَ يَوْمَئِذٍ بِجَهَنَّمَ يَوْمَئِذٍ يَتَذَكَّرُ الإِنسَانُ وَأَنَّى لَهُ الذِّكْرَى {٢٣} يَقُولُ يَا لَيْتَنِي قَدَّمْتُ لِحَيَاتِي {٢٤} فَيَوْمَئِذٍ لا يُعَذِّبُ عَذَابَهُ أَحَدٌ {٢٥} وَلا يُوثِقُ وَثَاقَهُ أَحَدٌ {٢٦} يَا أَيَّتُها النَّفْسُ المُطْمَئِنَّةُ {٢٧} ارْجِعِي إِلَى رَبِّكِ رَاضِيَةً مَّرضِيَّةً {٢٨} فَادْخُلِي فِي عِبَادِي {٢٩} وَادْخُلِي جَنَّتِي {٣٠}

■ New words

Nouns

odd	وَتر	even	شَفع
thinking, mind	حِجر	oath	قسَم
name of a place	إرم	a tribe	عاد
rock	صَخر	columns	عِماد
Pharaoh	فِرعون	valley	واد
mischief, iniquity	فَساد	pegs	أوتاد
watchful	بالمِرصاد	disaster, different kinds	سَوط
inheritance	تُراث	means of life	رِزق
devouring	لَمّ	eating, greed	أكل
much, abounding	جَمّ	love	حُبّ
angels	مَلَك	grinding	دَكّاً دَكّاً
remembrance	ذِكرى	in rows, (row after row)	صَفّاً صَفّاً
content, satisfied	مُطمَئنّ	binding	وِثاق
pleased with	مَرضي	well-pleased	راضي
		bondmen, honored slaves	عِباد

Verbs

to cut, cleave	جاب	to depart	سَرى – يسري
to pour	صبّ	to transgress	طغى – يطغى
to honor	أكرم – يُكرِم	to try, put to the test	ابتلى
to straiten, tighten	قَدَر	to be gracious to, to give gifts to	نعّم – ينعّم
to urge one another	تَحاضّ – يتحاضّ	to humiliate	أهان
to be ground	دُكّ	to like, love	أحبّ – يُحِبّ
to remember	تذكّر – يتذكّر	to be brought	جيء
to punish, torture	عذّب – يعذِّب	to send before	قدّم – يقدِّم
enter	دخَل – يدخُل	to be bound	أوثَق – يوثِق

Particles

like	مِثل	of, with, characterized by	ذي، ذات
O you (f.)	أيّتها	how، كيف	أنّى

Expression

I wish	يا ليتَني

■ Notes

1. Words are often shortened in the Qur'ān to preserve a rhyming scheme. In this *sūra*, the words بالواد and يسر are shortened forms of يسري and بالوادي.
2. Both the question word هل and the prefix أ are used to introduce questions that require yes/no answers. They share the same meaning and grammatical function. The only difference between them is that أ is attached to the following word, while هل is written separately.
3. The word ذو and its derivatives ذي and ذات (as well as ذوي and ذوات) can be translated into English as "of", "with", or "characterized by":

    ذي حِجر "the one characterized by, or the one with the mind or understanding"

    ذات العِماد "the one (f.) with the columns"

    ذي الأوتاد "the one with the pegs, who had the pegs"

    The difference between ذو and ذي is a difference of case (see Grammar appendix). The difference between both forms and ذات is that the latter refers to feminine nouns.

■ Exercise: Word analysis

Translate fully and then analyze the following words into a stem and affixes, giving the English translation of each element.

Stem + affixes	Translation	Word
		والليل
		جابوا
		فأكثروا
	truly in the ambush, wait	لبالمرصاد
		ابتلاه
		فأكرمه
		ونعّمه
		أكرمني
		أهانني
		تُكرمون
		وتأكلون
		وتُحبّون
		والملَك
		يتذكّر
		عذابه
		لحياتي
	so, enter!	فادخلي

▩ Words to remember

Write down the meanings of the following from memory.

....	ذي	....	قسَم
....	ذات	....	عاد
....	مِثل	....	خلق - يخلِق
....	واد	....	صَخر
....	أوتاد	....	فِرعون
....	فَساد	....	طغى - يطغى

أكرم	....	بالمرصاد	....
رِزق	....	نعّم	....
أكل	....	أهان	....
حُبّ	....	أحبّ	....
جيء	....	صَفّاً صَفّاً	....
ذِكرى	....	تذكّر – يتذكّر	....
قدّم – يقدّم	....	يا ليتَني	....
أوثَق – يوثِق	....	عذّب – يعذّب	....
أيّتها	....	وِثاق	....
راضي	....	مُطمَئنّ	....
دخَل – يدخُل	....	مَرضي	....
		عِباد	....

٨٨. سورة الغاشية، مكّيّة

بسم الله الرحمن الرحيم

هَل أَتاكَ حَديثُ الغاشِيَة {١} وُجوهٌ يَومَئِذٍ خاشِعَة {٢} عامِلَةٌ ناصِبَة {٣} تَصلى نارًا حامِيَة {٤} تُسقى مِن عَينٍ آنِيَة {٥} لَيسَ لَهُم طَعامٌ إلاّ مِن ضَريع {٦} لا يُسمِنُ وَلا يُغني مِن جوع {٧} وُجوهٌ يَومَئِذٍ ناعِمَة {٨} لِسَعيِها راضِيَة {٩} في جَنَّةٍ عالِيَة {١٠} لا تَسمَعُ فيها لاغِيَة {١١} فيها عَينٌ جارِيَة {١٢} فيها سُرُرٌ مَرفوعَة {١٣} وَأَكوابٌ مَوضوعَة {١٤} وَنَمارِقُ مَصفوفَة {١٥} وَزَرابِيُّ مَبثوثَة {١٦} أَفَلا يَنظرونَ إلى الإبِل كَيفَ خُلِقَت {١٧} وَإلى السَماء كَيفَ رُفِعَت {١٨} وَإلى الجِبالِ كَيفَ نُصِبَت {١٩} وَإلى الأرض كَيفَ سُطِحَت {٢٠} فَذَكِّر إنَّما أَنتَ مُذَكِّر {٢١} لَستَ عَلَيهِم بِمُصَيطِر {٢٢} إلاّ مَن تَوَلى وَكَفَر {٢٣} فَيُعَذِّبُهُ اللَهُ العَذابَ الأكبَر {٢٤} إنَّ إلَينا إيابَهُم {٢٥} ثُمَّ إنَّ عَلَينا حِسابَهُم {٢٦}

New words

Nouns

		overwhelming (Day of Resurrection)	غاشية
face	وَجه (ج. وُجوه)	downcast, humiliated	خاشِع
toiling	عامِل	weary	ناصِب
spring	عَين	boiling	آني
bitter thorn-fruit	ضَريع		

idle speech	لاغِية	calm, joyful	ناعِم
couches, thrones	سُرُر	running, gushing	جارِي
cups, goblets	أكواب	raised high	مَرفوع
cushions	نَمارق	set at hand	موضوع
rich, silken carpets	زَرابي	ranged, in rows	مصفوف
camels	إبِل	spread	مَبثوث
return	إياب	warder, dictator	مُسَيطِر
		reckoning	حِساب

Verbs

to be created	خُلِق	to nourish	أسمَن – يُسمِن
to be spread out	سُطِح	to be set up	نُصِب
		Remind! (imperative)	ذَكِّر!

Particles

| truly that (إنّ truly + ما that) | إنّما |

■ Grammar: Roots and patterns

Arabic vocabulary is traditionally divided into three categories: *verbs, nouns,* and *particles*. Particles are words or parts of words like prepositions, conjunctions, the definite article, question words, and other "function" elements. Verbs and nouns form the major categories, which include the great majority of words in the language. All verbs and nouns derive from roots of three- or, less commonly, four-letter roots.

Arabic has a system of word formation that is particularly helpful in acquiring new vocabulary. It is referred to as the *root and pattern system*: a limited number of roots combine with a limited set of patterns to produce the great majority of words.

Roots are the basic elements of meaning, and words derived from them, following specific patterns, represent extensions or modifications of the basic meaning of the root. For example, the root عبد has the basic meaning of *worshiping*. The following list includes the words you have seen that are derived from this root and their meanings:[1]

he worshiped	عَبَدَ
I worship	أَعبُدُ
you (m. pl.) worship	تعبُدون
worshiper	عابِد
slave	عَبْد
bondmen, human beings, honored slaves	عِباد

"Families" of words share the same root. All the members of the family of words in the above table share the the root ع.ب.د.

A distinction, whose significance will become more apparent as you know more Arabic, is made between roots on the one hand and stems on the other. The root is an idea or a concept from which stems are derived. To emphasize this fact about Arabic roots, they will appear in this book as strings of letters (three or four) separated by dots. Roots are the foundations of words.

One characteristic of roots is that they do not contain *alif*. If a word contains an *alif*, it is generally added as an affix, or it derives from و or ي at the root level. So in the verb أعطى "he gave", for example, the root is ع.ط.ي. A strong indication that the root has ي as opposed to the stem أعطى, with *alif maqsūra*, is that the the imperfect form of the verb is يعطي, with ي rather than *alif maqsūra*.

■ Exercise

The following words derive from ten roots. Group together the words that are based on the same root, identify the root, and give its general meaning in English. All the roots consist of three letters, except one. Separate the root letters by dots. The first group or family is identified for you:

---

[1] Other words derived from the same root that are not found in the *sūras* discussed in this book are:

place of worship	مَعبَد	worshiped	مَعْبود
slavery	عُبوديّة	places of worship	مَعابِد
piety, worship	تَعبُّد	he devoted himself to the service of God	تَعبَّد
enslavement	استِعباد	he enslaved	استعبَد
worship	عِبادة	pious, devout	مُتَعَبِّد

Words from the same family	مقابر، قبور
Root	ق.ب.ر
General meaning	grave

أرسل، مقابر، ثقُلت، زلزال، زلزال، أعمالهم، كافرون، كتاب، أنزلناه، جمَع، وعملوا، رسول، قُبور، كفروا، راضية، زلزل، أثقال، جمعاً، يعمل، رضي، كتُب، تنزّل

■ Patterns

As was pointed out above, most Arabic words are formed from roots following specific patterns. If we take the example of the derivatives of the root ع.ب.د presented above, we notice that the verb عبَدَ is created by inserting فتحة after the first and second consonants of the root, the word عابد is created by inserting ا between the first and second consonants and كسرة between the second and third consonants, and the word مَعْبود is created by prefixing م to the root and inserting و between its second and third consonants. Different patterns are associated with different meanings: the verb عبَدَ expresses past action performed by the third person singular, the word عابد refers to the doer of the action, the word معبود refers to the recipient of the action of the verb or its result, and the word مَعْبَد refers to the place where the activity is performed. The same extensions of meaning are found in other roots. So, from the root كتب "to write", the following words, among others, are derived:

he wrote	كتَبَ
writer	كاتِب
written	مَكتوب
office, place of writing	مَكْتَب

■ How knowledge of roots and patterns helps you learn Arabic

1. *Dictionary use.*
    Arabic dictionaries are arranged by root: all words derived from the same root are listed under that root. In addition, and this applies to verbs, most Arabic dictionaries written for foreign learners do not list the verbs themselves but

their pattern number. (This will be discussed in more detail when the verb forms are introduced.)

2. *Predicting pronunciation*

    If you recognize the pattern of a word, whether it is a verb or a noun, you can make sound predictions about its pronunciation, since all words of the same pattern share the same structure. For example, if you see the word يستكبر for the first time, you can predict that it is pronounced يَستَكبِر (yastakbir) based on words that you've already seen like يستغفر, which follows the same pattern. Predicting the correct pronunciation is important in a language like Arabic since short vowels are often not included in written texts.

3. *Predicting meaning*

    Knowledge of the word patterns is helpful in predicting the meanings of unfamiliar words of which you already know a relative. For instance, if you know the Arabic word حفظ "he protected" and you see the word حافظ for the first time, you can predict that its meaning will most likely be "protector", because you know that words that follow that pattern generally have the meaning of the doer of the action.

■ Grammar: The فعل skeleton

When discussing word derivation and word patterns, Arabic grammarians use the three letters ف.ع.ل to represent the three consonants of the triliteral root and ف.ع.ل.ل to represent those of a quadriliteral one: ف refers to the first consonant, ع to the second, and ل to the third, and the second ل to the fourth consonant in a four-consonant root. The pattern of a word consists of the root فعل and any consonants or vowels added to it.

Using the skeleton فعل, the above examples can be represented as follows:

فَعَل	عَبَد، كَتَب
فاعِل	عابِد، كاتِب
مَفعول	مَعبود، مَكتوب
مَفْعَل	مَعْبَد، مَكْتَب

■ Exercise: Active and passive participles

Some of the most common patterns in Arabic are the active participle فاعل and the passive participle مفعول. As was pointed out above, the active participle generally refers to the doer of the action of the verb, and the passive participle to the recipient of the action or its result. Not all active participles have the meaning of doer of the action and not all passive participles have the meaning of recipient or result; meanings of words change over time and original relationships are obscured.

The following table includes active and passive participles and the verbs from which they are derived. For each participle, indicate whether it is active or passive, and, based on the basic meaning given for the verb, predict the meaning of the participle. The first word is given as an example. The تاء مربوطة at the end of some words is a feminine ending.

English	Verb	Meaning	Active/Passive	Participle
to be humble	خشع	(a person who is) humble	active participle	خاشعة
to cover	غشي			غاشية
to own, be master	ملك			مالك
to be angry	غضب			المغضوب
to become dark	غسق			غاسِق
to envy	حسَد			حاسِد
to disbelieve	كفَر			الكافرون
to insult	شنأ			شانئك
to eat, devour	أكل			مأكول
to knock, strike	قَرَع			القارعة
to scatter	بَثَّ			المبثوث
to card	نفَش			المنفوش
to be pleased	رضي			راضية
to become hot	حَمي			حامية
to flow	جرى			جارية
to raise	رفَع			مرفوعة
to put, place	وضَع			موضوعة
to arrange in rows	صَفَّ			مصفوفة
Extra credit				
to be pleased	رضي			مَرضِيّة

◼ Words to remember

Write down the meanings of the following from memory.

....	وُجوه	....	غاشية
....	عامِل	....	خاشِع
....	ناعِم	....	عَين
....	لاغِية	....	سَعي
....	مَرفوع	....	جاري
....	ذَكِّر	....	خُلِق
....	تَوَلّى	....	إنّما
		....	حِساب

٨٧. سورة الأعلى، مكّية

بسم الله الرحمن الرحيم

سَبِّحِ اسمَ رَبِّكَ الأَعلى {١} الّذي خَلَقَ فَسَوَّى {٢} والّذي قَدَّرَ فَهَدى {٣} والّذي
أَخرَجَ المَرعى {٤} فَجَعَلَهُ غُثاءً أَحوى {٥} سَنُقرِؤُكَ فَلا تَنسى {٦} الّا ما شاءَ
اللَّهُ إِنَّهُ يَعلَمُ الجَهرَ وما يَخفى {٧} وَنُيَسِّرُكَ لِليُسرى {٨} فَذَكِّر إِن نَفَعَتِ
الذِّكرى {٩} سَيَذَّكَّرُ مَن يَخشى {١٠} وَيَتَجَنَّبُها الأَشقى {١١} الّذي يَصلى
النارَ الكُبرى {١٢} ثُمَّ لا يَموتُ فيها ولا يَحيى {١٣} قَد أَفلَحَ مَن تَزَكّى {١٤}
وَذَكَرَ اسمَ رَبِّهِ فَصَلّى {١٥} بَل تُؤثِرونَ الحَياةَ الدُّنيا {١٦} والآخِرَةُ خَيرٌ وَأَبقى
{١٧} إِنَّ هَذا لَفي الصُّحُفِ الأولى {١٨} صُحُفِ إِبراهيمَ وَموسى {١٩}

▪ New words

....

Nouns

pasturage	مَرعى	the most high	أَعلى
dark	أَحوى	stubble	غُثاء
reminder	ذِكرى	what is apparent	جَهر
more lasting	أَبقى	wretched	أَشقى
		scriptures	صُحُف

Verbs

to bring out	أَخرَج – يُخرِج	to measure	قدَّر – يقدِّر
to forget	نَسِي – يَنسى	to make (someone) recite	أَقرأَ – يُقرِى
to profit, benefit	نَفَع – ينفَع	to be hidden	خَفِي – يَخفى
to fear	خَشِي – يَخشى	to be reminded	تَذَكَّر – يتَذَكَّر
to purify oneself	تَزَكَّى – يتَزَكَّى	to be avoided	تَجَنَّب – يتَجَنَّب
		to prefer	أَثَر – يُؤثِر

■ Notes

The word سَيَذَّكَّر is missing the letter ت, which is assimilated to the following ذ. This is why the latter is doubled.

■ Exercise: Roots and families

The following words derive from 14 roots. Group together the words that are based on the same root, identify the root, and give its general meaning in English. All the roots consist of three letters, except one.

تعلمون، وأرسل، المستقيم، ربّك، زلزَلَت، الكافرون، كاذبة، خالدين، ورضوا، كتاب، تنزّل، الأمين، أسفل، الحاكمين، علّم، كفروا، يكذّب، رضي، كتب، زلزالها، آمنوا، يعلم، كذّب، تقويم، راضية، أنزلناه، سافلين، يكذّبك، قيّمة، بربّ، رسول، أحكم

■ Grammar: Root types

Three-letter roots can be divided into five different types that behave in distinct ways. *Sound* roots have three consonants in the three letter positions, no doubling of any two consonants, and no و or ي in any of these positions. Roots like ع.ب.د "to worship", ك.ف.ر "to disbelieve", and ن.ع.م "to make soft, comfortable" are sound roots.

Remember

1. roots do not have *alifs*,
2. *hamza* is considered a consonant, so a root like ق.ر.أ "to read" is a sound root.[2]

Hollow roots have و or ي in the second root slot. The و or ي appears as ا in the perfect tense of the verb: ك.و.ن "to be", ق.و.ل "to say", ن.و.م "to sleep", س.ي.ر "to travel".

Lame roots are characterized by the presence of ي or و as their third or final element. The ي or و appears as ا or ى in the perfect form of the verb. Examples of lame roots are ص.ل.و "to pray", ت.ل.و "to recite", and ر.م.ي "to throw".

Assimilated roots have و in the first root slot, as in و.ج.د "to find", and و.ق.ي "to protect".

Doubled roots have the same consonant in second and third positions: ح.ب.ب "to like, love", ر.د.د "to return (something)".

Whereas persons are indicated simply by attaching an affix to verbs based on sound roots, certain adjustments are made to verbs derived from the other types of roots when the same affixes are attached, as shown in the following table. عبد "he worshiped", قال "he said", رمى "he threw", وجد "he found", ردّ "he returned (something)". P = perfect, Imp = imperfect.

		he	she	they (m.)	they (f.)	you (m. sg.)	you (m. pl.)	I	we
sound	P	عبد	عبدَت	عبدوا	عبدنَ	عبدتَ	عبدتُم	عبدتُ	عبدنا
	Imp	يعبد	تعبد	يعبدون	يعبدنَ	تعبُد	تعبدون	أعبد	نعبد
hollow	P	قال	قالَت	قالوا	قُلنَ	قلت	قلتُم	قلتُ	قلنا
	Imp	يقول	تقول	يقولون	يقُلنَ	تقول	تقولون	أقول	نقول
lame	P	رمى	رمَت	رموا	رمينَ	رميتَ	رميتُم	رميتُ	رمينا
	Imp	يرمي	ترمي	يرمون	يرمينَ	ترمي	ترمون	أرمي	نرمي
assimilated	P	وجد	وجدت	وجدوا	وجدنَ	وجدتَ	وجدتُم	وجدتُ	وجدنا
	Imp	يجد	تجد	يجدون	يجدنَ	تجد	تجدون	أجد	نجد
doubled	P	ردّ	ردّت	ردّوا	رددنَ	رددتَ	رددتُم	رددتُ	رددنا
	Imp	يردُّ	تردُّ	يردّون	يردُدنَ	تردّ	تردّون	أُردّ	نردّ

---

[2] In a few cases, which will be noted later in the book, roots with an initial أ (*hamza*), like أ.خ.ذ "to take," behave like assimilated roots.

■ Exercise

Translate the following verbs into English, then identify their stems, their roots and indicate for each root what type it is. Follow the examples.

Root type	Root	Stem	Translation	Verb
hollow	ع.و.ذ	عاذ	I seek refuge	أعوذ
lame	ص.ل.ي	صلا	he will be burned	سيصلى
				يدخلون
doubled	د.ع.ع	دَعّ	he repels	يدعّ
				ويمنعون
				يجعل
				وعملوا
				زرتم
				تعلمون
			we open up	نشرح
				ووضعنا
				ووجدك
				وتكون
				ثقلت
				خفّت
				يصدر
				كفروا

Remember

1.   roots do not have *alifs*,
2.   *hamza* is considered a consonant, so a root like ﻕ.ﺭ.ﺃ "to read" is a sound root.[2]

Hollow roots have ﻭ or ﻱ in the second root slot. The ﻭ or ﻱ appears as ﺍ in the perfect tense of the verb: ﻙ.ﻭ.ﻥ "to be", ﻕ.ﻭ.ﻝ "to say", ﻥ.ﻭ.ﻡ "to sleep", ﺱ.ﻱ.ﺭ "to travel".

Lame roots are characterized by the presence of ﻱ or ﻭ as their third or final element. The ﻱ or ﻭ appears as ﺍ or ﻯ in the perfect form of the verb. Examples of lame roots are ﺹ.ﻝ.ﻭ "to pray", ﺕ.ﻝ.ﻭ "to recite", and ﺭ.ﻡ.ﻱ "to throw".

Assimilated roots have ﻭ in the first root slot, as in ﻭ.ﺝ.ﺩ "to find", and ﻭ.ﻕ.ﻱ "to protect".

Doubled roots have the same consonant in second and third positions: ﺡ.ﺏ.ﺏ "to like, love", ﺭ.ﺩ.ﺩ "to return (something)".

Whereas persons are indicated simply by attaching an affix to verbs based on sound roots, certain adjustments are made to verbs derived from the other types of roots when the same affixes are attached, as shown in the following table. عبد "he worshiped", قال "he said", رمى "he threw", وجد "he found", ردّ "he returned (something)". P = perfect, Imp = imperfect.

		he	she	they (m.)	they (f.)	you (m. sg.)	you (m. pl.)	I	we
sound	P	عبد	عبدَت	عبدوا	عبدنَ	عبدتَ	عبدتُم	عبدتُ	عبدنا
	Imp	يعبد	تعبد	يعبدون	يعبدنَ	تعبُد	تعبدون	أعبد	نعبد
hollow	P	قال	قالَت	قالوا	قُلنَ	قلتَ	قلتُم	قلتُ	قلنا
	Imp	يقول	تقول	يقولون	يقُلنَ	تقول	تقولون	أقول	نقول
lame	P	رمى	رمَت	رموا	رمينَ	رميتَ	رميتُم	رميتُ	رمينا
	Imp	يرمي	ترمي	يرمون	يرمينَ	ترمي	ترمون	أرمي	نرمي
assimilated	P	وجد	وجدت	وجدوا	وجدنَ	وجدتَ	وجدتُم	وجدتُ	وجدنا
	Imp	يجد	تجد	يجدون	يجدنَ	تجد	تجدون	أجد	نجد
doubled	P	ردّ	ردّت	ردّوا	رددنَ	رددتَ	رددتُم	رددتُ	رددنا
	Imp	يردّ	تردّ	يردّون	يردُدنَ	تردّ	تردّون	أردّ	نردّ

---

[2] In a few cases, which will be noted later in the book, roots with an initial ﺃ (*hamza*), like ﺃ.ﺥ.ﺫ "to take," behave like assimilated roots.

■ **Exercise**

....

Translate the following verbs into English, then identify their stems, their roots and indicate for each root what type it is. Follow the examples.

Root type	Root	Stem	Translation	Verb
hollow	ع.و.ذ	عاذ	I seek refuge	أعوذ
lame	ص.ل.ي	صلا	he will be burned	سيصلى
				يدخلون
doubled	د.ع.ع	دَعّ	he repels	يدعّ
				ويمنعون
				يجعل
				وعملوا
				زرتم
				تعلمون
			we open up	نشرح
				ووضعنا
				ووجدك
				وتكون
				ثقلت
				خفّت
				يصدر
				كفروا

Root type	Root	Stem	Translation	Verb
			she flows	تجري
			Did you see?	أرأيتَ
			Read!	اقرأ
				خلقنا
				ورفعنا
				يجدكَ
				ووجدك

■ Words to remember

Write down the meanings of the following from memory.

سبّح – يسبِّح	أعلى ....
هَدى – يَهدي	أخرَج – يُخرِج ....
مَرعى	أقرأ – يُقرِئ ....
نَسِي – يَنسى	نَفَع – ينفَع ....
ذِكرى	تَذَكّر – يتَذَكّر ....
خَشِي – يَخشى	تَجنّب – يَتَجنّب ....
أشقى	تَزكّى – يتَزكّى ....
آثَر – يُؤثِر	أبقى ....
صُحُف	

بسم الله الرحمن الرحيم

والسَّماء والطارِق {١} وَما أَدراكَ ما الطارِق {٢} النَجمُ الثاقِب {٣} إن كُلُّ نَفسٍ لَمّا عَلَيها حافِظ {٤} فَلَينظُرِ الإنسان مِمَّ خُلِق {٥} خُلِقَ مِن ماء دافِق {٦} يَخرُجُ مِن بَينِ الصُّلبِ والتَرائِب {٧} إنَّهُ عَلى رَجعِهِ لَقادِر {٨} يَومَ تُبلى السَرائِر {٩} فَما لَهُ مِن قُوَّةٍ ولا ناصِر {١٠} والسَّماء ذاتِ الرَجعِ {١١} والأرض ذاتِ الصَّدعِ {١٢} إنَّهُ لَقَولٌ فَصل {١٣} وَما هُوَ بالهَزل {١٤} إنَّهُم يَكيدونَ كَيدا {١٥} وَأَكيدُ كَيدا {١٦} فَمَهِّلِ الكافِرينَ أَمهِلهُم رُوَيدا {١٧}

■ New words

Nouns

night-comer (the bright star)	طارِق
star	نَجم
piercing	ثاقِب
protector	حافِظ
water	ماء
gushing forth	دافِق
backbone	صُلب
ribs	تَرائِب
bringing back	رَجع
secrets	سَرائِر

power	قُوّة
helper	ناصِر
rain that returns again	رَجع
splitting	صَدع
conclusiveness, separation of truth from falsehood	فَصل
amusement, pleasantry	هَزل
a plot	كَيد
a while	رُوَيداً

Verbs

to be examined	بُلِيَ – يُبلى
to plot	كاد – يَكيد
to give a respite	مَهَّل – يُمَهِّل
to deal gently	أَمهَل – يُمهِل

Particle

from what	مِمَّ = مِن ما

■ Exercise 1: Active participles; roots

There are seven occurrences of active participles in this سورة following the pattern فاعِل. Make a list of these participles and write down their meanings in English and identify their roots. Do all the participles share the meaning of doer of an action? How many root types are there?

■ Exercise 2: Roots and families

The following words are based on 19 roots. Group together the words that are based on the same root, identify the root, indicate its type (sound, hollow, lame, assimilated, doubled), and give its general translation in English.

خلقنا، أغنى، يدخلون، حافظ، مأكول، كيداً، أكرمني، التَكاثُر، أكرم، الرُجعى، اقترب، عبداً،

والِد، مرحمة، البلد، ونعّمه، مقربة، يوثِق، تُكرمون، راضية، يكيدون، مرفوعة، مصفوفة،

الرحمن، ولد، رجعه، رُفِعت، صَفّاً، مرضيّة، فأكثروا، تأكلون، البلاد، ناعمة، أكلاً، استغنى،

ادخلي، يُخلَق، محفوظ، الرحيم، وثاقه، نعمة، فأكرمه، ارجعي، وأكيد، عبادي، النعيم

■ Exercise 3: Opposites

Copy each of the words in the second row under its opposite in the first.

أ	شَفع	أكرَم	دخل	قدّم	كفر	أعلى	جَهر	يُسرى	يموت	دُنيا
ب	قدَر	أسفَل	آخِرة	ما يَخفى	وَتر	عُسرى	خرج	يَحيا	أخِّر	آمَن

■ Words to remember

Write down the meanings of the following from memory.

	حافظ		نَجم
....	خُلِق	....	مِّم
....	رَجع	....	مَاء
....	ناصِر	....	قُوّة
....	كَيد	....	كاد
....	أمهَل	....	مَهَّل

٨٥. سورة البروج، مكّية

بسم الله الرحمن الرحيم

والسَماء ذاتِ البُروج {١} واليَوم المَوعود {٢} وَشاهِدٍ وَمَشهود {٣} قُتِلَ أَصحابُ الأُخدود {٤} النار ذاتِ الوَقود {٥} إذ هُم عَلَيها قُعود {٦} وَهُم عَلى ما يَفعَلونَ بالمُؤمِنينَ شُهود {٧} وَما نَقَموا مِنهُم الاّ أَن يُؤمِنوا باللهِ العَزيزِ الحَميد {٨} الّذي لَهُ مُلكُ السَماوات والأرض واللَهُ عَلى كُلِّ شَيءٍ شَهيد {٩} إنَّ الّذينَ فَتَنوا المُؤمِنينَ والمُؤمِنات ثُمَّ لَم يَتوبوا فَلَهُم عَذابُ جَهَنَّمَ وَلَهُم عَذابُ الحَريق {١٠} إنَّ الّذينَ آمَنوا وَعَمِلوا الصالِحات لَهُم جَنّاتٌ تَجري مِن تَحتِها الأنهار ذَلِكَ الفَوزُ الكَبيرُ {١١} إنَّ بَطشَ رَبِّكَ لَشَديد {١٢} إنَّهُ هُوَ يُبدِئُ وَيُعيد {١٣} وَهُوَ الغَفورُ الوَدود {١٤} ذو العَرشِ المَجيد {١٥} فَعّالٌ لِما يُريد {١٦} هَل أَتاكَ حَديثُ الجُنود {١٧} فِرعَونَ وَثَمود {١٨} بَلِ الّذينَ كَفَروا في تَكذيب {١٩} واللَهُ مِن وَرائِهِم مُحيط {٢٠} بَل هُوَ قُرآنٌ مَجيد {٢١} في لَوحٍ مَحفوظ {٢٢}

■ New words

Nouns

mansions (of the stars), big stars	بُروج
promised (Day of Resurrection)	مَوعود
witness, witnessing day (Friday)	شاهِد (ج. شُهود)
witnessed day (the Day of Arafat)	مَشهود
owner, person of	صاحب (ج. أصحاب)
ditch	أُخدود
supplied (with fuel)	وَقود

people (sitting)	قُعود
Almighty	عزيز
Witness	شَهيد
burning fire	حَريق
success	فَوز
punishment	بَطش
forgiving	غَفور
full of love	وَدود
throne	عَرش
glorious	مَجيد
doer	فَعّال
hosts	جُنود
denial	تَكذيب
encompassing	مُحيط
tablet	لَوح
guarded, preserved	مَحفوظ

Verbs

to be cursed, destroyed	قُتِل – يُقتَل
to do	فعَل – يفعَل
To resent, have (something) against	نَقَم – ينقِم
to persecute, put into trial	فتَن – يفتِن
to repent	تاب – يتوب
to begin, produce	أبدأ – يُبدِئ
to repeat, reproduce	أعاد – يُعيد
to will, intend	أراد – يُريد

■ Exercise: Roots and patterns

For the words in the following table:

a. give an English translation,
b. identify the stem and give its pattern using فعل,
c. identify the root.

Follow the example.

Root	Pattern	Stem	Translation	
أ.م.ن	مُفعِل	مؤمِن	the believers (f.)	المُؤمِنات
				المَوعود
				وشاهد
				مَشهود
				العزيز
				الحميد
				المؤمِنين
				شَهيد
		صالحة		الصالِحات
				الكبير
ش.د.د				لَشَديد
				فَعّال
				مَجيد
				مَحفوظ

a. How many patterns are there? What are they?
b. What is common to the members of each pattern?

■ Exercise: Roots and families

The following words are based on 13 roots. Group together the words that are based on the same root, identify the root, indicate its type, and give its general meaning in English.

الكبير، مَحفوظ، سيذّكر، كيداً، آمنوا، عذابه، الرجع، شاهد، يتذكّر، يقدر، يفعلون، الكُبرى،
لليُسرى، حافِظ، المؤمنين، يعذّبه، وذكر، ونيسّرك، عاملة، فمهِّل، والمؤمنات، الذِكرى، مشهود،
فعل، مذكّر، شهود، يكيدون، رجعه، يعذّب، لقادر، وعملوا، الأكبر، أمهِل، شهيد

■ **Words to remember**

Write down the meanings of the following from memory.

مَشهود	....	شاهِد	....
أصحاب	....	قُتِل – يُقتَل	....
عزيز	....	فعَل – يفعَل	....
فتَن – يفتِن	....	شَهيد	....
غَفور	....	تاب – يتوب	....
فَعّال	....	عَرش	....
جُنود	....	أراد – يُريد	....
مَحفوظ	....	تَكذيب	....

بسم الله الرحمن الرحيم

إِذَا السَّمَاءُ انشَقَّت ﴿١﴾ وَأَذِنَت لِرَبِّهَا وَحُقَّت ﴿٢﴾ وَإِذَا الْأَرْضُ مُدَّت ﴿٣﴾ وَأَلْقَت مَا فِيهَا وَتَخَلَّت ﴿٤﴾ وَأَذِنَت لِرَبِّهَا وَحُقَّت ﴿٥﴾ يَا أَيُّهَا الْإِنسَانُ إِنَّكَ كَادِحٌ إِلَى رَبِّكَ كَدْحًا فَمُلَاقِيهِ ﴿٦﴾ فَأَمَّا مَنْ أُوتِيَ كِتَابَهُ بِيَمِينِهِ ﴿٧﴾ فَسَوْفَ يُحَاسَبُ حِسَابًا يَسِيرًا ﴿٨﴾ وَيَنقَلِبُ إِلَى أَهْلِهِ مَسْرُورًا ﴿٩﴾ وَأَمَّا مَنْ أُوتِيَ كِتَابَهُ وَرَاءَ ظَهْرِهِ ﴿١٠﴾ فَسَوْفَ يَدْعُو ثُبُورًا ﴿١١﴾ وَيَصْلَى سَعِيرًا ﴿١٢﴾ إِنَّهُ كَانَ فِي أَهْلِهِ مَسْرُورًا ﴿١٣﴾ إِنَّهُ ظَنَّ أَن لَّن يَحُورَ ﴿١٤﴾ بَلَى إِنَّ رَبَّهُ كَانَ بِهِ بَصِيرًا ﴿١٥﴾ فَلَا أُقْسِمُ بِالشَّفَقِ ﴿١٦﴾ وَاللَّيْلِ وَمَا وَسَقَ ﴿١٧﴾ وَالْقَمَرِ إِذَا اتَّسَقَ ﴿١٨﴾ لَتَرْكَبُنَّ طَبَقًا عَن طَبَقٍ ﴿١٩﴾ فَمَا لَهُمْ لَا يُؤْمِنُونَ ﴿٢٠﴾ وَإِذَا قُرِئَ عَلَيْهِمُ الْقُرْآنُ لَا يَسْجُدُونَ ﴿٢١﴾ بَلِ الَّذِينَ كَفَرُوا يُكَذِّبُونَ ﴿٢٢﴾ وَاللَّهُ أَعْلَمُ بِمَا يُوعُونَ ﴿٢٣﴾ فَبَشِّرْهُم بِعَذَابٍ أَلِيمٍ ﴿٢٤﴾ الَّا الَّذِينَ آمَنُوا وَعَمِلُوا الصَّالِحَاتِ لَهُمْ أَجْرٌ غَيْرُ مَمْنُونٍ ﴿٢٥﴾

■ New words

Nouns

working, returning	كادِح
work, return	كَدح
meeting	مُلاقي
destruction	ثُبور
blazing, scorching fire	سَعير
looking, beholding	بصير
afterglow of sunset	شَفَق
stage, plane	طَبَق
painful	أَليم

Verbs

to be split asunder	انشَقّ – ينشَقّ
to listen and obey, be attentive	أَذِن – يأَذَن
to be afraid, to be obligated to do	حُقّ – يُحَقّ
to be stretched	مُدّ – يُمَدّ
to cast out	ألقى – يُلقي
to become empty	تَخَلّى – يتخَلّى
to settle an account	حاسَب – يُحاسِب
to return	انقَلَب – ينقَلِب
to invoke	دعا – يدعو
to return	حار – يحور
to gather in darkness, to enshroud	وَسَق
to be at the full	اتّسَق
to ride	ركِب – يركَب
to prostrate, worship	سَجَد – يسجُد
to gather, hide	أوعى – يوعي
to give tidings to	بَشَّر – يُبَشِّر

Exercise: Roots and stems

Translate the following words into English fully, then identify their roots, their stems, and indicate their patterns, using the فعل skeleton. Follow the examples.

Pattern	Stem	Root	Translation	
انفعل	انشقّ	ش.ق.ق	she was split asunder	انشقّت
				وأذنت
				كادح
				كتابه
				حساباً
	حاسَب			يحاسَب
				وينقلب
				مسروراً
				سعيراً
	حار			يحور
				بصيراً
				يسجُدون
				كفروا
				يُكذّبون
			with torture	بعذاب
فعيل				أليم
	آمن			آمنوا
				وعملوا
				الصالحات
مفعول				ممنون

Words to remember

Write down the meanings of the following words from memory.

....	أَذِن – يأَذَن	....	انشَقّ – ينشَقّ
....	مُلاقي	....	أَلقى – يُلقي
....	انقَلَب – ينقَلِب	....	حاسَب – يُحاسِب
....	سَعير	....	دعا – يدعو
....	بصير	....	أَقسَم
....	بَشَّر – يُبَشِّر	....	سَجَد – يسجُد
		....	أَليم

بسم الله الرحمن الرحيم

وَيْلٌ لِّلْمُطَفِّفِينَ {١} الَّذِينَ إِذَا اكْتَالُوا عَلَى النَّاسِ يَسْتَوْفُونَ {٢} وَإِذَا كَالُوهُمْ أَو
وَزَنُوهُمْ يُخْسِرُونَ {٣} أَلَا يَظُنُّ أَولَئِكَ أَنَّهُم مَّبْعُوثُونَ {٤} لِيَوْمٍ عَظِيمٍ {٥} يَوْمَ
يَقُومُ النَّاسُ لِرَبِّ العَالَمِينَ {٦} كَلَّا إِنَّ كِتَابَ الفُجَّارِ لَفِي سِجِّينٍ {٧} وَمَا أَدْرَاكَ
مَا سِجِّينٌ {٨} كِتَابٌ مَّرْقُومٌ {٩} وَيْلٌ يَوْمَئِذٍ لِّلْمُكَذِّبِينَ {١٠} الَّذِينَ يُكَذِّبُونَ
بِيَوْمِ الدِّينِ {١١} وَمَا يُكَذِّبُ بِهِ إِلَّا كُلُّ مُعْتَدٍ أَثِيمٍ {١٢} إِذَا تُتْلَى عَلَيْهِ آيَاتُنَا
قَالَ أَسَاطِيرُ الأَوَّلِينَ {١٣} كَلَّا بَلْ رَانَ عَلَى قُلُوبِهِم مَّا كَانُوا يَكْسِبُونَ {١٤}
كَلَّا إِنَّهُمْ عَن رَّبِّهِمْ يَوْمَئِذٍ لَّمَحْجُوبُونَ {١٥} ثُمَّ إِنَّهُمْ لَصَالُو الجَحِيمِ {١٦} ثُمَّ
يُقَالُ هَذَا الَّذِي كُنتُم بِهِ تُكَذِّبُونَ {١٧} كَلَّا إِنَّ كِتَابَ الأَبْرَارِ لَفِي عِلِّيِّينَ {١٨}
وَمَا أَدْرَاكَ مَا عِلِّيُّونَ {١٩} كِتَابٌ مَّرْقُومٌ {٢٠} يَشْهَدُهُ المُقَرَّبُونَ {٢١} إِنَّ الأَبْرَارَ
لَفِي نَعِيمٍ {٢٢} عَلَى الأَرَائِكِ يَنظُرُونَ {٢٣} تَعْرِفُ فِي وُجُوهِهِمْ نَضْرَةَ النَّعِيمِ
{٢٤} يُسْقَوْنَ مِن رَّحِيقٍ مَّخْتُومٍ {٢٥} خِتَامُهُ مِسْكٌ وَفِي ذَلِكَ فَلْيَتَنَافَسِ
المُتَنَافِسُونَ {٢٦} وَمِزَاجُهُ مِن تَسْنِيمٍ {٢٧} عَيْنًا يَشْرَبُ بِهَا المُقَرَّبُونَ {٢٨} إِنَّ
الَّذِينَ أَجْرَمُوا كَانُوا مِنَ الَّذِينَ آمَنُوا يَضْحَكُونَ {٢٩} وَإِذَا مَرُّوا بِهِمْ يَتَغَامَزُونَ
{٣٠} وَإِذَا انقَلَبُوا إِلَى أَهْلِهِمُ انقَلَبُوا فَكِهِينَ {٣١} وَإِذَا رَأَوْهُمْ قَالُوا إِنَّ هَؤُلَاء
لَضَالُّونَ {٣٢} وَمَا أُرْسِلُوا عَلَيْهِمْ حَافِظِينَ {٣٣} فَالْيَوْمَ الَّذِينَ آمَنُوا مِنَ الكُفَّارِ
يَضْحَكُونَ {٣٤} عَلَى الأَرَائِكِ يَنظُرُونَ {٣٥} هَلْ ثُوِّبَ الكُفَّارُ مَا كَانُوا يَفْعَلُونَ
{٣٦}

■ New words

Nouns

he who gives less in measure and weight, defrauder	مُطَفِّف
resurrected	مَبعوث
disbelievers, sinners, evil-doers	فُجَّار
record, register	كتاب
inscribed, written	مَرقوم
that who denies	مُكَذِّب
transgressor	مُعتَدي
sinner, criminal	أَثيم
tales, fables	أَساطير
ancients, men of old	أَوّل (ج. أَوّلين)
covered, veiled	مَحجوب
burned (see Cases)	صالي (ج. صالون)
righteous	أَبرار
highest place	عِلِّيِّين، عِلِّيّون
that who is nearest, brought near	مُقَرَّب
thrones, couches	أَرائك
brightness, radiance	نضرة
pure wine	رَحيق
sealed	مَختوم
seal, last part of	خِتام
musk	مِسك
that who strives	مُتَنافِس
mixing	مِزاج
spring	عَين
jesting	فَكِه
gone astray	ضالّ (ج. ضالّون)

Verbs

to take the measure	اكتال
to demand full measure	استوفى – يستوفي
to weigh	وزن – يزِن
to give less	أخسَر – يُخسِر
to be recited	تُلِي – يُتلى
to be covered with sins and evil deeds	ران
to earn	كسِب – يكسَب
to attest, bear witness	شَهِد – يشهَد
to be given to drink	سُقِي – يُسقى
to strive	تنافس – يتنافس
to commit a crime	أجرَم – يُجرِم
to wink at one another	تغامَز – يتغامَز
to return	انقلَب – ينقلِب
to be paid for	ثُوِّب – يُثَوَّب

◼ Exercise

....

Translate the following verbs fully into English, then identify their roots, their stems, and their patterns using فعل. Follow the examples.

Pattern	Stem	Root	Meaning	
افتعل	اكتال	ك.ي.ل	they took the measure	اكتالوا
استفعل	استوفى		they demand full measure	يستوفون
			they gave them the measure	كالوهم
فعل	وزن			وَزَنوهم
				يُخسِرون
				يقوم

Pattern	Stem	Root	Meaning	
فَعّل				يُكَذِّبون
				يَكسَبون
فعل	كان			كُنتُم
				يَشهَده
				تَعرِف
تَفاعَل	تنافس		so let him compete	فليَتنافَس
				يَشرَب
أَفعَل				أجرَموا
				يَضحَكون
				مَرّوا
				يَتَغامَزون
	انقلب			انقلبوا
				يَنظُرون
				يَفعَلون

▮ Grammar: Roots, stems, and patterns; forms of the verb

One feature of Arabic grammar that is particularly helpful to the learner is that the thousands of Arabic verbs follow a surprisingly small number of patterns, namely 14. Ten of these patterns are quite common; the rest are of limited occurrences. Only those forms that are found in the *sūras* presented in this book will be introduced here.

The most common form is the basic one, represented in Arabic grammar by the three basic letters of the root فعل, with no doubling of any of its consonants. We have seen many examples of this form, such as خَلق "he created", حسد "he envied", كسب "he earned". The imperfect of فعل is يَفعل, as in يخلق، يحسد, and يكسب.

In addition to the basic فعل form, this *sūra* contains examples of another six commonly used forms, as the following table shows. The verbs are shown in their imperfect as well as their perfect tenses.

Examples		Forms	
Imperfect	Perfect	Imperfect	Perfect
يكيل	كال	يفعَل	فعل
يكتال	اكتال	يفتعل	افتعل
يستوفي	استوفى	يستفعل	استفعل
يكذِّب	كذَّب	يُفعِّل	فعَّل
يتَنافس	تنافس	يتَفاعَل	تفاعل
يُجرِم	أجرَم	يُفعِل	أفعل
ينقلِب	انقلب	ينفعِل	انفعل

In place of فعل and its derivatives, Western scholars of Arabic use a system of roman numerals I–X and QI–QIV (for quadriliteral roots) to refer to the different verb forms. According to this system, فعَل is Form I, أفعَل is Form IV, etc. The following table shows the forms listed above in both traditions, the Arabic and the Western. The forms have been reordered to reflect a numeral ascending order.

Arabic System	Western System
فعل/يفعل	I
فعَّل/يُفعِّل	II
أفعل/يُفعِل	IV
تفاعل/يتَفاعَل	VI
انفعل/ينفعِل	VII
افتعل/يفتعل	VIII
استفعل/يستفعل	X

■ Notes on the above forms

The following table shows the distinguishing feature of each of the forms in the above table and examples of it that you have already seen.

Examples	Distinguishing feature	Form	
	three consonants of the root + short vowels	فعل/يفعل	I
ودّع/يودّع، علّم/يعلّم	doubling of the middle consonant	فعّل/يُفعّل	II
أطعم/يُطعِم، أدرى/يُدري	prefixing أ before the first consonant of the root in the perfect and replacing it with the subject marker and ضمّة in the imperfect	أفعل/يُفعِل	IV
تواصى/يتواصى	adding ا between first and second consonants and prefix ت before the first consonant	تفاعل/يتَفاعَل	VI
انقلب/ينقلب	prefixing ان before the first consonant of the root in the perfect and dropping ا in the imperfect	انفعل/ينفعِل	VII
اقتحم/يقتحم	prefixing ا before the first consonant of the root and infixing ت between first and second consonant in the perfect, and dropping ا in the imperfect	افتعل/يفتعل	VIII
استغفر/يستتغفر	prefixing است before the first consonant of the root in the perfect and dropping ا in the imperfect	استفعل/يستفعل	X

Notice that the أ of أفعل (Form IV) in the perfect can be confused with the أ of the first person singular (I) in the imperfect. So a verb like أعبد could theoretically be a Form IV (أفعل) verb, or a Form I (فعل) in the imperfect with the subject أ "I". You will learn ways to tell the two forms apart in time, but for now your only clues come from the context.

■ Exercise

The following verbs found in the first eight *sūras* of the book belong to four verb forms: I (فعل), II (فعّل), IV (أفعل), and X (استفعل). For each verb, give a full English translation, then give the root, the stem, and the form using فعل and the roman numeral.

Remember that the stem corresponds to the form translated into English *he + simple past tense*, so the stem of the verb نستعين "we seek help" is استعان "he sought help". In general, a ي or a و that shows up as the second or third root consonant in the imperfect shows up as *alif* in the perfect.

Form and #	Stem	Root	English translation	Verb
				نعبد
	استعان		we seek help	نستعين
				أنعمتَ
				أعوذ
			and he perished	وتبّ
				أغنى
		ص.ل.ي		سيَصلى
				يدخلون
			so glorify	فسبّح
				أعبد
				عبدتم
	أعطى			أعطيناك
Extra credit				
				جاء

■ Words to remember

Write down the meanings of the following from memory.

....	كال – يكيل	....	اكتال – يكتال
....	أخسَر – يُخسِر	....	وزِن – يزِن
....	فُجّار	....	مَبعوث
....	مُكَذِّب	....	كتاب
....	أثيم	....	مُعتَدي
....	آية (ج. آيات)	....	تُلِي – يُتلى
....	أوّل (ج. أوّلين)	....	أساطير

صالي (ج. صالون)	....	كسِب – يكسَب	....
شَهِد – يشهَد	....	أبرار	....
سُقي – يُسقى	....	مُقَرَّب	....
خِتام	....	مَختوم	....
تنافس – يتنافس	....	مِسك	....
عَين	....	مُتَنافِس	....
تغامَز – يتغامَز	....	أجرَم – يُجرِم	....
ضالّ (ج. ضالّون)	....	انقَلَب – ينقَلِب	....
		ثوَّب – يُثوَّب	....

بسم الله الرحمن الرحيم

إذا السَّماءُ انفَطَرَت {١} وَإذا الكَواكِبُ انتَثَرَت {٢} وَإذا البِحارُ فُجِّرَت {٣} وَإذا القُبورُ بُعثِرَت {٤} عَلِمَت نَفسٌ ما قَدَّمَت وَأَخَّرَت {٥} يا أَيُّها الإنسانُ ما غَرَّكَ بِرَبِّكَ الكَريمِ {٦} الَّذي خَلَقَكَ فَسَوّاكَ فَعَدَلَكَ {٧} في أَيِّ صورَةٍ ما شاءَ رَكَّبَكَ {٨} كَلّا بَل تُكَذِّبونَ بِالدِّينِ {٩} وَإنَّ عَلَيكُم لَحافِظينَ {١٠} كِرامًا كاتِبينَ {١١} يَعلَمونَ ما تَفعَلونَ {١٢} إنَّ الأبرارَ لَفي نَعيمٍ {١٣} وَإنَّ الفُجّارَ لَفي جَحيمٍ {١٤} يَصلَونَها يَومَ الدِّينِ {١٥} وَما هُم عَنها بِغائِبينَ {١٦} وَما أَدراكَ ما يَومُ الدِّينِ {١٧} ثُمَّ ما أَدراكَ ما يَومُ الدِّينِ {١٨} يَومَ لا تَملِكُ نَفسٌ لِّنَفسٍ شَيئًا، وَالأمرُ يَومَئِذٍ لِلَّهِ {١٩}

New words

Nouns

stars, planets	كَواكِب
sea	بَحر (ج. بِحار)
grave	قَبر (ج. قُبور)
form	صورة
guardian	حافِظ
honorable, generous	كَريم (ج. كِرام)
writing down	كاتِب
command, decision	أمر

Verbs

to be cleft asunder	انفطر – ينفطِر
to be dispersed, scattered	انتثَّر – ينتَثر
to be poured forth, burst forth	فُجِّر – يُفَجَّر
turned upside down	بُعثِر – يُبَعثر
to send forward, before	قَدَّم – يُقَدِّم
to leave behind	أخَّر – يؤَخِّر
to make (someone) careless	غَرَّ – يَغُرَّ
to give due proportion	عَدَل – يعدِل
to will	شاء – يشاء
to cast, put together	ركَّب – يركِّب
to possess	ملَك – يملِك

▣ Grammar: Form Q1

As was pointed out above, a minority of roots in Arabic consist of four letters and a few verbs are based on such roots. The form to which they belong is called Q1. Among the four-letter verbs you have already seen are وسوس "to whisper", زلزل "to shake violently", بعثر "to scatter".

▣ Exercise 1: Verb forms

The following verbs belong to the following six forms: I, II, IV, VII, VIII, Q1. For each verb, give a full English translation, then identify the root, the stem, and the form. Some cells are filled in.

Form and #	Stem	Root	Translation	
			she was cleft asunder	انفطَرَت
VIII ،افتعل	انتثر	ن.ث.ر	she was dispersed	انتَثَّرَت
			she was poured forth	فُجِّرَت
			she was scattered	بُعثِرَت
				قدَّمَت

Form and #	Stem	Root	Translation	
		أ.خ.ر	she delayed	أخَّرَت
	غرّ			غَرَّك
				خلقَك
		س.و.ي		فسوَّاك
				فعدلك
				ركّبك
	كذّب			تُكَذِّبون
				يعلَمون
				تفعَلون
	أدرى			أدراك
				تَملِك
Extra credit				
				يصلَونها
				شاءَ

Exercise 2: Noun patterns

For the words in the table, write a full English translation, identify the root and the pattern, using فعل, and then answer the questions below.

Pattern	Stem	Root	Translation	
فعيل				الكَريم
			truly (the) keepers	لحافِظين
				كاتِبين
				نَعيم
		ب.ر.ر		الأبرار
فُعّال				الفُجّار
فاعل	غائب	غ.ي.ب		بغائبين

a.   How many different patterns are there?
b.   What is common to the members of each pattern?

■ Exercise 3: Roots and families

The following words derive from 14 roots. Group together the words that are based on the same root, identify the root, and give its general meaning in English. All the roots consist of three letters each. Each root has at least two words based on it.

كالوهم، مختوم، يسجدون، كتابه، يكذّبون، علّيّون، ينظرون، كِراماً، كاتبين، المتنافسون، وزنوهم، ختامه، للمكذّبين، الكافرين، بيمينه، موازين، لصالو، ميمنة، يحاسب، يكذّب، اسجد، حساباً، وسق، تكذّبون، اتّسق، اكتالوا، فلينظر، فليتنافس، انقلبوا، طبقاً، علّيّين، يصلونها، الكفّار، طبق، الكريم

■ Words to remember

Write down the meanings of the following from memory.

....	بَحر (ج. بِحار)	....	كَواكِب
....	بُعثِر – يُبَعثَر	....	قَبر (ج. قُبور)
....	أخَّر – يُؤخِّر	....	قَدَّم – يُقَدِّم
....	صورة	....	عَدَل – يعدِل
....	ركَّب – يركِّب	....	شاء – يشاء
....	كَريم (ج. كِرام)	....	حافِظ
....	ملَك – يملِك	....	كاتِب
		....	أمر

٨١. سورة التكوير، مكّية

بسم الله الرحمن الرحيم

إذا الشَمسُ كُوِّرَت {١} وَإذا النُّجومُ انكَدَرَت {٢} وَإذا الجِبالُ سُيِّرَت {٣} وَإذا العِشارُ
عُطِّلَت {٤} وَإذا الوُحوشُ حُشِرَت {٥} وَإذا البِحارُ سُجِّرَت {٦} وَإذا النُّفوسُ زُوِّجَت
{٧} وَإذا المَوؤودَةُ سُئِلَت {٨} بِأَيِّ ذَنبٍ قُتِلَت {٩} وَإذا الصُّحُفُ نُشِرَت {١٠}
وَإذا السَماءُ كُشِطَت {١١} وَإذا الجَحيمُ سُعِّرَت {١٢} وَإذا الجَنّةُ أُزلِفَت {١٣}
عَلِمَت نَفسٌ ما أَحضَرَت {١٤} فَلا أُقسِمُ بِالخُنَّس {١٥} الجَوارِ الكُنَّس {١٦}
وَاللَيلِ إذا عَسعَسَ {١٧} وَالصُّبحِ إذا تَنَفَّسَ {١٨} إنَّهُ لَقَولُ رَسولٍ كَريم {١٩}
ذي قُوّةٍ عِندَ ذي العَرشِ مَكين {٢٠} مُطاعٍ ثَمَّ أَمين {٢١} وَما صاحِبُكُم بِمَجنون
{٢٢} وَلَقَد رَآهُ بِالأُفُقِ المُبين {٢٣} وَما هُوَ عَلى الغَيبِ بِضَنين {٢٤} وَما هُوَ بِقَولِ
شَيطانٍ رَجيم {٢٥} فَأَينَ تَذهَبون {٢٦} إن هُوَ الّا ذِكرٌ لِلعالَمين {٢٧} لِمَن شاءَ
مِنكُم أَن يَستَقيم {٢٨} وَما تَشاؤونَ إلّا أَن يَشاءَ اللَهُ رَبُّ العالَمين {٢٩}

New words

Nouns

stars	نُجوم
pregnant she-camels	عِشار
wild beasts	وُحوش
girl-child buried alive	مَوؤودة
sin	ذَنب
planets (that recede)	خُنَّس

stars, planets	جَواري
that which moves swiftly and hides itself, that rises and sets	كُنَّس
of high rank, established	مَكين
obeyed	مُطاع
companion	صاحِب
mad	مجنون
horizon	أُفُق
clear	مُبين
(the) unseen	غَيب
avid, withholding knowledge	ضَنين
Satan, the devil	شَيطان
outcast, worthy to be stoned	رَجيم
reminder	ذِكر

Verbs

to be wound around, lose its light, and be overthrown	كُوِّر
to fall	انكَدَر
to be moved to pass away, moved	سُيِّر
to be neglected, abandoned	عُطِّل
to be gathered, herded together	حُشِر
to become like blazing fire, overflow, rise	سُجِّر
to be reunited, joined together	زُوِّج
to be asked, questioned	سُئِل
to be laid open	نُشِر
to be stripped off, torn away	كُشِطَ
lighted, to be kindled to a fierce blaze	سُعِّر

to be brought near	أُزلِف
to bring, make ready	أحضَر – يُحضِر
to depart, close	عَسْعَس
to brighten, to breathe	تنَفَّس – يتنفَّس
to walk straight	استقام – يستَقيم

▪ Grammar: Form V

So far, you've been introduced to the following verb forms:

Q1	X	VIII	VII	VI	IV	II	I
فعلل – يفعلل	استفعل/ يستفعل	افتعل/ يفتعل	انفعل/ ينفعِل	تفاعل/ يتَفاعَل	أفعل/ يُفعِل	فعّل/ يُفعِّل	فعل/ يفعل
وَسوَس – يُوسوِس	استغفر – يَستغفِر	اقتحم – يقتحم	انقلب – يَنقلب	تَواصى – يتَواصى	أطعم – يُطعِم	علّم – يعلّم	عبَد – يعبد

Another commonly used verb form is Form V (تفعَّل – يتفعَّل). Examples of this form that we have seen are تفرّق "to be divided", تولّى "to turn away, go away".

▪ Grammar: More on the passive

It was pointed out above that a verb can be changed from the active voice to a passive voice through an internal vowel change, as follows (فتحة – فتحة is changed ضمّة – كسرة to):

Active	Passive
he scattered بَعثَر	he (it) was scattered بُعثِر
he obtained حَصَّل	he (it) was obtained حُصِّل

In the first exercise below, you are asked to change a number of passive verbs, of which there are many in this *sūra*, into their active counterparts.

Exercises

1. Translate the following verbs, then identify their roots, write down their stems, and indicate their forms, using the فعل skeleton and the form number. Follow the notes about active–passive conversion presented above. The stem of a verb is the third person masculine singular active form of it. Follow the examples. The verbs belong to the following seven forms: I, II, IV, V, VII, X, Q1.

Form and #	Stem	Root	Translation	
فعّل، II	كَوَّر	ك.و.ر	she was wound around	كُوِّرَت
	انكدَر			انكدَرَت
				سُيِّرَت
				عُطِّلَت
				حُشِرَت
	زَوَّج			زُوِّجَت
	سأل			سُئِلَت
				قُتِلَت
				نُشِرَت
			she was made like a blazing fire	سُعِّرَت
	أزلَف		she was brought near	أُزلِفَت
أفعل، IV				أُحضِرَت
	أقسم		I swear	أقسِم
				عَسعَس
				تَنَفَّس
				تَذهَبون
	استقام		he becomes straight	يستَقيم
			you (pl.) will, desire	تشاؤون
		ش.ي.ء		يشاء
Extra credit				
				رأه

2. For the words in the table, write a full English translation, identify the root and the pattern, using فعل, and then answer the questions below.

Pattern	Stem	Root	Translation	
				النُّجوم
				الجِبال
				العِشار
				الوُحوش
				البِحار
				النُّفوس
				السماء
				الجحيم
				رسول
				بضنين
				رجيم

a. How many different patterns are there?
b. What is common to the members of each pattern?
c. (Extra credit) What is common to all these words in terms of their word or syllable structure? (Hint: focus on the stem and the pattern)

3. What is the function of the prefix ب in the following verses, if there is any?

١. وما صاحبكم بمجنون {التكوير:٢٢}.

٢. وما هو على الغيب بضنين {التكوير:٢٤}.

٣. وما هو بقول شيطان رجيم {التكوير:٢٥}.

٤. وَمَا هُم عَنهَا بِغَائِبِين {الانفطار:١٦}.

■ Words to remember

Write down the meanings of the following from memory.

....	سُيِّر – يُسَيَّر	....	نُجوم
....	حَشِر – يُحشَر	....	وُحوش
....	سُئِل – يُسأَل	....	زَوَّج – يُزَوِّج
....	سُعِّر – يُسَعَّر	....	ذَنب
....	تَنَفَّس – يتنفَّس	....	أحضَر – يُحضِر
....	مُطاع	....	مَكين
....	مجنون	....	صاحِب
....	مُبين	....	أُفُق
....	شَيطان	....	غَيب
....	ذِكر	....	رَجيم
		....	استقام – يستَقيم

Lesson Fifteen	الدرس رقم ١٥
	٨٠. سورة عبس، مكّيّة

بسم الله الرحمن الرحيم

عَبَسَ وَتَوَلَّى {١} أَن جَاءَهُ الأَعْمَى {٢} وَمَا يُدْرِيكَ لَعَلَّهُ يَزَّكَّى {٣} أَو يَذَّكَّرُ فَتَنفَعَهُ الذِّكْرَى {٤} أَمَّا مَنِ استَغْنَى {٥} فَأَنتَ لَهُ تَصَدَّى {٦} وَمَا عَلَيكَ أَلَّا يَزَّكَّى {٧} وَأَمَّا مَن جَاءَكَ يَسْعَى {٨} وَهُوَ يَخْشَى {٩} فَأَنتَ عَنهُ تَلَهَّى {١٠} كَلَّا إِنَّهَا تَذْكِرَةٌ {١١} فَمَن شَاءَ ذَكَرَهُ {١٢} فِي صُحُفٍ مُّكَرَّمَةٍ {١٣} مَّرْفُوعَةٍ مُّطَهَّرَةٍ {١٤} بِأَيدِي سَفَرَةٍ {١٥} كِرَامٍ بَرَرَةٍ {١٦} قُتِلَ الإِنسَانُ مَا أَكْفَرَهُ {١٧} مِن أَيِّ شَيءٍ خَلَقَهُ {١٨} مِن نُّطْفَةٍ خَلَقَهُ فَقَدَّرَهُ {١٩} ثُمَّ السَّبِيلَ يَسَّرَهُ {٢٠} ثُمَّ أَمَاتَهُ فَأَقْبَرَهُ {٢١} ثُمَّ إِذَا شَاءَ أَنشَرَهُ {٢٢} كَلَّا لَمَّا يَقْضِ مَا أَمَرَهُ {٢٣} فَلْيَنظُرِ الإِنسَانُ إِلَى طَعَامِهِ {٢٤} أَنَّا صَبَبْنَا المَاءَ صَبًّا {٢٥} ثُمَّ شَقَقْنَا الأَرْضَ شَقًّا {٢٦} فَأَنبَتْنَا فِيهَا حَبًّا {٢٧} وَعِنَبًا وَقَضْبًا {٢٨} وَزَيتُونًا ونَخْلًا {٢٩} وَحَدَائِقَ غُلْبًا {٣٠} وَفَاكِهَةً وَأَبًّا {٣١} مَّتَاعًا لَّكُم ولأَنعَامِكُم {٣٢} فَإِذَا جَاءَتِ الصَّاخَّةُ {٣٣} يَوْمَ يَفِرُّ المَرْءُ مِن أَخِيهِ {٣٤} وَأُمِّهِ وَأَبِيهِ {٣٥} وَصَاحِبَتِهِ وَبَنِيهِ {٣٦} لِكُلِّ امْرِئٍ مِّنهُم يَومَئِذٍ شَأْنٌ يُغْنِيهِ {٣٧} وُجُوهٌ يَومَئِذٍ مُّسْفِرَةٌ {٣٨} ضَاحِكَةٌ مُّسْتَبْشِرَةٌ {٣٩} وَوُجُوهٌ يَومَئِذٍ عَلَيهَا غَبَرَةٌ {٤٠} تَرْهَقُهَا قَتَرَةٌ {٤١} أُولَئِكَ هُمُ الكَفَرَةُ الفَجَرَةُ {٤٢}

◼ New words

Nouns

to frown	عَبَس
honored	مُكَرَّم
exalted	مَرفوع
purified	مُطَهَّر
hand	يَد (ج. أيدي)
scribes (angels)	سَفَرة
honorable, noble	كَريم (ج. كِرام)
righteous, obedient	بَرَرة
ungrateful	أكفَر
drop of seed, semen drop	نُطفة
way, path	سَبيل
pouring (المفعول المطلق see)	صَبّ
splitting	شَقّ
grapes	عِنَب
green fodder, clover plants	قَضب
date-palms	نَخل
gardens	حَدائق
of thick foliage, dense	غُلب
fruit	فاكِهة
grasses, herbage	أَبّ
provision and benefit	مَتاع
cattle	أنعام
the Shout, Day of Resurrection's second blowing of Trumpet	صاخّة
to flee	فَرَّ – يفِرّ

man	مَرء
wife	صاحِبة
child	ابن (ج. بَني)
man	امرئ
concern (enough)	شَأن
bright	مُسفِر
rejoicing at good news	مُستَبشِر
dust	غَبَرة
darkness	قَتَرة
disbelievers, wicked	فَجَرة

Verbs

to tell, inform	أدرى – يُدري
to become pure	تزكّى – يتزكّى
to pay regard, to attend	تصدّى – يتصدّى
to run, come with earnest purpose	سَعى – يسعى
to be neglectful, distracted	تلَهّى – يتلَهّى
to proportion	قَدَّر
to make easy	يَسَّر
to cause to die	أمات
to put in the grave	أقبَر
to bring to life, resurrect	أنشَر
to do	قضى – يقضي
to pour	صَبّ – يصُبّ
to split	شَقَّق
to make grow	أنبَت
to make careless or heedless	أغنى – يُغني
to veil, cover	رهَق – يرهَق

Particles

because	أَن
not (see Negation)	لّا

■ Exercise 1: Word study

1. Translate the following verbs, then identify their roots, write down their stems, and indicate their forms, using the فعل skeleton and the form number. Refer to the *sūra* if you are not sure about the meaning or pronunciation of any of the verbs. The verbs belong to the following five forms: I, II, IV, V, and X. Some of these verbs are shortened in the *sūra*; their fuller forms are shown in parenthesis.

Form and #	Stem	Root	Translation	
		و.ل.ي		وتولّى
		ج.ي.ء		جاءه
	أدرى			يُدريك
				فتنفعه
	استغنى			استغنى
				يَسعى
				يخشى
				قُتِل
				خلقه
				فقدّره
				يسّره
		م.و.ت		أماته
				فأقبره
				أنشره
				أمَره
	نظر			فلينظر
		ص.ب.ب		صببنا

Form and #	Stem	Root	Translation	
				شققنا
				فأنبتنا
	فَرّ			يفِرّ
	رَهَق			تَرهَقها
		ق.ض.ي		يَقضِ (يَقضي)
	تصدّى	ص.د.ي		تصدّى (تتصدّى)
				يزّكّى (يتزكى)
				يذّكّر (يتذكّر)
				تَلَهّى (تتلهّى)

2. Identify the two features that the following adjectives have in common in terms of form and meaning. Using the skeleton فعل will make the forms of these words clearer.

٨٠ – عبس	الأعمى، أكفره
٩٦ – العلق	الأكرم
٩٥ – التين	أحسن، أسفل، أحكم
٩٢ – الليل	الأشقى، أتقى
٨٨ – الغاشية	الأكبر
٨٧ – الأعلى	الأعلى، أبقى

Exercise 2: Roots and families

The following words derive from 16 roots. Group together the words that are based on the same root, identify the root, and give its general meaning in English. All the roots consist of three letters each. Each root has at least two words based on it.

صبينا، جاءه، مبعوثون، ذِكر، أكفره، شقّاً، جاءك، صبّاً، مستبشرة، صاحبته، كِرام، يذّكّر، النفوس، يسيراً، فبشّرهم، تشاؤون، يسّره، الأبرار، نفس، يشاء، بررَة، نعيم، الذِكرى، صاحبكم، شققنا، بُعثِرَت، ولأنعامكم، جاءت، الكفرة، تذكِرة، تنفّس، يعلمون، للعالمين، مكرّمة، ذكره

■ Words to remember

Write down the meanings of the following from memory.

....	تزكّى – يتزكّى	....	أدرى – يُدري
....	مُكَرَّم	....	سَعى – يسعى
....	مُطَهَّر	....	مَرفوع
....	كَريم (ج. كِرام)	....	يَد (ج. أيدي)
....	أكفَر	....	بَرَرة
....	قَدَّر – يقدِّر	....	نُطفة
....	يَسَّر – يُيَسِّر	....	سَبيل
....	أقبَر – يُقبِر	....	أمات – يُميت
....	صَبّ – يصُبّ	....	قضى – يقضي
....	عِنَب	....	شَقّ – يشُقّ
....	حَدائق	....	نَخل
....	مَتاع	....	فاكِهة
....	فَرّ – يفِرّ	....	أنعام
....	صاحِبة	....	مَرء
....	امرئٍ	....	ابن (ج. بَني)
....	أغنى – يُغني	....	شَأن
....	مُستَبشِر	....	مُسفِر
		....	فَجَرة

بسم الله الرحمن الرحيم

وَالنَّازِعَاتِ غَرْقًا {١} وَالنَّاشِطَاتِ نَشْطًا {٢} وَالسَّابِحَاتِ سَبْحًا {٣} فَالسَّابِقَاتِ سَبْقًا {٤} فَالْمُدَبِّرَاتِ أَمْرًا {٥} يَوْمَ تَرْجُفُ الرَّاجِفَةُ {٦} تَتْبَعُهَا الرَّادِفَةُ {٧} قُلُوبٌ يَوْمَئِذٍ وَاجِفَةٌ {٨} أَبْصَارُهَا خَاشِعَةٌ {٩} يَقُولُونَ أَئِنَّا لَمَرْدُودُونَ فِي الْحَافِرَةِ {١٠} أَئِذَا كُنَّا عِظَامًا نَخِرَةً {١١} قَالُوا تِلْكَ إِذًا كَرَّةٌ خَاسِرَةٌ {١٢} فَإِنَّمَا هِيَ زَجْرَةٌ وَاحِدَةٌ {١٣} فَإِذَا هُم بِالسَّاهِرَةِ {١٤} هَلْ أَتَاكَ حَدِيثُ مُوسَى {١٥} إِذْ نَادَاهُ رَبُّهُ بِالْوَادِ الْمُقَدَّسِ طُوًى {١٦} اذْهَبْ إِلَى فِرْعَوْنَ إِنَّهُ طَغَى {١٧} فَقُلْ هَل لَّكَ إِلَى أَن تَزَكَّى {١٨} وَأَهْدِيَكَ إِلَى رَبِّكَ فَتَخْشَى {١٩} فَأَرَاهُ الْآيَةَ الْكُبْرَى {٢٠} فَكَذَّبَ وَعَصَى {٢١} ثُمَّ أَدْبَرَ يَسْعَى {٢٢} فَحَشَرَ فَنَادَى {٢٣} فَقَالَ أَنَا رَبُّكُمُ الْأَعْلَى {٢٤} فَأَخَذَهُ اللَّهُ نَكَالَ الْآخِرَةِ وَالْأُولَى {٢٥} إِنَّ فِي ذَلِكَ لَعِبْرَةً لِّمَن يَخْشَى {٢٦} أَأَنتُمْ أَشَدُّ خَلْقًا أَمِ السَّمَاءُ بَنَاهَا {٢٧} رَفَعَ سَمْكَهَا فَسَوَّاهَا {٢٨} وَأَغْطَشَ لَيْلَهَا وَأَخْرَجَ ضُحَاهَا {٢٩} وَالْأَرْضَ بَعْدَ ذَلِكَ دَحَاهَا {٣٠} أَخْرَجَ مِنْهَا مَاءَهَا وَمَرْعَاهَا {٣١} وَالْجِبَالَ أَرْسَاهَا {٣٢} مَتَاعًا لَّكُمْ وَلِأَنْعَامِكُمْ {٣٣} فَإِذَا جَاءَتِ الطَّامَّةُ الْكُبْرَى {٣٤} يَوْمَ يَتَذَكَّرُ الْإِنسَانُ مَا سَعَى {٣٥} وَبُرِّزَتِ الْجَحِيمُ لِمَن يَرَى {٣٦} فَأَمَّا مَن طَغَى {٣٧} وَآثَرَ الْحَيَاةَ الدُّنْيَا {٣٨} فَإِنَّ الْجَحِيمَ هِيَ الْمَأْوَى {٣٩} وَأَمَّا مَنْ خَافَ مَقَامَ رَبِّهِ وَنَهَى النَّفْسَ عَنِ الْهَوَى {٤٠} فَإِنَّ الْجَنَّةَ هِيَ الْمَأْوَى {٤١} يَسْأَلُونَكَ عَنِ السَّاعَةِ أَيَّانَ مُرْسَاهَا {٤٢} فِيمَ أَنتَ مِن ذِكْرَاهَا {٤٣} إِلَى رَبِّكَ مُنتَهَاهَا {٤٤} إِنَّمَا أَنتَ مُنذِرُ مَن يَخْشَاهَا {٤٥} كَأَنَّهُمْ يَوْمَ يَرَوْنَهَا لَمْ يَلْبَثُوا إِلَّا عَشِيَّةً أَوْ ضُحَاهَا {٤٦}

■ New words

Nouns

those who drag forth, pull out	نازعة
destruction, with great violence	غَرق
meteor, one who takes out	ناشطة
taking out	نَشط
lone star, that which swims along	سابِحة
swimming, floating	سَبح
that (angel) which hastens, presses forward	سابقة
hastening, pressing forward	سَبق
one who governs, arranges	مُدَبِّر
event, command	أمر
the first trump, the earth and the mountains	راجِفة
second (blowing of the Trumpet)	رادِفة
that which beats painfully, that which shakes with fear and anxiety	واجِف
eyes	أبصار
one who is restored	مَردود
first state, former state	حافِرة
bones	عِظام
crumbled	نَخِر
proceeding, return	كَرّة
vain, losing	خاسِر
shout	زَجرة
awakened, alive	ساهِرة
vale, valley	واد

to disobey	عَصى
example, punishment	نَكال
lesson, instructive admonition	عِبرة
harder, more difficult	أشَدّ
creating	خلق
height	سَمك
to make dark, cover with darkness	أغطَش
morning, forenoon	ضُحى
to make fast, fix firmly	أرسى
disaster, catastrophe	طامّة
(place of) standing	مَقام
lust, evil desires	هَوى
port, appointed hour	مَرسى
term	مُنتَهى
warner	مُنذِر
evening, afternoon	عَشِيّة

Verbs

to resound, to shake violently	رجَف – يرجُف
to follow	تبِع – يتبَع
to rebel, transgress	طَغى
to show	أرى
to turn away, turn his back	أدبَر
to hasten, strive hard	سَعى – يسعى
to gather	حَشَر – يحشُر
to summon, cry out	نادى – ينادي

to spread	دَحا
to stand forth, to be made apparent in full view	بُرِّز
to choose, prefer	أَثَر
to restrain	نَهى
to tarry	لَبِث – يَلبَث

Particle

when	أيّان

■ Grammar: Form III

The penultinate verb form that will be introduced in this book is Form III, which has the shape فاعَل in the perfect and يُفاعِل in the imperfect. The following table includes all the verb forms introduced along with their distinguishing features and the meanings or grammatical functions traditionally associated with each, if such meanings or grammatical functions exist.

Meaning/Grammatical function	Distinguishing feature	Form	
none	three consonants of the root + short vowels	فعل/يفعل	I
often intensive or causative of I	doubling of the middle consonant	فعّل/يُفعِّل	II
often associative	inserting ا between the first and second consonants of the root	فاعَل – يُفاعِل	III
often causative of I	prefixing أ before the first consonant of the root in the perfect and replacing it with the subject marker and ضمّة in the imperfect	أفعل/يُفعِل	IV
often passive/ reflexive of II	doubling of the middle consonant of the root, and prefixing تـ before the first consonant	تَفَعَّل – يتفعَّل	V

often reflexive of III	adding ا between first and second consonants and prefixing ت before the first consonant	تفاعل/يتَفاعَل	VI
often passive of I	prefixing ان before the first consonant of the root in the perfect and dropping ا in the imperfect	انفعل/ينفعِل	VII
often passive/ reflexive of I	prefixing ا before the first consonant of the root and infixing ت between first and second consonant in the perfect, and dropping ا in the imperfect	افتعل/يفتعل	VIII
often passive/ reflexive of IV	prefixing است before the first consonant of the root in the perfect and dropping ا in the imperfect	استفعل/يستفعل	X
none	four consonants of the root + the short vowels فتحة – فتحة	فعلَ – يُفعلِل	Q1

■ Exercise 1: Word study

1. Analyze the following words into a stem and affixes, giving the English equivalent of each unit. Follow the examples in the table.

Stem + affixes	Word
plural marker ات، ال the، و and، ناشطة meteor (stem)	والناشطات
her ها، she ت، he followed (stem) تبع	تتبعها
	والسابحات
	أبصارها
	يقولون
	قالوا
	فأخذه

2. Translate the following verbs, then identify their roots, write down their stems, and indicate their forms, using the فعل skeleton and the form number. Refer to the *sūra* if you are not sure about the meaning or pronunciation of any of the verbs.

Form and #	Stem	Root	Translation	
أفعل، IV	آتى			أتاك
	نادى			ناداه
	هدى			وأَهديكَ
				فتخشى
أفعل، IV				فأراه
				يقولون
				فَكذَّب
				أدبر
				فحشر
				فنادى
أفعل، IV	أرسى	ر.س.و/ ر.س.ي	He made her fast	أرساها
				وأخْرَج
				رفع
				يتَذكّر
				يسألونك
				يلبثوا
				وأغطش

3. Translate the following nouns, then identify their roots, write down their stems, and indicate their patterns. The first one is given as an example.

Pattern	Stem	Root	Translation	
مفعل	مرعا (مرعى)	ر.ع.ي	and her pasture	ومرعاها
				والجِبال
				ولأنعامكم
				مُرساها
				مُنتَهاها

Exercise 2: Roots and families

The following words are based on 19 roots. Group together the words that are based on the same root, identify the root, and give its general meaning in English.

معاشاً، يُخسِرون، لَمردودون، نجعل، والسابحات، تُؤثِرون، الأولى، لابثين، فسوّاك، وآثَر، زُوِّجَت، فسوّاها، شداد، سبقاً، ترجف، أرساها، المرعى، يخشاها، مقام، يخشى، بعذاب، أشدّ، يتذكّر، فتخشى، يلبَث، خاسرة، أزواجاً، الراجفة، وذِكراها، يستقيم، سبحاً، فالسابقات، رددناه، وجعلنا، عيشة، شديد، مَرساها

Words to remember

Write down the meanings of the following words from memory.

....	سَبح	....	سابِحة
....	تبِع - يتبَع	....	أمر
....	مَردود	....	أبصار
....	خاسِر	....	عِظام
....	طَغى	....	واد
....	عَصى	....	أرى
....	سَعى - يسعى	....	أدبَر
....	نادى - ينادي	....	حَشَر - يحشُر
....	ضُحى	....	عِبرة
....	خلق	....	أشَدّ
....	آثَر	....	بُرِّز
....	نَهى	....	مَقام
....	مُنذِر	....	هَوى
		....	لبِث - يلبَث
		....	عَشِيّة

بسم الله الرحمن الرحيم

عَمَّ يَتَساءلون {١} عَنِ النَّبَإِ العَظيم {٢} الَّذي هُم فيه مُختَلِفون {٣} كلّا سَيَعلَمون {٤} ثُمَّ كلّا سَيَعلَمون {٥} أَلَم نَجعَل الأرض مِهادا {٦} والجبالَ أوتادا {٧} وَخَلَقناكُم أزواجا {٨} وَجَعَلنا نومَكُم سُباتا {٩} وَجَعَلنا اللَّيلَ لِباسا {١٠} وَجَعَلنا النَّهارَ مَعاشا {١١} وَبَنينا فَوقَكُم سَبعًا شِدادا {١٢} وَجَعَلنا سِراجًا وَهّاجا {١٣} وَأَنزَلنا مِنَ المُعصِراتِ ماء ثَجّاجا {١٤} لِنُخرِجَ بِه حَبّا وَنَباتا {١٥} وَجَنّاتٍ ألفافا {١٦} إِنَّ يَومَ الفَصلِ كانَ ميقاتا {١٧} يَومَ يُنفَخُ في الصورِ فَتَأتونَ أفواجا {١٨} وَفُتِحَتِ السَّماءُ فَكانَت أبوابا {١٩} وَسُيِّرَتِ الجبالُ فَكانَت سَرابا {٢٠} إِنَّ جَهَنَّمَ كانَت مِرصادا {٢١} لِلطّاغينَ مَآبا {٢٢} لابِثينَ فيها أحقابا {٢٣} لا يَذوقونَ فيها بَردًا ولا شَرابا {٢٤} الّا حَميمًا وَغَسّاقا {٢٥} جَزاءً وِفاقا {٢٦} إِنَّهُم كانوا لا يَرجونَ حِسابا {٢٧} وَكَذَّبوا بِآياتِنا كِذّابا {٢٨} وَكُلَّ شَيءٍ أحصَيناهُ كِتابا {٢٩} فَذوقوا فَلَن نَزيدَكُم الّا عَذابا {٣٠} إِنَّ لِلمُتَّقينَ مَفازا {٣١} حَدائِقَ وَأعنابا {٣٢} وَكَواعِبَ أترابا {٣٣} وَكَأسًا دِهاقا {٣٤} لا يَسمَعونَ فيها لَغوًا ولا كِذّابا {٣٥} جَزاءً مِّن رَّبِّكَ عَطاءً حِسابا {٣٦} رَبِّ السَّماواتِ والأرضِ وَما بَينَهُما الرحمَنِ لا يَملِكونَ مِنهُ خِطابا {٣٧} يَومَ يَقومُ الرّوحُ والملائكةُ صَفًّا لا يَتَكَلَّمونَ الّا مَن أَذِنَ لَهُ الرحمَنُ وَقالَ صَوابا {٣٨} ذَلِكَ اليَومُ الحَقُّ فَمَن شاء اتَّخَذَ إلى رَبِّهِ مَآبا {٣٩} إِنّا أَنذَرناكُم عَذابًا قَريبًا يَومَ يَنظُرُ المَرءُ ما قَدَّمَت يَداهُ وَيَقولُ الكافِرُ يا لَيتَني كُنتُ تُرابا {٤٠}

New words

Nouns

tidings, news	نَبأ
awful, great	عَظيم
an expanse, bed	مِهاد
bulwarks, pegs	أوتاد
pair	زَوج (ج. أزواج)
repose, rest	سُبات
cloak, covering	لِباس
livelihood	مَعاش
seven	سَبع
strong (heavens)	شِداد
lamp	سِراج
dazzling, shining	وَهّاج
rainy cloud	مُعصِرة
abundant	ثَجّاج
thick foliage, thick growth	ألفاف
decision	فَصل
fixed time	مِيقات
Trumpet	صور
to be set in motion, be moved away	سُيِّر
mirage	سَراب
ambush	مِرصاد
rebellious, transgressor	طاغي
home, dwelling place	مآب
abiding	لابِث
ages	أحقاب

drink	شَراب
boiling water	حَميم
paralyzing cold, dirty wound discharges	غَسّاق
proportioned, exact	وِفاق
denying, belying strongly	كِذّاب
duteous	مُتَّقي
achievement, success	مَفاز
young, full-breasted or mature maidens	كَواعِب
of equal age	أتراب
cup	كَأس
full	دِهاق
vain discourse; dirty, false, evil talk	لَغو
gift	عَطاء
conversing, speaking	خِطاب
Spirit; Gabriel or another angel	روح
arrayed, in rows	صَفّ
right	صَواب
dust	تُراب

Verbs

to ask one another	تَساءَل – يتَساءَل
to be blown	نُفِخ – يُنفَخ
to look for	رَجا – يَرجو
to record	أحصى
to taste	ذاق – يذوق
to increase	زاد – يَزيد
to seek	اتَّخَذ
to warn	أنذَر

Particle

about what	عَمَّ = عن ما

◼ Exercise 1: Word study

1. Translate the following nouns and adjectives, then identify their roots, write down their stems, and indicate their patterns.

Pattern	Stem	Root	Translation	
				مختلفون
				المُعصِرات
	أوتاد		pegs	أوتاداً
				أزواجاً
				ألفافاً
				أفواجاً
		ب.و.ب		أبواباً
				أحقاباً

These words belong to three different patterns. How can the pattern with the largest number of examples be described in terms of meaning or grammatical function?

   1. Analyze the following words into a stem and affixes and give an English translation of each element.

plural marker ين ،the ال ،to ل ،pious, God-fearing مُتّقي	للمُتّقين
	السماوات
	الرحمن

2. Translate the following verbs, then identify their roots, write down their stems, and indicate their forms, using the فعل skeleton and the form number.

   The table gives an idea of the typical frequency of verb forms in Qur'ānic Arabic. You will notice that Form I, فعل, is by far the most common verb form. Indeed this form is the most common in all varieties of Arabic.

   According to the table, which forms occupy second and third positions?

Form and #	Stem	Root	Translation	
	تَساءل			يَتَساءلون
				سيعلمون
				نجعل
فعل، I				وخلقناكم
				وجعلنا
	أنزل			وأَنزلنا
	بنى			وبنينا
				وأَنزلنا
				لِنُخْرِج
		ك.و.ن		كان
	نَفَخ			يُنفَخ
	أتى			فتأتون
	فَتَح			وفُتِحَت
				فكانَت
	سَيَّر			وسُيِّرَت
				يذوقون
				كانوا
	رجا	ر.ج.و		يَرجون
				وكذّبوا
أفعل، IV	أحصى			أحصيناه
		ذ.و.ق		فذوقوا
	زاد	ز.ي.د		نزيدكم
				يسمَعون
				يَملِكون
				يقوم

Form and #	Stem	Root	Translation	
تفعّل، V				يتكلّمون
	أذِن			أذِن
				وقال
	شاء	ش.و.ء		شاء
	اتّخذ	أخذ		اتّخذ
	أنذر			أنذرناكم
				يَنظُر
				قَدَّمَت
				ويقول
				كُنتُ

Exercise 2: Roots and families

The following words are based on 13 roots. Group together the words that are based on the same root, identify the root, and give its general meaning in English.

مرصاداً، كِذّاباً، تملك، يتساءلون، منذر، أوتي، عظاماً، خلقه، وأخرج، فأنبتنا، فسوّاك، مأكول، تشاءون، وتأكلون، فكذّب، فسوّاها، فتأتون، يسألونك، لبالمرصاد، سُئلت، فأنذرتكم، خلقك، لنخرج، سوّى، يشاء، نباتاً، أكلاً، أتاك، وكذّبوا، يملكون، لتسألَنّ، خلقنا، يخرج، خلق، شيئاً، السائل، العظيم، وخلقناكم، السائل

Exercise 3: Opposites

Write each of the words in row ب under its opposite in row أ. The first one is given as an example.

آخِرة	أعلى	أطاع	كذّب	أمات	أبرار	قدّم	جنّة	تَحت	أ
								فوق	
أحيا	جحيم	أسفل	فوق	عصى	أولى	أشرار	أخّر	آمَن	ب

■ Words to remember

Write down the meanings of the following words from memory.

تساءل – يتساءل	....	عَمّ	....
عَظيم	....	نَبَأ	....
لِباس	....	زَوج (ج. أزواج)	....
سَبع	....	مَعاش	....
سِراج	....	شِداد	....
مِيقات	....	وَهّاج	....
صُور	....	نُفِخ – يُنفَخ	....
سُيِّر	....	أتى – يأتي	....
لابِث	....	طاغي	....
حَميم	....	شَراب	....
كِذّاب	....	رَجا – يَرجو	....
ذاق – يذوق	....	أحصى	....
كَأس	....	مُتَّقي	....
عَطاء	....	لَغو	....
روح	....	خِطاب	....
صَواب	....	صَفّ	....
أنذَر	....	اتَّخَذ	....
تُراب	....	يا لَيتَني	....

بسم الله الرحمن الرحيم

يس {١} والقُرآنِ الحَكيم {٢} إِنَّكَ لَمِنَ المُرسَلين {٣} عَلى صِراطٍ مُستَقيم {٤} تَنزيلَ العَزيزِ الرَحيم {٥} لِتُنذِرَ قَومًا ما أُنذِرَ آباؤُهُم فَهُم غافِلون {٦} لَقَد حَقَّ القَولُ عَلى أَكثَرِهِم فَهُم لا يُؤمِنون {٧} إِنّا جَعَلنا في أَعناقِهِم أَغلالاً فَهِيَ إِلى الأَذقانِ فَهُم مُقمَحون {٨} وَجَعَلنا مِن بَينِ أَيديهِم سَدًّا وَمِن خَلفِهِم سَدًّا فَأَغشَيناهُم فَهُم لا يُبصِرون {٩} وَسَواءٌ عَلَيهِم أَأَنذَرتَهُم أَم لَم تُنذِرهُم لا يُؤمِنون {١٠} إِنَّما تُنذِرُ مَنِ اتَّبَعَ الذِّكرَ وَخَشِيَ الرَحمَنَ بِالغَيبِ فَبَشِّرهُ بِمَغفِرَةٍ وَأَجرٍ كَريم {١١} إِنّا نَحنُ نُحيي المَوتى وَنَكتُبُ ما قَدَّموا وَآثارَهُم وَكُلَّ شَيءٍ أَحصَيناهُ في إِمامٍ مُبين {١٢} واضرِب لَهُم مَثَلاً أَصحابَ القَريَةِ إِذ جاءَها المُرسَلون {١٣} إِذ أَرسَلنا إِلَيهِمُ اثنَينِ فَكَذَّبوهُما فَعَزَّزنا بِثالِثٍ فَقالوا إِنّا إِلَيكُم مُرسَلون {١٤} قالوا ما أَنتُم إِلّا بَشَرٌ مِثلُنا وَما أَنزَلَ الرَحمَنُ مِن شَيءٍ إِن أَنتُم إِلّا تَكذِبون {١٥} قالوا رَبُّنا يَعلَمُ إِنّا إِلَيكُم لَمُرسَلون {١٦} وَما عَلَينا إِلّا البَلاغُ المُبين {١٧} قالوا إِنّا تَطَيَّرنا بِكُم لَئِن لَم تَنتَهوا لَنَرجُمَنَّكُم وَلَيَمَسَّنَّكُم مِنّا عَذابٌ أَليم {١٨} قالوا طائِرُكُم مَعَكُم أَئِن ذُكِّرتُم بَل أَنتُم قَومٌ مُسرِفون {١٩}

■ New words

Nouns

wise, full of wisdom	حَكيم
messenger, one who is sent	مُرسَل
revelation, (something) sent down	تَنزيل
heedless	غافِل
necks	أعناق
iron collars	أغلال
with heads raised up, stiff-necked	مُقمَح
behind	خَلف
barrier	سَدّ
the same	سَواء
reminder (the Qur'ān)	ذِكر
unseen, in secret	غَيب
forgiveness	مَغفِرة
dead (plural)	مَوتى
traces, footprints	آثار
book	إمام
town, city	قَرية
two	اثنَين
third	ثالِث
conveyance (of a message)	بَلاغ
clear	مُبين
torture, torment	عَذاب
evil omen	طائِر
transgressing all bounds, forward	مُسرِف

Verbs

to prove true	حَقَّ – يحِقّ
to cover	أغشى
to see	أبصَر – يُبصِر
to follow	اتَّبَع
bring to life	أحيا – يُحيي
to record with numbers	أحصى – يُحصي
to reinforce	عَزَّز
to see an evil omen	تَطَيَّر
to cease, desist	انتَهى – ينتَهي
to stone	رجَم – يرجُم
to touch, befall	مَسّ – يَمَسّ
to remind	ذَكَّر – يُذَكِّر

Particle

أ yes/no question particle + إن if	أإن (أئَن)

Expressions

before, between the hands	بَين أيدي
to give as an example	ضرَب – يضرِب مثَلا
you are only . . . (human beings)	ما أنتُم الا . . . (بشر)

■ Exercise: Word study

1. For the following nouns and adjectives, give a full English translation, then identify the root, the stem, and the pattern, using the فعل skeleton.

Pattern	Stem	Root	Translation	
				الحَكيم
				المُرسَلين
				الرَحيم
				أعناقهم
				الأذقان
			most of them	أكثرهم
				أغلالاً
				مُقْمَحون
				كَريم
				وآثارهم
				أصحاب
				المُرسَلون
				أليم
				مُسرِفون
				المُبين

How many patterns are there? What meaning/grammatical function is associated with each?

2. Translate the following verbs, then identify their roots, stems, and forms, using the فعل skeleton and the form number. Refer to the part of the *sūra* discussed in this section if you are not sure about any of the verbs.

Form and #	Stem	Root	Translation	
				لتُنذِر
				يُؤمِنون
				وجَعلنا
	أغشى			فأغشيناهم
	أبصر			يُبصِرون

Form and #	Stem	Root	Translation	
				أَأَنذَرتَهم
				تُنذِرهم
				فَبَشّرْهُ
	أحيا			نُحيي
				قدّموا
				أحصيناه
	ضرب			واضرِب
				أرسلنا
				فكذّبوهما
				فعزّزنا
				فقالوا
				أنزَل
				تَكذِبون
				تطَيّرنا
	انتهى			تنتهوا
	رجم			لنرجُمنّكم
	مسّ			وليمسّنّكم
	ذكّر			ذُكِّرتُم
Extra credit				
		ت.ب.ع		اتّبَع

Words to remember

Write down the meanings of the following words from memory.

....	مُرسَل	....	حَكيم
....	غافِل	....	تَنزيل
....	أعناق	....	حَقَّ – يحِقّ

	خَلف		بَين أيدي
....	أبصَر - يُبصِر	....	أغشى
....	اتَّبَع	....	سَواء
....	مَغفِرة	....	ذِكر
....	مَوتى	....	أحيا - يُحيي
....	أحصى - يُحصي	....	آثار
....	قَرية	....	ضرَب - يضرِب مثَلاً
....	عَزَّز	....	اثنَين
....	ما أنتُم الا . . .	....	ثالِث
....	بَلاغ	....	بَشَر
....	انتَهى - ينتَهي	....	مُبين
....	ذَكَّر - يُذَكِّر	....	عَذاب

٣٦. سورة يس
٢

وَجاءَ مِن أَقصى المَدينَةِ رَجُلٌ يَسعى قالَ يا قَومِ اتَّبِعوا المُرسَلينَ {٢٠} اتَّبِعوا مَن لا يَسأَلُكُم أَجرًا وَهُم مُهتَدونَ {٢١} وَما لِي لا أَعبُدُ الَّذي فَطَرَني وَإِلَيهِ تُرجَعونَ {٢٢} أَأَتَّخِذُ مِن دونِهِ آلِهَةً إِن يُرِدنِ الرَحمَنُ بِضُرٍّ لا تُغنِ عَنّي شَفاعَتُهُم شَيئًا وَلا يُنقِذونِ {٢٣} إِنّي إِذًا لَفي ضَلالٍ مُبينٍ {٢٤} إِنّي آمَنتُ بِرَبِّكُم فَاسمَعونِ {٢٥} قيلَ ادخُلِ الجَنَّةَ قالَ يا لَيتَ قَومي يَعلَمونَ {٢٦} بِما غَفَرَ لي رَبّي وَجَعَلَني مِنَ المُكرَمينَ {٢٧} وَما أَنزَلنا عَلى قَومِهِ مِن بَعدِهِ مِن جُندٍ مِّنَ السَماءِ وَما كُنّا مُنزِلينَ {٢٨} إِن كانَت إِلّا صَيحَةً واحِدَةً فَإِذا هُم خامِدونَ {٢٩} يا حَسرَةً عَلى العِبادِ ما يَأتيهِم مِن رَسولٍ إِلّا كانوا بِهِ يَستَهزِؤونَ {٣٠} أَلَم يَرَوا كَم أَهلَكنا قَبلَهُم مِّنَ القُرونِ إِنَّهُم إِلَيهِم لا يَرجِعونَ {٣١} وَإِن كُلٌّ لَّمّا جَميعٌ لَّدَينا مُحضَرونَ {٣٢} وَآيَةٌ لَهُمُ الأَرضُ المَيتَةُ أَحيَيناها وَأَخرَجنا مِنها حَبًّا فَمِنهُ يَأكُلونَ {٣٣} وَجَعَلنا فيها جَنّاتٍ مِن نَخيلٍ وَأَعنابٍ وَفَجَّرنا فيها مِنَ العُيونِ {٣٤} لِيَأكُلوا مِن ثَمَرِهِ وَما عَمِلَتهُ أَيديهِم أَفَلا يَشكُرونَ {٣٥}

New words

Nouns

farthest part	أَقصى
town, city	مَدينة
rightly guided	مُهتَدي
to create	فَطَر
gods	اَلِهة
harm	ضُرّ
intercession	شَفاعة
honored	مُكرَم
host	جُند
sending down	مُنزِل
shout	صَيحة
still, dead, destroyed	خامِد
alas, anguish	حَسرة
mankind, bondmen	عِباد
generations	قُرون
brought	مُحضَر
dead	مَيت
to cause to gush forth	فَجَّر
springs of water	عُيون
fruit	ثَمَر

Verbs

to run	سَعى – يَسعى
to return (someone or something)	أرجَع – يُرجِع
to intend, wish	أراد – يُريد
to be of use, avail	أغنى – يُغني
to save	أنقَذ – يُنقِذ
to forgive, pardon	غَفَر
to mock	استَهزأ – يستَهزِئ
to destroy	أهلَك
to give thanks	شَكَر – يشكُر

Particles

besides, in place of	دون
then, therefore, in that case	إذاً (إذَن)
before	لَدى

Expression

everyone of them, all, without exception	إن كُلٌّ لَمّا جَميع

■ Note

A number of words appear in shortened forms in the *sūra*. The following table shows these forms along with their unabbreviated shapes:

Shortened	Regular
يُردِنِ	يُردني
تُغنِ	تُغني
يُنقِذونِ	يُنقِذوني
فاسمعونِ	فاسمعوني

Exercise 1: Word study

1. For the following nouns and adjectives, give a full English translation, then identify the root, the stem, and the pattern, using the فعل skeleton.

Pattern	Stem	Root	Translation	
				شفاعتهم
				بربّكم
				المُكرَمين
				مُنزلين
				خامِدون
				القُرون
				مُحضَرون
				وأعناب
				العُيون

How many patterns are there? What meaning/grammatical function is associated with each?

2. Translate the following verbs, then identify their roots, stems, and forms, using the فعل skeleton and the form number. Refer to the part of the *sūra* discussed in this section if you are not sure about any of the verbs.

Form and #	Stem	Root	Translation	
				اتّبعوا
	اتّخذ			أأتّخذ
	أراد			يُردن(ي) = يُريدني
	أغنى			تُغنِ(ي)
أفعل، IV				يُنقِذون(ي)
				آمنتُ
	سمع			فاسمعون(ي)
				كُنّا
				وجعلني

Form and #	Stem	Root	Translation	
				أَنزَلنَا
				يَستَهزِئُون
				أَهلَكنَا
				يَرجِعون
	أحيا			أَحيَيناها
				وَفَجّرنا

■ Grammar: Initial weak (assimilated) roots in Form VIII

Words like تقوى "piety, fear of Allah" and المتّقون "those who fear Allah" are sometimes assumed to be based on the same root. However, an examination of verb forms, particularly roots with an initial weak letter (و, أ, or ي) in Form VIII, shows a process of assimilation that is quite regular, in which the initial weak letter is assimilated to the ت of Form VIII. This results in a doubled ت. The process can be shown as follows, where three initial-weak roots are contrasted with a sound root.

Final shape	Assimilation	Form VIII افتعل	Roots
اجتنب	none	اجتنب	ج.ن.ب
اتّخذ	أ changes to ت	اوتخذ	أ.خ.ذ
اتّقى	و changes to ت	اوتقى	و.ق.ي
اتّسق	و changes to ت	اوتسق	و.س.ق

Note that the Form VIII verb اتّبع "to follow" has ت as its first root consonant, which merges with the the ت of Form VIII. ت.ب.ع is a sound root that follows the regular rules of verb derivation. The word تقوى is derived from the root و.ق.و so a verb like اتّقى could in theory be derived from either و.ق.و or و.ق.ي. The Form VIII of both is identical. The similarity in meaning often results in confusing the origins of the words derived from the two roots.

■ Exercise 2: Roots and families

The following words are based on 14 roots. Group together the words that are based on the same root, identify the root, and give its general meaning in English.

قُرآن، مُرسَلِين، الحاكِمِين، آمنتُ، وجعلنا، تنذر، اتّبع، ذُكِّرتُم، بشَر، الأكرَم، تكذِبون، مُنزِلِين، يَعلَمون، تَطَيَّرنا، حكيم، اقرأ، يُؤمنون، اتّبعوا، الذِكر، المُكرَمِين، أأنذرتهم، أحكم، وجعلني، المرسَلون، فبشِّره، فكذّبوهما، أنزلنا، أرسلنا، أنذِر، يجعل، الذِكرى، كريم، أنزل، طائركم، لتنذر، منازل، تنذرهم، يعلم، طيراً

■ Words to remember

Write down the meanings of the following words from memory.

....	سَعى – . . .	....	مَدينة
....	أرجَع – يُرجِع	....	مُهتَدي
....	آلِهة	....	دون
....	أغنى – يُغني	....	أراد – يُريد
....	إذَن	....	أنقَذ – يُنقِذ
....	غَفَر	....	يا لَيتَ . . .
....	مُنزِل	....	مُكرَم
....	استَهزأ – يستَهزِئ	....	عِباد
....	لَدى	....	أهلَك
....	مَيت	....	مُحضَر
....	عُيون	....	فَجَّر
		....	شَكَر – يشكُر

سُبحانَ الَّذي خَلَقَ الأزواجَ كُلَّها مِمّا تُنبِتُ الأرضُ وَمِن أنفُسِهِم وَمِمّا لا يَعلَمون {٣٦} وَآيَةٌ لَهُم اللَّيلُ نَسلَخُ مِنهُ النَّهارَفَإذا هُم مُظلِمون {٣٧} والشَّمسُ تَجري لِمُستَقَرٍّ لَها ذَلِكَ تَقديرُ العَزيزِ العَليمِ {٣٨} والقَمَرَ قَدَّرناهُ مَنازِلَ حَتّى عادَ كالعُرجونِ القَديمِ {٣٩} لا الشَّمسُ يَنبَغي لَها أن تُدرِكَ القَمَرَ ولا اللَّيلُ سابِقُ النَّهارِ وَكُلٌّ في فَلَكٍ يَسبَحون {٤٠} وَآيَةٌ لَهُم أَنّا حَمَلنا ذُرِّيَّتَهُم في الفُلكِ المَشحونِ {٤١} وَخَلَقنا لَهُم مِن مِثلِهِ ما يَركَبون {٤٢} وَإن نَشَأ نُغرِقهُم فَلا صَريخَ لَهُم وَلا هُم يُنقَذون {٤٣} اِلّا رَحمَةً مِنّا وَمَتاعًا إلى حينٍ {٤٤} وَإذا قيلَ لَهُمُ اتَّقوا ما بَينَ أَيديكُم وَما خَلفَكُم لَعَلَّكُم تُرحَمون {٤٥} وَما تَأتيهِم مِّن آيَةٍ مِّن آياتِ رَبِّهِم الّا كانوا عَنها مُعرِضينَ {٤٦} وَإِذا قيلَ لَهُم أَنفِقوا مِمّا رَزَقكُمُ اللَّهُ قالَ الَّذينَ كَفَروا لِلَّذينَ آمَنوا أَنُطعِمُ مَن لَّو يَشاء اللَّهُ أَطعَمَهُ إن أنتُم الّا في ضَلالٍ مُبينٍ {٤٧} وَيَقولونَ مَتى هَذا الوَعدُ إن كُنتُم صادِقينَ {٤٨} ما يَنظُرونَ الّا صَيحَةً واحِدَةً تَأخُذُهُم وَهُم يَخِصِّمون {٤٩} فَلا يَستَطيعونَ تَوصِيَةً وَلا إلى أَهلِهِم يَرجِعون {٥٠}

■ New words

Nouns

in darkness	مُظلِم
fixed course, resting-place	مُستَقَرّ
decree, measuring	تَقدير
to measure, to appoint	قَدَّر
mansions	مَنازِل
dried, curved date stalk, shriveled palm-leaf	عُرجون
outstripping	سابِق
ship, orbit	فَلَك
offspring	ذُرِّيّة
laden	مَشحون
shout, help	صَريخ
mercy	رَحمة
enjoyment, comfort	مَتاع
turning away	مُعرِض
promise	وَعد
bequest	تَوصِية

Verbs

to produce, grow	أنبَت – يُنبِت
to withdraw, strip	سَلَخ – يسلَخ
to run	جَرى – يَجري
to return	عاد
to be for	انبَغى – يَنبَغي
to overtake	أدرَك – يُدرِك

float	سَبَحَ – يَسبَح
to bear	حَمَل
to ride	ركِب – يَركَب
to will	شاء – يشاء
to drown	أغرَق – يُغرِق
to save	أنقَذ – يُنقِذ
to spend	أنفَق
to dispute	خَصَّم – يَخصِّم

Particle

like	مِثل

Expressions

for a while	الى حين
you are only . . . , you are nothing but . . .	إن أنتُم الاّ . . .

▪ Exercise 1: Word study

1. For the following nouns and adjectives, give a full English translation, then identify the root, the stem, and the pattern, using the فعل skeleton.

Pattern	Stem	Root	Translation	
				مُظلِمون
				العَزيز
				القَديم
				المَشحون
				مُعرِضين
				مُبين
				صادِقين

How many patterns are there? What meaning/grammatical function is associated with each?

2. Translate the following verbs, then identify their roots, stems, and forms, using the فعل skeleton and the form number. Refer to the part of the *sūra* discussed in this section if you are not sure about any of the verbs.

Form and #	Stem	Root	Translation	
				يَعلَمون
				تُنبِتُ
				تَجري
				قَدَّرناه
				تُدرِك
				يَسبَحون
				وخلَقنا
				يَركَبون
				نُغرِقُهُم
				يُنقذ
				أنفِقوا
				رزَقكم
				أنُطعِم
				يستطيعون
Extra credit				
				تأتيهم
				اتّقوا

■ Grammar: Active and passive participles

When سورة الغاشية was discussed, a large number of active and passive participles were presented. The active participle is generally defined as the doer of an action, and the passive participle as the recipient or the result of the action. So عابِد refers to a worshiper, while معبود refers to the thing that is worshiped.

عابد and معبود, which follow the patterns of فاعل and مفعول, are the active and passive participles of Form I verbs. Active and passive participles of verbs derived from other forms follow different patterns, which are shown in the following table along with the active and passive participles of Form I verbs. (The table shows only the participles of the examples are found in the book. Participles of which no examples are found are marked with an x.)

Passive participle		Active participle		Verb form	
eaten مَأْكول	مَفْعول	unbeliever كافِر	فاعِل	فعل – يفعل	I
made close مُقَرَّب	مُفَعَّل	reminder مُذكِّر	مُفَعِّل	فعّل – يُفَعِّل	II
x	مُفاعَل	someone meeting مُلاقِي	مُفاعِل	فاعَل – يُفاعِل	III
sent, a messenger مُرسَل	مُفعَل	polytheist مُشرِك	مُفعِل	أَفْعَل – يُفعِل	IV
x	x	x	مُتَفَعِّل	تَفَعَّل – يتفعّل	V
x	x	someone competing مُتنافِس	مُتَفاعِل	تَفاعَل – يَتَفاعَل	VI
x	x	someone ceasing, leaving مُنفَكّ	مُنفَعِل	انفَعَل – ينفَعِل	VII
end point, term مُنتَهى	مُفتَعَل	different مُختَلِف	مُفتَعِل	افتَعَل – يفتَعِل	VIII
resting place مُستقَرّ	مستفعَل	someone rejoicing at good news مُستَبشِر	مُستَفعِل	استفعَل – يستفعِل	X
x	مُفَعْلَل	someone dominating مُصيطِر	مُفَعلِل	فعلل – يُفعلِل	Q1

■ Exercise 2

With reference to the above table, indicate whether each of the following participles is active or passive, write down the source verb of the participle as well as its form and number. Follow the example.

Source verb and its form	Active or passive	Participle
استقام، استفعل X	active	المُستقيم (الفاتحة ٦)
	passive	للمصلّين (الماعون ٤)
أوقد،		المُوقَدة (الهمزة ٦)
أغار،		فالمُغيرات (العاديات ٣)
		مُخلِصين (البيّنة ٥)
	active	للمطفّفين (المطفّفين ١)
		مُعتَدي (المطفّفين ١٢)
		مُقْمَحون (يس ٨)
		المُرسَلون (يس ١٣)
		المشحون (يس ٤١)
		مُعرِضين (يس ٤٦)
		صادِقين (يس ٤٨)
أطاع،		مُطاع (التكوير ٢١)
		المُبين (التكوير ٢٣)
اهتدى	active	مُهتَدون (يس ٢١)

◼ Words to remember

Write down the meanings of the following words from memory.

مُظلِم	....	أنبَت ‑ يُنبِت	....
مُستَقَرّ	....	جَرى ‑ يَجري	....
قَدَّر	....	تَقدير	....
أدرَك ‑ يُدرِك	....	عاد	....
فَلَك	....	سابِق	....
حَمَل	....	سَبَح ‑ يَسبَح	....
ركِب ‑ يَركَب	....	مِثل	....
أنقَذ ‑ يُنقِذ	....	شاء ‑ يشاء	....
مَتاع	....	رَحمة	....
مُعرِض	....	الى حين	....
إن أنتُم الاّ . . .	....	أنفَق	....
		وَعد	....

وَنُفِخَ في الصُّورِ فَإذا هُم مِّنَ الأَجداثِ إلى رَبِّهِم يَنسِلون {٥١} قالوا يا وَيلَنا مَن بَعَثَنا من مَرقَدِنا هَذا ما وَعَدَ الرَّحمَنُ وَصَدَقَ المُرسَلون {٥٢} إن كانَت الاّ صَيحَةً واحِدَةً فَإذا هُم جَميعٌ لَّدَينا مُحضَرون {٥٣} فاليَومَ لا تُظلَمُ نَفسٌ شَيئًا ولا تُجزَونَ الا ما كُنتُم تَعمَلون {٥٤} إنَّ أَصحابَ الجَنَّةِ اليَومَ في شُغُلٍ فاكِهون {٥٥} هُم وَأَزواجُهُم في ظِلالٍ عَلى الأَرائكِ مُتَّكِئون {٥٦} لَهُم فيها فاكِهَةٌ وَلَهُم ما يَدَّعون {٥٧} سَلامٌ قولاً مِن رَبٍّ رَحيم {٥٨} وامتازوا اليَومَ أَيُّها المُجرِمون {٥٩} أَلَم أَعهَد إلَيكُم يا بَني آدَمَ أَن لا تَعبُدوا الشَّيطانَ إنَّهُ لَكُم عَدُوٌّ مُبين {٦٠} وَأَن اعبُدوني هَذا صِراطٌ مُّستَقيم {٦١} وَلَقَد أَضَلَّ مِنكُم جِبِلاًّ كَثيرًا أَفَلَم تَكونوا تَعقِلون {٦٢} هَذِهِ جَهَنَّمُ الَّتي كُنتُم توعَدون {٦٣} اصلَوها اليَومَ بِما كُنتُم تَكفُرون {٦٤} اليَومَ نَختِمُ عَلى أَفواهِهِم وَتُكَلِّمُنا أَيديهِم وَتَشهَدُ أَرجُلُهُم بِما كانوا يَكسِبون {٦٥} وَلَو نَشاءُ لَطَمَسنا عَلى أَعيُنِهِم فاستَبَقوا السِراطَ فَأَنّى يُبصِرون {٦٦} وَلَو نَشاء لَمَسَخناهُم عَلى مَكانَتِهِم فَما استَطاعوا مُضِيًّا ولا يَرجِعون {٦٧} وَمَن نُعَمِّرهُ نُنَكِّسهُ في الخَلقِ أَفلا يَعقِلون {٦٨}

New words

Nouns

Trumpet	صور
graves	أجداث
place of sleep	مَرقَد
to speak the truth	صَدَق
brought	مُحضَر
busy	في شُغُل
happy, joyful	فاكِه
shade	ظِلال
reclining	مُتَّكِئ
fruits	فاكِهة
word	قَول
criminal, disbeliever, sinner, wicked, guilty	مُجرِم
enemy, foe	عَدُوّ
to lead astray	أَضَلَّ
multitude	جِبِلّ
mouths	أفواه
legs, feet	أرجُل
to wipe out, blind, quench	طَمَس
to transform (into animals, objects)	مَسَخ
going forward	مُضِيّ
creation	خَلق

Verbs

to blow	نفَخَ – ينفُخ
to come out quickly	نَسَل – يَنسِل
to raise up, out of	بَعَث
to requite	جَزِي – يَجزِي
to ask (for)	ادَّعى – يَدَّعي
to be apart, distinguished	إمتاز – يمتاز
to command, charge	عهَد – يَعهَد
to promise	وَعَد – يَعِد
to seal up	خَتَم – يختِم
to earn	كسَب – يكسِب
to struggle	استَبَق
to see	أبصَر – يُبصِر
to have a long life, to go into old age	عَمَّر – يُعَمِّر
to reverse	نَكَّس – يُنَكِّس

Particle

how, then how	أنَّى

Expression

Woe to us	يا ويلَنا

■ Exercise: Word study

1. For the following nouns and adjectives, give a full English translation, then identify the root, the stem, and the pattern, using the فعل skeleton. How many patterns are there? What meaning/grammatical function is associated with each?

Pattern	Stem	Root	Translation	
				مرقَدنا
				مُحضَرون
				المُرسَلون
				أصحاب
				فاكِهون
				وأزواجهم
				رَحيم
				المُجرِمون
				مُستَقيم
				أفواهـهم

2. Translate the following verbs, then identify their roots, stems, and forms, using the فعل skeleton and the form number. Refer to the part of the *sūra* discussed in this section if you are not sure about any of the verbs.

Form and #	Stem	Root	Translation	
	ادّعى	د.ع.و		يَدّعون
		م.ي.ز		وامتازوا
				تَكونوا
				تَكفُرون
				تعقلون
				أعبدوني
	وعد			توعَدون
				وتُكَلِّمنا
		س.ب.ق		فاستبقوا
				يُبصِرون

Form and #	Stem	Root	Translation	
فعل، I				لِسِخناهم
				استطاعوا
		ع.م.ر		نُعَمِّره
فعّل، II				نُنَكِّسْه

■ Words to remember

Write down the meanings of the following words from memory.

....	صور	....	نفَخ – ينفُخ
....	بَعَث	....	يا ويلَنا
....	جَزي – يَجزي	....	صَدَق
....	فاكِهة	....	في شُغُل
....	مُجرِم	....	قَول
....	أضَلَّ	....	عَدُوّ
		....	وَعَد – يَعِد

وَما عَلَّمْناهُ الشِّعرَ وَما يَنْبَغي لَهُ إِن هُوَ الا ذِكرٌ وَقُرآنٌ مُبين {٦٩} لِيُنذِرَ مَن كانَ حَيًّا وَيَحِقَّ القَولُ عَلى الكافِرين {٧٠} أَوَلَم يَرَوا أَنّا خَلَقنا لَهُم مِمّا عَمِلَت أَيدينا أَنعامًا فَهُم لَها مالِكون {٧١} وَذَلَّلناها لَهُم فَمِنها رَكوبُهُم وَمِنها يَأكُلون {٧٢} وَلَهُم فيها مَنافِعُ وَمَشارِبُ أَفلا يَشكُرون {٧٣} وَاتَّخَذوا مِن دونِ اللَّهِ آلِهَةً لَعَلَّهُم يُنصَرون {٧٤} لا يَستَطيعونَ نَصرَهُم وَهُم لَهُم جُندٌ مُحضَرون {٧٥} فَلا يَحزُنكَ قَولُهُم إِنّا نَعلَمُ ما يُسِرّونَ وَما يُعلِنون {٧٦} أَوَلَم يَرَ الإنسانُ أَنّا خَلَقناهُ مِن نُطفَةٍ فَإِذا هُوَ خَصيمٌ مُبين {٧٧} وَضَرَبَ لَنا مَثَلاً وَنَسِيَ خَلقَهُ قالَ مَن يُحيي العِظامَ وَهِيَ رَميم {٧٨} قُل يُحييها الَّذي أَنشَأَها أَوَّلَ مَرَّةٍ وَهُوَ بِكُلِّ خَلقٍ عَليم {٧٩} الَّذي جَعَلَ لَكُم مِّنَ الشَّجَرِ الأَخضَرِ نارًا فَإِذا أَنتُم مِّنهُ توقِدون {٨٠} أَوَلَيسَ الَّذي خَلَقَ السَّماواتِ والأرضَ بِقادِرٍ عَلى أَن يَخلُقَ مِثلَهُم بَلى وَهُوَ الخَلّاقُ العَليم {٨١} إِنَّما أَمرُهُ إِذا أَرادَ شَيئًا أَن يَقولَ لَهُ كُن فَيَكون {٨٢} فَسُبحانَ الَّذي بِيَدِهِ مَلَكوتُ كُلِّ شَيءٍ وَإِلَيهِ تُرجَعون {٨٣}

New words

Nouns

poetry	شِعر
reminder	ذِكر
living, alive	حَيّ
owner	مالك
riding	رُكوب
benefits	مَنافِع
drinks	مَشارِب
help	نَصر
opponent	خَصيم
to forget	نَسِي
bones	عِظام
dust, something that has rotted away	رَميم
All-Knowing	عَليم
trees	شَجَر
green	أخضَر
able	قادِر
Creator	خَلاّق

Verbs

to be suitable for	إنبَغى – يَنبَغي
to subdue	ذَلَّ
to be grateful, give thanks	شَكَر – يَشكُر
to help	نَصَر – يَنصُر
to grieve	حَزَن – يَحزُن
to conceal	أسَرَّ – يُسِرّ
to reveal, proclaim	أعلَن – يُعلِن
to create, produce	أنشَأ
to kindle	أوقَد – يُوقِد

Particle

yes, indeed	بَلى

■ Exercise 1: Nouns

....

For the following nouns, give a full English translation, then identify the root, the stem, and the pattern, using the فعل skeleton. Indicate how many patterns the nouns belong to and what meaning/grammatical function is associated with each pattern.

Pattern	Stem	Root	Translation	
				الكافِرين
				أنعاماً
				مالِكون
				مَنافِع
				مَشارِب
				مُحضَرون
				خَصيم
				رَميم
				الأخضَر
				بِقادِر
				الخَلّاق
				العَليم

■ Exercise 2: Participles

....

The following participles, found in the last two parts of سورة يس are all derived from Form IV verbs. For each of them, indicate whether it is active or passive and what the source verb is. Follow the example.

أرسل	passive	المُرسَلون
		مُحضَرون
		المُجرِمون
		مُبين

■ Exercise 3: Verbs

....

Translate the following verbs, then identify their roots, stems, and forms, using the فعل skeleton and the form number. Refer to the part of the *sūra* discussed in this section if you are not sure about any of the verbs.

Form and #	Stem	Root	Translation	
				علّمناه
				ينبغي
				لِيُنذِر
				ويَحِقّ
				يَروا
				وذلّلناها
				واتّخذوا
				يستَطيعون
				يُسيِّرون
				يُعلِنون
				يَرَ
				يُحييها
				أنشأها
				توقِدون
				أراد

■ Exercise 4: Roots and families

The following words are based on 19 roots. Group together the words that are based on the same root, identify the root, and give their general meaning in English.

تُرحَمون، حَقّ، خلفكم، وخلقنا، أحييناها، القديم، العِباد، أَتّخذ، ضَلال، ضَلّ، يأكلون، وأزواجهم، خلقه، قدّموا، يُحييها، يخْلق، أعبد، ليأكلوا، أضلّ، يرجعون، صادِقين، الأزواج، يركبون، أنطعِم، الخلّاق، وصدَق، تكفُرون، تقدير، وعزّزنا، اعبدوني، تأخذهم، قدّرناه، العزيز، ويحقّ، رحمة، تعبدوا، الكافِرون، عليم، خلقناه، علّمناه، أطعمه، تُرجَعون، ركوبهم، نُحيي، خلفهم

■ Words to remember

Write down the meanings of the following words from memory.

....	نَصْر	....	نَصَر – يَنصُر
....	أَسَرَّ – يُسِرّ	....	حَزَن – يَحزُن
....	نَسِي	....	أعلَن – يُعلِن
....	عَليم	....	عِظام
....	قادِر	....	شَجَر
....	خَلّاق	....	بَلى

بِسم اللهِ الرَّحمَنِ الرَّحيم

كهيعص {١} ذِكرُ رَحمَةِ رَبِّكَ عَبدَهُ زَكَرِيّا {٢} إذ نادى رَبَّهُ نِداء خَفيّا {٣}
قالَ رَبِّ إنّي وَهَنَ العَظمُ مِنّي واشتَعَلَ الرَّأسُ شَيبًا وَلَم أَكُن بِدُعائِكَ رَبِّ شَقيّا
{٤} وَإنّي خِفتُ المَوالِيَ مِن وَرائي وَكانَتِ امرَأَتي عاقِرًا فَهَب لي مِن لَدُنكَ وَلِيّا
{٥} يَرِثُني وَيَرِثُ مِن آلِ يَعقوبَ واجعَلهُ رَبِّ رَضِيّا {٦} يا زَكَرِيّا إنّا نُبَشِّرُكَ
بِغُلامٍ اسمُهُ يَحيى لَم نَجعَل لَهُ مِن قَبلُ سَمِيّا {٧} قالَ رَبِّ أَنّى يَكونُ لي غُلامٌ
وَكانَتِ امرَأَتي عاقِرًا وَقَد بَلَغتُ مِنَ الكِبَرِ عِتِيّا {٨} قالَ كَذَلِكَ قالَ رَبُّكَ هُوَ عَلَيَّ
هَيِّنٌ وَقَد خَلَقتُكَ مِن قَبلُ وَلَم تَكُ شَيئا {٩} قالَ رَبِّ اجعَل لي آيَةً قالَ آيَتُكَ
أَلّا تُكَلِّمَ النّاسَ ثَلاثَ لَيالٍ سَوِيّا {١٠} فَخَرَجَ عَلى قَومِهِ مِنَ المِحرابِ فَأَوحى
إلَيهِم أَن سَبِّحوا بُكرَةً وَعَشِيّا {١١} يا يَحيى خُذِ الكِتابَ بِقُوَّةٍ وَآتَيناهُ الحُكمَ
صَبِيّا {١٢} وَحَنانًا مِن لَدُنّا وَزَكاةً وَكانَ تَقِيّا {١٣} وَبَرًّا بِوالِدَيهِ وَلَم يَكُن جَبّارًا
عَصِيّا {١٤} وَسَلامٌ عَلَيهِ يَومَ وُلِدَ وَيَومَ يَموتُ وَيَومَ يُبعَثُ حَيّا {١٥}

◾ New words

Nouns

mention	ذِكر
mercy	رَحمة
call, cry	نِداء
secret	خَفِيّ
bone(s)	عَظم (ج. عِظام)
head	رَأس
gray hair	شَيب
invocation, prayer	دُعاء
unblessed	شَقِيّ
relatives, kinfolk	مَوالي
barren	عاقِر
heir, successor	وَلِيّ
posterity, house of	آل
well-pleased, acceptable	رَضِيّ
son	غُلام
of the same name	سَمِيّ
old age	كِبَر
extremity, infirmity	عِتِيّاً
easy	هَيِّن
complete, with no bodily defect	سَوِيّ
praying place, sanctuary	مِحراب
morning, break of day	بُكرة
afternoon, fall of night	عَشِيّاً
fast, with strength	قُوّة
wisdom	حُكم

child	صَبِيّ
sympathy, mercy, compassion	حَنان
righteous, devout	تَقِيّ
dutiful	بَرّ
arrogant	جَبّار
disobedient, rebellious	عَصِيّ

Verbs

to grow feeble	وَهَن
to spread, shine	اشتَعَل
to fear، خِفتُ I was afraid	خافَ
to give، هَبْ! Give!	وَهَب – يهب = أعطى – يُعطي
to inherit	وَرِثَ – يَرِث
to give glad tidings	بَشَّر – يُبَشِّر
to reach	بَلَغ
you were not (see note below)	(لَم) تَكُ
to glorify	سبّح – يُسَبِّح

Particles

Yourself, Your presence	لَدُنك
on me, for me	عَلَيَّ
that not	ألّا = أنْ لا

■ Note

تَكُ is a shortened form of تكُنْ, which itself is a shortened form of تكون. (More on this in the Grammar appendix under Moods of the verb.)

▨ Exercise 1: Verbs

Identify any eight verbs in the following four verses, and for each verb:

a. give the full English translation (of the verb and all affixes),
b. identify the root, the stem, and the form, using فعل and the form number.

Follow the example. There is a total of five verbs besides the one given in the example.

Form and #	Stem	Root	Translation	
II ،فعّل	بشّر	ب.ش.ر	we give you (m. sg.) glad tidings	نُبشّرك

١. قالَ رَبِّ إنّي وَهَنَ العَظمُ مِنّي واشتَعَلَ الرَّأسُ شَيبًا وَلَم أَكُن بِدُعائِكَ رَبِّ شَقِيًّا {٤}

٢. يا زَكَرِيّا إنّا نُبَشِّرُكَ بِغُلام اسمُهُ يَحيى لَم نَجعَل لَهُ مِن قَبلُ سَمِيًّا {٧}

٣. فَخَرَجَ عَلى قَومِهِ مِنَ المِحرابِ فَأَوحى إلَيهِم أَن سَبِّحوا بُكرَةً وَعَشِيًّا {١١}

٤. وَسَلامٌ عَلَيهِ يَومَ وُلِدَ وَيَومَ يَموتُ وَيَومَ يُبعَثُ حَيًّا {١٥}

▨ Exercise 2: Moods of the verb

With reference to the section on Moods of the imperfect verb in the Grammar appendix, and for each of the following verbs:

a. give a full English translation,
b. indicate what mood it is in,
c. explain the mood assignment.

The number in parenthesis indicates the verse number in the part of سورة مريم presented above. Follow the examples.

Reason for mood assignment	Mood	Translation	Verb
governed by لم	jussive	I am	أكن (٤)
not governed by anything	declarative	he inherits me	يَرِثُني (٦)
			وَيَرِثُ (٦)
			نُبشِّرُكَ (٧)

Reason for mood assignment	Mood	Translation	Verb
			نَجعَل (٧)
			يَكونُ (٨)
			تكُ (تكن) (٩)
			تُكلِّمَ (١٠)
			يَموتُ (١٥)
			يُبعَثُ (١٥)

■ Words to remember

Write down the meanings of the following words from memory.

....	نِداء	....	رَحمة
....	عَظم	....	خَفِيّ
....	دُعاء	....	رَأس
....	خافَ (خفتُ)	....	شَقِيّ
....	وَهَب (هَب)	....	عاقِر
....	وَرِثَ – يَرِث	....	وَلِيّ
....	رَضِيّ	....	آل
....	غُلام	....	بَشَّر – يُبَشِّر
....	كِبَر	....	بَلَغ
....	هَيِّن	....	عَلِيّ
....	ألّا	....	لَم تَكُ
....	سبَّح – يُسَبِّح	....	سَوِيّ
....	حُكم	....	قُوّة
....	تَقِيّ	....	صَبِيّ
....	جَبّار	....	بَرّ
		....	عَصِيّ

واذكُر في الكِتابِ مَريَمَ إِذِ انتَبَذَت مِن أَهلِها مَكانًا شَرقِيًّا {١٦} فاتَّخَذَت مِن دونِهِم حِجابًا فَأَرسَلنا إِلَيها روحَنا فَتَمَثَّلَ لَها بَشَرًا سَوِيًّا {١٧} قالَت إِنّي أَعوذُ بِالرَحمَنِ مِنكَ إِن كُنتَ تَقِيًّا {١٨} قالَ إِنَّما أَنا رَسولُ رَبِّكِ لِأَهَبَ لَكِ غُلامًا زَكِيًّا {١٩} قالَت أَنّى يَكونُ لي غُلامٌ وَلَم يَمسَسني بَشَرٌ وَلَم أَكُ بَغِيًّا {٢٠} قالَ كَذَلِكِ قالَ رَبُّكِ هُوَ عَلَيَّ هَيِّنٌ وَلِنَجعَلَهُ آيَةً لِلنّاسِ وَرَحمَةً مِنّا وَكانَ أَمرًا مَقضِيًّا {٢١} فَحَمَلَتهُ فانتَبَذَت بِهِ مَكانًا قَصِيًّا {٢٢} فَأَجاءَها المَخاضُ إِلى جِذعِ النَّخلَةِ قالَت يا لَيتَني مِتُّ قَبلَ هَذا وَكُنتُ نَسيًا مَنسِيًّا {٢٣} فَناداها مِن تَحتِها أَلّا تَحزَني قَد جَعَلَ رَبُّكِ تَحتَكِ سَرِيًّا {٢٤} وَهُزّي إِلَيكِ بِجِذعِ النَّخلَةِ تُساقِط عَلَيكِ رُطَبًا جَنِيًّا {٢٥} فَكُلي واشرَبي وَقَرّي عَينًا فَإِمّا تَرَيِنَّ مِنَ البَشَرِ أَحَدًا فَقولي إِنّي نَذَرتُ لِلرَحمَنِ صَومًا فَلَن أُكَلِّمَ اليَومَ إِنسِيًّا {٢٦} فَأَتَت بِهِ قَومَها تَحمِلُهُ قالوا يا مَريَمُ لَقَد جِئتِ شَيئًا فَرِيًّا {٢٧} يا أُختَ هارونَ ما كانَ أَبوكِ امرَأَ سَوءٍ وَما كانَت أُمُّكِ بَغِيًّا {٢٨}

New words

Nouns

east, facing east	شَرقي
screen, seclusion	حِجاب
complete, in all respects, perfect	سَوِيّ
righteous, faultless	زَكِيّ
unchaste	بَغِيّ
decreed, ordained	مَقضِيّ
far	قَصِيّ
labor, pain of childbirth	مَخاض
trunk	جِذع
palm-tree	نَخلة
nothing	نَسْي
forgotten	مَنسِيّ
stream, rivulet	سَرِيّ
dates	رُطَب
fresh; ripe	جَنِيّ
fast	صَوم
human being, mortal	إنسِيّ
mighty, amazing	فَرِيّاً
man	امرأ
adultery, wickedness	سوء

Verbs

to withdraw in seclusion	انتَبَذ
to appear, assume the likeness of	تَمَثَّل
to touch	مَسَّ
to drive to, bring to	أجاء
to grieve	حَزِنَ – يحزَن
to shake	هزَّ – يهُزّ
to let fall, cause to fall	ساقَط – يُساقِط
Eat (f. sg.)! كُلِي، to eat	أكل – يأكُل
to drink	شرِب – يشرَب
to vow	نَذَر

Expression

to be happy, be consoled	قرَّ – يَقَرَّ عَيناً

■ Exercise 1: Verb forms

Find ten verbs in the following four verses, and for each verb:

a. give the full English translation (of the verb and all affixes),
b. identify the root, the stem, and the form, using فعل and the form number.

١. فَاتَّخَذَت مِن دُونِهِم حِجَابًا فَأَرسَلنَا إِلَيهَا رُوحَنَا فَتَمَثَّلَ لَهَا بَشَرًا سَوِيًّا {١٧}

٢. فَنَادَاهَا مِن تَحتِهَا أَلاَّ تَحزَنِي قَد جَعَلَ رَبُّكِ تَحتَكِ سَرِيًّا {٢٤}

٣. فَكُلِي وَاشرَبِي وَقَرِّي عَينًا فَإِمَّا تَرَينَّ مِنَ البَشَرِ أَحَدًا فَقُولِي إِنِّي نَذَرتُ لِلرَّحمَنِ صَومًا فَلَن أُكَلِّمَ اليَومَ إِنسِيًّا {٢٦}

٤. فَأَتَت بِهِ قَومَهَا تَحمِلُهُ قَالُوا يَا مَريَمُ لَقَد جِئتِ شَيئًا فَرِيًّا {٢٧}

Exercise 2: Moods of the verb

With reference to the section on Moods in the Grammar appendix, and for each of the following verbs:

a. give a full English translation,
b. indicate what mood it is in,
c. explain the mood assignment.

The number in parenthesis indicates the verse number in the part of سورة مريم presented above. Follow the examples.

Reason for mood assignment	Mood	Translation	Verb
	declarative		أعوذُ (١٨)
	subjunctive		لأهبَ (١٩)
			يكون (٢٠)
			ولنجعله (٢١)
			تُساقِط (٢٥)
			أكلّم (٢٦)
	declarative		تحمله (٢٧)

Exercise 3: The imperative

This part of سورة مريم includes a number of verbs in the imperative mood. For those verbs in the table below, all of which are in the imperative mood, give a full English translation, then provide the third person masculine singular active conjugation in the perfect and imperfect. (Refer to the discussion of the Imperative in the Grammar appendix.) Follow the example.

Simple perfect/imperfect conjugation	Translation	Verb
ذكر – يذكر	and you (m. sg.) mention!	واذكُر
	(that) you (f. sg.) (do not) become sad!	(أَلّا) تَحزَني
		وَهُزّي
أكل – يأكل		فَكُلي
		واشرَبي
		وَقَرّي
		فَقولي

▮ Words to remember

Write down the meanings of the following words from memory.

....	حِجاب	....	شَرقي
....	زَكِيّ	....	سَوِيّ
....	قَصِيّا	....	بَغِيّ
....	نَخلة	....	أجاء
....	مَنسِيّ	....	نَسِيَ
....	هزّ – يهُزّ	....	حَزِن – يحزَن
....	شرِب – يشرَب	....	أكل – يأكُل (كُلي)
....	صَوم	....	نَذَر
		....	امرأ

فَأَشَارَت إِلَيهِ قَالوا كَيفَ نُكَلِّمُ مَن كَانَ في المَهدِ صَبيًّا {٢٩} قَالَ إِنِّي عَبدُ اللَّهِ آتانيَ الكِتابَ وَجَعَلَني نَبيًّا {٣٠} وَجَعَلَني مُبارَكًا أَينَ ما كُنتُ وَأَوصاني بِالصَّلاةِ والزَّكاةِ ما دُمتُ حَيًّا {٣١} وَبَرًّا بِوالِدَتي وَلَم يَجعَلني جَبّارًا شَقيًّا {٣٢} والسَّلامُ عَلَيَّ يَومَ وُلِدتُ وَيَومَ أَموتُ وَيَومَ أُبعَثُ حَيًّا {٣٣} ذَلِكَ عيسى ابنُ مَريَمَ قَولَ الحَقِّ الَّذي فيهِ يَمتَرونَ {٣٤} ما كانَ لِلَّهِ أَن يَتَّخِذَ مِن وَلَدٍ سُبحانَهُ إِذا قَضى أَمرًا فَإِنَّما يَقولُ لَهُ كُن فَيَكونُ {٣٥} وَإِنَّ اللَّهَ رَبّي وَرَبُّكُم فاعبُدوهُ هَذا صِراطٌ مُستَقيمٌ {٣٦} فاختَلَفَ الأَحزابُ مِن بَينِهِم فَوَيلٌ لِلَّذينَ كَفَروا مِن مَشهَدِ يَومٍ عَظيمٍ {٣٧} أَسمِع بِهِم وَأَبصِر يَومَ يَأتونَنا لَكِنِ الظالِمونَ اليَومَ في ضَلالٍ مُبينٍ {٣٨} وَأَنذِرهُم يَومَ الحَسرَةِ إِذ قُضِيَ الأَمرُ وَهُم في غَفلَةٍ وَهُم لا يُؤمِنونَ {٣٩} إِنّا نَحنُ نَرِثُ الأَرضَ وَمَن عَلَيها وَإِلَينا يُرجَعونَ {٤٠} واذكُر في الكِتابِ إِبراهيمَ إِنَّهُ كانَ صِدّيقًا نَبيًّا {٤١} إِذ قالَ لِأَبيهِ يا أَبَتِ لِمَ تَعبُدُ ما لا يَسمَعُ وَلا يُبصِرُ وَلا يُغني عَنكَ شَيئًا {٤٢}

New words

Nouns

cradle	مَهد
child, young boy	صَبِيّ
blessed	مُبارَك
sects	أحزاب
meeting	مَشهَد
polytheist, evil-doer	ظالِم
state of carelessness	غَفلة
man of truth, saint	صِدِّيق

Verbs

to point	أشار
to talk to	كَلَّم – يُكلِّم
to enjoin	أوصى
to decree	قَضى
to differ	اختَلَف
as long as I . . . . . . ، ما دمتُ، as long as	ما دام
to doubt or dispute	امترى – يَمتَري

Expression

O my father	يا أَبَتِ

Exercise 1: Verb forms

Identify ten verbs in the following four verses, and for each verb:

a. give the full English translation (of the verb and all affixes),
b. identify the root, the stem, and the form, using فعل and the form number.

١. وَجَعَلَنِي مُبَارَكًا أَيْنَ مَا كُنتُ وَأَوْصَانِي بِالصَّلَاةِ وَالزَّكَاةِ مَا دُمْتُ حَيًّا {۳۱}

٢. مَا كَانَ لِلَّهِ أَن يَتَّخِذَ مِن وَلَدٍ سُبْحَانَهُ إِذَا قَضَى أَمْرًا فَإِنَّمَا يَقُولُ لَهُ كُن فَيَكُونُ {۳٥}

٣. وَأَنذِرْهُمْ يَوْمَ الْحَسْرَةِ إِذْ قُضِيَ الْأَمْرُ وَهُمْ فِي غَفْلَةٍ وَهُمْ لَا يُؤْمِنُونَ {۳۹}

٤. إِذْ قَالَ لِأَبِيهِ يَا أَبَتِ لِمَ تَعْبُدُ مَا لَا يَسْمَعُ وَلَا يُبْصِرُ وَلَا يُغْنِي عَنكَ شَيْئًا {٤۲}

■ Exercise 2: خَفِيًّا and شَقِيًّا

In the first 33 verses of سورة مريم there are many words that belong to the same pattern as the words خَفِيًّا and شَقِيًّا found in the first and second verses:

a.   find at least another ten words that share the same structure,
b.   identify the pattern using the فعل skeleton,
c.   what do these words have in common in terms of their meaning and/or grammatical function?
d.   in spite of superficial differences, this pattern is really part of a larger, more familiar one. Can you identify it?

■ Exercise 3: Moods of the verb

For each of the following verbs:

a.   give a full English translation,
b.   indicate what mood it is in,
c.   explain the mood assignment.

The number in parentheses indicates the verse number in the part of سورة مريم presented above. Follow the examples.

Reason for mood assignment	Mood	Translation	Verb
neutral, not governed by a particle	declarative		نكلّم (۲۹)
governed by لم	jussive		يجعلني (۳۲)
			يمتَرون (۳٤)
			يتّخذ (۳٥)
			يقول (۳٥)
			يأتوننا (۳۸)

Reason for mood assignment	Mood	Translation	Verb
	declarative		يؤمنون (٣٩)
			نرِث (٤٠)
			يرجِعون (٤٠)
	declarative		تعبُد (٤٢)
			يسمع (٤٢)
			يُبصِر (٤٢)

▪ Exercise 4: Cases

The word غلام "boy, son" appears as غلام in Q19: 7, غلامٌ in Q19: 8), غلاماً in Q19: 19, and غلامٌ in Q19: 20). With reference to the section on Cases in the Grammar appendix, indicate the case of each occurrence of غلام and explain the case assignment. For example, the first occurrence is in المجرور because it is preceded/governed by a preposition.

▪ Words to remember

Write down the meanings of the following words from memory.

....	كَلَّم – يُكلِّم	....	أشَار
....	صَبِيّ	....	مَهد
....	أوصى	....	مُبارَك
....	قَضى	....	ما دام – يَدوم
....	أحزاب	....	اختَلَف
....	ظالِم	....	مَشهَد
....	وَرِث – يَرِث	....	غَفلة
....	يا أبَتِ	....	صِدِّيق

الدرس رقم ٢٦

١٩. سورة مريم

٤

يا أَبَتِ إِنّي قَد جاءَني مِنَ العِلمِ ما لَم يَأتِكَ فَاتَّبِعني أَهدِكَ صِراطًا سَوِيًّا {٤٣} يا أَبَتِ لا تَعبُدِ الشَّيطانَ إِنَّ الشَّيطانَ كانَ لِلرَّحمَنِ عَصِيًّا {٤٤} يا أَبَتِ إِنّي أَخافُ أَن يَمَسَّكَ عَذابٌ مِنَ الرَّحمَنِ فَتَكونَ لِلشَّيطانِ وَلِيًّا {٤٥} قالَ أَراغِبٌ أَنتَ عَن آلِهَتي يا إِبراهيمُ لَئِن لَم تَنتَهِ لَأَرجُمَنَّكَ وَاهجُرني مَلِيًّا {٤٦} قالَ سَلامٌ عَلَيكَ سَأَستَغفِرُ لَكَ رَبّي إِنَّهُ كانَ بي حَفِيًّا {٤٧} وَأَعتَزِلُكُم وَما تَدعونَ مِن دونِ اللَّهِ وَأَدعو رَبّي عَسى أَلّا أَكونَ بِدُعاءِ رَبّي شَقِيًّا {٤٨} فَلَمّا اعتَزَلَهُم وَما يَعبُدونَ مِن دونِ اللَّهِ وَهَبنا لَهُ إِسحَقَ وَيَعقوبَ وَكُلًّا جَعَلنا نَبِيًّا {٤٩} وَوَهَبنا لَهُم مِن رَحمَتِنا وَجَعَلنا لَهُم لِسانَ صِدقٍ عَلِيًّا {٥٠} وَاذكُر فِي الكِتابِ موسى إِنَّهُ كانَ مُخلَصًا وَكانَ رَسولًا نَبِيًّا {٥١} وَنادَيناهُ مِن جانِبِ الطّورِ الأَيمَنِ وَقَرَّبناهُ نَجِيًّا {٥٢} وَوَهَبنا لَهُ مِن رَحمَتِنا أَخاهُ هارونَ نَبِيًّا {٥٣} وَاذكُر فِي الكِتابِ إِسماعيلَ إِنَّهُ كانَ صادِقَ الوَعدِ وَكانَ رَسولًا نَبِيًّا {٥٤} وَكانَ يَأمُرُ أَهلَهُ بِالصَّلاةِ وَالزَّكاةِ وَكانَ عِندَ رَبِّهِ مَرضِيًّا {٥٥}

■ New words

Nouns

rebel	عَصِيّ
rejecting	راغِب عَن
safely; for a long while	مَلِيّ
gracious	حَفِيّ
unblessed	شَقِيّ
high	عَلِيّ
side, slope	جانِب
mount	طُور
right (side)	أَيمَن
a talk, communion	نَجِيّ
promise	وَعد

Verbs

to overtake	مَسّ – يمَسّ
to stone	رَجَم – يرجُم
to depart, get away from	هَجَر – يهجُر
to ask forgiveness	استَغفَر – يستَغفِر
to turn away from, withdraw	اعتَزَل – يعتَزِل
to make (someone) draw near	قَرَّب

Particle

(not لا + to أَن) not to	أَلّا

■ Exercise 1: Verb forms

Identify any ten verbs in the following five verses, and for each verb:

a. give the full English translation (of the verb and all affixes),
b. identify the root, the stem, and the form, using فعل and the form number.

١. يَا أَبَتِ إِنِّي قَدْ جَاءَنِي مِنَ الْعِلْمِ مَا لَمْ يَأْتِكَ فَاتَّبِعْنِي أَهْدِكَ صِرَاطًا سَوِيًّا {٤٣}

٢. قَالَ سَلَامٌ عَلَيْكَ سَأَسْتَغْفِرُ لَكَ رَبِّي إِنَّهُ كَانَ بِي حَفِيًّا {٤٧}

٣. وَأَعْتَزِلُكُمْ وَمَا تَدْعُونَ مِنْ دُونِ اللَّهِ وَأَدْعُو رَبِّي عَسَى أَلَّا أَكُونَ بِدُعَاءِ رَبِّي شَقِيًّا {٤٨}

٤. فَلَمَّا اعْتَزَلَهُمْ وَمَا يَعْبُدُونَ مِنْ دُونِ اللَّهِ وَهَبْنَا لَهُ إِسْحَقَ وَيَعْقُوبَ وَكُلًّا جَعَلْنَا نَبِيًّا {٤٩}

٥. وَنَادَيْنَاهُ مِنْ جَانِبِ الطُّورِ الْأَيْمَنِ وَقَرَّبْنَاهُ نَجِيًّا {٥٢}

▇ Exercise 2: Moods

For each of the following verbs:

a. give a full English translation,
b. indicate what mood it is in,
c. explain the mood assignment.

The number in parenthesis indicates the verse number in the part of سورة مريم presented above. Follow the examples.

Reason for mood assignment	Mood	Translation	Verb
	jussive		أَهْدِكَ (٤٣)
			تَعْبُدَ (٤٤)
			أَخَافُ (٤٥)
			يَمَسَّكَ (٤٥)
			لَأَرْجُمَنَّكَ (٤٦)
			سَأَسْتَغْفِرُ (٤٧)
			وَأَعْتَزِلُكُمْ (٤٨)
			تَدْعُونَ (٤٨)
	subjunctive		أَكُونَ (٤٨)
			يَعْبُدُونَ (٤٩)
			يَأْمُرُ (٥٥)

■ Exercise 3: Roots and families

The following words are based on 18 roots. Group together the words that are based on the same root, identify the root, and give its general meaning in English.

فَكُلي، اتّقوا، اسمِع، وآتيناه، فجعلهم، أَأَتّخذ، مِثلنا، فاعبدوه، ليَأكلوا، يسمَع، كُنتُم، يدّعون، مثله، ونَسِي، تقيّاً، نجعل، نكلّم، مَشارِب، العظم، الأشقى، وتكلّمنا، وكانَت، العِظام، فتمثَّل، واشرَبي، اجعل، عَظيم، مَنسيّاً، فأَتَت، شقيّاً، يأكلون، ولنجعله، آتاني، يُبصِر، مُرسَلون، مكانتهم، بدُعائك، وأبصِر، يأتيهم، فحملته، وجعلني، نَسيّاً، كُن، واجعله، يأتوننا، فيكون، يجعلني، تكلّم، فاتّخذت، فأَرسلنا، حملنا، يتّخذ، اتّقوا، تعبد، فتكون

■ Words to remember

Write down the meanings of the following words from memory.

	مَسّ – يمَسّ		عَصِيّ
....		....	
	هَجَر – يهجُر		رَجَم – يرجُم
....		....	
	أَلاّ		استَغفَر – يستَغفِر
....		....	
	عَلِيّ		شَقِيّ
....		....	
	أَيمَن		جانِب
....		....	
	وَعد		قَرَّب
....		....	

واذكُر في الكتاب إدريسَ إنَّهُ كانَ صِدّيقًا نَبِيًّا {٥٦} وَرَفَعناهُ مَكانًا عَلِيًّا {٥٧} أولَئكَ الَّذينَ أنعَمَ اللَّهُ عَلَيهِم مِّنَ النَّبِيّينَ مِن ذُرِّيَّةِ آدَمَ وَمِمَّن حَمَلنا مَعَ نوحٍ وَمِن ذُرِّيَّةِ إبراهيمَ وَإسرائيلَ وَمِمَّن هَدَينا واجتَبَينا إذا تُتلى عَلَيهِم آياتُ الرَّحمَنِ خَرّوا سُجَّدًا وَبُكِيًّا {٥٨} فَخَلَفَ مِن بَعدِهِم خَلفٌ أضاعوا الصَّلاةَ واتَّبَعوا الشَّهَواتِ فَسَوفَ يَلقَونَ غَيًّا {٥٩} إلّا مَن تابَ وَآمَنَ وَعَمِلَ صالِحًا فَأولَئكَ يَدخُلونَ الجَنَّةَ وَلا يُظلَمونَ شَيئًا {٦٠} جَنّاتِ عَدنٍ الَّتي وَعَدَ الرَّحمَنُ عِبادَهُ بِالغَيبِ إنَّهُ كانَ وَعدُهُ مَأتِيًّا {٦١} لا يَسمَعونَ فيها لَغوًا إلّا سَلامًا وَلَهُم رِزقُهُم فيها بُكرَةً وَعَشِيًّا {٦٢} تِلكَ الجَنَّةُ الَّتي نورِثُ مِن عِبادِنا مَن كانَ تَقِيًّا {٦٣} وَما نَتَنَزَّلُ إلّا بِأَمرِ رَبِّكَ لَهُ ما بَينَ أَيدينا وَما خَلفَنا وَما بَينَ ذَلِكَ وَما كانَ رَبُّكَ نَسِيًّا {٦٤} رَبُّ السَّماواتِ والأرضِ وَما بَينَهُما فاعبُدهُ واصطَبِر لِعبادته هل تَعلَمُ لَهُ سَمِيًّا {٦٥} وَيَقولُ الإنسانُ أَئِذا ما مِتُّ لَسَوفَ أُخرَجُ حَيًّا {٦٦} أوَلا يَذكُرُ الإنسانُ أَنّا خَلَقناهُ مِن قَبلُ وَلَم يَكُ شَيئًا {٦٧}

◼ New words

Nouns

man of truth, saint	صِدِّيق
high	عَلِيّ
prostrate, adoring	سُجَّد
weeping	بُكِيّ
posterity, later generation	خَلَف
lust	شَهوة
deception	غَيّ
will come to pass, sure of fulfillment	مَأتِيّ
morning	بُكرة
afternoon, evening	عَشِيّ
pious, devout	تَقِيّ
forgetful	نَسِيّ
similar, to be named the same as	سَمِيّ

Verbs

to guide	هَدى
to choose	اجتَبى
to recite	تَلى – يَتلو
to fall down	خَرّ
to succeed	خَلَف
to meet	لَقِي – يَلقى
to cause to inherit, give as inheritance	أورَث – يورِث
to be patient, steadfast	اصطَبَر

◾ Exercise 1: Verb forms

Identify ten verbs in the following five verses, and for each verb:

a.   give the full English translation (of the verb and all affixes),

b.   identify the root, the stem, and the form, using فعل and the form number.

١.   أُولَـٰئِكَ الَّذِينَ أَنعَمَ اللَّهُ عَلَيهِم مِّنَ النَّبِيِّينَ مِن ذُرِّيَّةِ آدَمَ وَمِمَّن حَمَلنَا مَعَ نُوحٍ وَمِن
ذُرِّيَّةِ إِبرَاهِيمَ وَإِسرَائِيلَ وَمِمَّن هَدَينَا وَاجتَبَينَا إِذَا تُتلَىٰ عَلَيهِم آيَاتُ الرَّحمَـٰنِ خَرُّوا
سُجَّدًا وَبُكِيًّا {٥٨}

٢.   فَخَلَفَ مِن بَعدِهِم خَلفٌ أَضَاعُوا الصَّلَاةَ وَاتَّبَعُوا الشَّهَوَاتِ فَسَوفَ يَلقَونَ غَيًّا {٥٩}

٣.   إِلَّا مَن تَابَ وَآمَنَ وَعَمِلَ صَالِحًا فَأُولَـٰئِكَ يَدخُلُونَ الجَنَّةَ وَلَا يُظلَمُونَ شَيئًا {٦٠}

٤.   رَبُّ السَّمَاوَاتِ وَالأَرضِ وَمَا بَينَهُمَا فَاعبُدهُ وَاصطَبِر لِعِبَادَتِهِ هَل تَعلَمُ لَهُ سَمِيًّا {٦٥}

٥.   أَوَلَا يَذكُرُ الإِنسَانُ أَنَّا خَلَقنَاهُ مِن قَبلُ وَلَم يَكُ شَيئًا {٦٣}

◾ Exercise 2: منسِيًّا and مَقضِيًّا, etc.

The words مَقضِيًّا, منسِيًّا, مَرضِيًّا, and مَأتِيًّا are participles. Before looking at the answer below, can you tell whether they are active or passive participles, and which verbs they are derived from?

Answer: They are passive participles from the Form I verbs قضى, نسِي, رضِي, and أتى. Form I passive participles based on lame roots take the form مَفعِيّ instead of the regular مَفعُول.

◾ Exercise 3: Noun types

The following nouns and adjectives appear in the last three parts of سورة مريم. Study them and answer the questions. Do not look at the answer to question c. below until you have thought the questions through and done your best at answering them.

a.   For each noun or adjective, identify the root, the stem, and the pattern using فعل.

مستقيم، عظيم، الظالمون، الكتاب، الحسرة، صادق، الأمر، عباد، راغب، غفلة، صدّيق،
رحمتنا، عبادة، الوعد، نبيّاً، ربّه، الأرض، شقيّاً، شيئاً، تقيّاً، الشهوات، مأتيّاً، الجنّة،
رَسولاً، بالغيب، مُبين

b.   These words can be divided into two major groups, depending on their structure and general meanings, as follows:

Group 1

مستقيم، عظيم، الظالمون، الكتاب، صادق، عِباد، راغب، صِدّيق، عبادة، نبيّاً، شَقيّاً، شيئاً، تَقيّاً، مَأتِيّاً، رَسولاً، مُبين

Group 2

الحسرة، الأمر، غفلة، رحمتنا، الوعد، ربّه، الأرض، شيئاً، الشهوات، الجنّة، بالغيب

c.   What is common to each group in terms of structure and general meaning?

Answer: The words in Group 1 can be described as derived. كتاب is derived from the verb كتب, and ظالم from ظلم. But words like ربّ, أمر, and أرض are not derived from other words. They can be described as primary words. Some of the oldest words in Arabic that go back to Semitic roots shared by other Semitic languages belong in this category. Unlike derived words and like Form I verbs, they lack a pattern-meaning association.

■ Words to remember

Write down the meanings of the following words from memory.

....	عَلِيّ	....	صِدّيق
....	تَلى – يَتلو	....	هَدى
....	سُجَّد	....	خَرّ
....	خَلَف	....	بُكِيّ
....	شَهوة	....	خَلَف
....	مَأتِيّ	....	لَقِي – يَلقى
....	عَشِيّ	....	بُكرة
....	تَقِيّ	....	أورَث – يورِث
....	اصطَبَر	....	نَسِيّ
....	يَك	....	سَمِيّ

فَوَرَبِّكَ لَنَحشُرَنَّهُم وَالشَّياطِينَ ثُمَّ لَنُحضِرَنَّهُم حَولَ جَهَنَّمَ جِثِيًّا {٦٨} ثُمَّ لَنَنزِعَنَّ مِن كُلِّ شِيعَةٍ أَيُّهُم أَشَدُّ عَلَى الرَّحمَنِ عِتِيًّا {٦٩} ثُمَّ لَنَحنُ أَعلَمُ بِالَّذِينَ هُم أَولَى بِها صِلِيًّا {٧٠} وَإِن مِنكُم إِلَّا وَارِدُها كانَ عَلَى رَبِّكَ حَتمًا مَقضِيًّا {٧١} ثُمَّ نُنَجِّي الَّذِينَ اتَّقَوا وَنَذَرُ الظَّالِمِينَ فِيها جِثِيًّا {٧٢} وَإِذا تُتلَى عَلَيهِم آياتُنا بَيِّناتٍ قالَ الَّذِينَ كَفَرواللَّذِينَ آمَنوا أَيُّ الفَرِيقَينِ خَيرٌ مَقامًا وَأَحسَنُ نَدِيًّا {٧٣} وَكَم أَهلَكنا قَبلَهُم مِّن قَرنٍ هُم أَحسَنُ أَثاثًا وَرِئيًا {٧٤} قُل مَن كانَ فِي الضَّلالَةِ فَليَمدُد لَهُ الرَّحمَنُ مَدًّا حَتَّى إِذا رَأَوا ما يوعَدونَ إِمّا العَذابَ وَإِمّا السّاعَةَ فَسَيَعلَمونَ مَن هُوَ شَرٌّ مَكانًا وَأَضعَفُ جُندًا {٧٥} وَيَزِيدُ اللَّهُ الَّذِينَ اهتَدَوا هُدًى وَالباقِياتُ الصّالِحاتُ خَيرٌ عِندَ رَبِّكَ ثَوابًا وَخَيرٌ مَرَدًّا {٧٦} أَفَرَأَيتَ الَّذِي كَفَرَ بِآياتِنا وَقالَ لَأوتَيَنَّ مالًا وَوَلَدًا {٧٧} أَطَّلَعَ الغَيبَ أَمِ اتَّخَذَ عِندَ الرَّحمَنِ عَهدا {٧٨} كَلَّا سَنَكتُبُ ما يَقولُ وَنَمُدُّ لَهُ مِنَ العَذابِ مَدّا {٧٩} وَنَرِثُهُ ما يَقولُ وَيَأتِينا فَردا {٨٠}

■ New words

Nouns

on their knees, crouching	جِثِيّ
sect	شِيعة
obstinate, stubborn in rebellion	عِتِيّ
most worthy	أَوْلى
being burned	صِلِيّ
passing over, approaching	وارِد
decree, ordinance	حَتْم
fixed, must be accomplished	مَقْضِيّ
clear	بَيِّنة
group, party	فَرِيق
position	مَقام
station, imposing	نَدِيّ
goods, gear	أَثاث
outward appearance	رِئْيّ
error	ضَلالة
to extend, prolong	مَدَّ – يمُدُّ
extending	مَدّ
either, whether	إمّا
the Hour (of Doom)	الساعة
reward	ثَواب
resort	مَرَدّ
alone	فَرْد

Verbs

to gather together, assemble	حَشَر – يَحشُر
to bring	أحضَر – يُحضِر
to drag out, pluck out	نَزَع – يَنزِع
to save, rescue	نَجّى – يُنَجّي
to leave[1]	يَذَر
to be guided to the right way	اهتَدى – يَهتَدي
to be given	أُوتِي – يُؤتى
to know, to be aware of	اطَّلَع

■ Exercise 1: Roots

This part of the *sūra* has a large number of verbs whose roots might not be readily recognizable. The following table shows seven verbs and four roots. Fill in the three missing roots.

و.ق.ي	they feared Allah	اتّقوا
و.ذ.ر	and we leave	ونذر
ت.ل.و	(they) are recited	تُتلى
	they were rightly guided	اهتدوا
أ.ت.ي	I will surely give	لأوتينّ
	he undertook	اتّخذ
	we inherit him	ونرثه

---

[1] This verb does not have a form in the perfect tense. It has an imperfect (يذر) and an imperative form (ذر).

■ Exercise 2: Verb forms

Identify ten verbs in the following five verses, and for each verb:

a. give the full English translation (of the verb and all affixes),
b. identify the root, the stem, and the form, using فعل and the form number.

١. ثُمَّ نُنَجِّي الَّذِينَ اتَّقَوا وَنَذَرُ الظالِمِينَ فيها جِثِيًّا {٧٢}

٢. قُل مَن كانَ في الضَّلالَةِ فَلْيَمدُد لَهُ الرَّحمَنُ مَدًّا حَتَّى إذا رَأَوا ما يوعَدونَ إمّا العَذابَ وَإمّا السّاعَةَ فَسَيَعلَمونَ مَن هُوَ

٣. شَرٌّ مَكانًا وَأَضعَفُ جُندا {٧٥} وَيَزيدُ اللَّهُ الَّذِينَ اهتَدَوا هُدًى والباقياتُ الصّالِحاتُ خَيرٌ عِندَ رَبِّكَ ثَوابًا وَخَيرٌ مَرَدًّا {٧٦}

٤. كَلّا سَنَكتُبُ ما يَقولُ وَنَمُدُّ لَهُ مِنَ العَذابِ مَدًّا {٧٩}

٥. وَنَرِثُهُ ما يَقولُ وَيَأتينا فَردا {٨٠}

■ Exercise 3: Cases

The word رَبّ "Lord" occurs 11 times in the following verses of Q19: 3, 9, 19, 24, 36, 64 (twice), 65, 68, 71, and 76. Make a list of these occurrences, then for each one, give an English translation of the whole word, indicate what case it is in, and the reason for the case assignment. Follow the example. (Ignore the one occurrence in verse 10, where رَبّ is a shortened form of رَبِّي "my Lord". The possessive ي obscures the case marker.)

Reason for case assignment	Case	Translation	Noun or adjective	Verse #
object of the verb نادى	accusative	his Lord	رَبّه	3

Words to remember

Write down the meanings of the following words from memory.

أحضَر – يُحضِر	....	حَشَر – يَحشُر	....
أُولى	....	شيعة	....
وارِد	....	صِلِيّ	....
مَقضِيّ	....	خَتم	....
بَيِّنة	....	نَجّى – يُنَجِّي	....
مَقام	....	فَريق	....
ضَلالة	....	أثاث	....
إمّا	....	مَدَّ – يمُدّ	....
اهتَدى – يَهتَدي	....	الساعة	....
أُتِي – يُؤتى	....	ثَواب	....
		فَرد	....

وَاتَّخَذُوا مِن دُونِ اللَّهِ آلِهَةً لِيَكُونُوا لَهُم عِزًّا {٨١} كَلَّا سَيَكفُرُونَ بِعِبادَتِهِم وَيَكُونُونَ عَلَيهِم ضِدًّا {٨٢} أَلَم تَرَ أَنَّا أَرسَلنا الشَّياطينَ عَلَى الكافِرينَ تَؤُزُّهُم أَزًّا {٨٣} فَلا تَعجَل عَلَيهِم إِنَّما نَعُدُّ لَهُم عَدًّا {٨٤} يَومَ نَحشُرُ المُتَّقينَ إِلَى الرَّحمَنِ وَفدا {٨٥} وَنَسوقُ المُجرِمينَ إِلَى جَهَنَّمَ وِردا {٨٦} لا يَملِكونَ الشَّفاعَةَ إِلّا مَنِ اتَّخَذَ عِندَ الرَّحمَنِ عَهدًا {٨٧} وَقالوا اتَّخَذَ الرَّحمَنُ وَلَدا {٨٨} لَقَد جِئتُم شَيئًا إِدًّا {٨٩} تَكادُ السَّماواتُ يَتَفَطَّرنَ مِنهُ وَتَنشَقُّ الأَرضُ وَتَخِرُّ الجِبالُ هَدًّا {٩٠} أَن دَعَوا لِلرَّحمَنِ وَلَدا {٩١} وَما يَنبَغي لِلرَّحمَنِ أَن يَتَّخِذَ وَلَدا {٩٢} إِن كُلُّ مَن فِي السَّماواتِ والأَرضِ إِلّا آتِي الرَّحمَنِ عَبدا {٩٣} لَقَد أَحصاهُم وَعَدَّهُم عَدًّا {٩٤} وَكُلُّهُم آتيهِ يَومَ القِيامَةِ فَردا {٩٥} إِنَّ الَّذينَ آمَنوا وَعَمِلوا الصالِحاتِ سَيَجعَلُ لَهُمُ الرَّحمَنُ وُدًّا {٩٦} فَإِنَّما يَسَّرناهُ بِلِسانِكَ لِتُبَشِّرَ بِهِ المُتَّقينَ وَتُنذِرَ بِهِ قَومًا لُدًّا {٩٧} وَكَم أَهلَكنا قَبلَهُم مِن قَرنٍ هَل تُحِسُّ مِنهُم مِن أَحَدٍ أَو تَسمَعُ لَهُم رِكزا {٩٨}

■ New words

....

Nouns

power	عِزّ
opponent	ضِدّ
number, sum	عَدّ
(like a) delegation, goodly company	وَفد
in a thirsty state; weary herd	ورد
intercession	شَفاعة
terrible, evil	إِدّ
in ruins	هَدّ
counting, numbering	عَدّ
coming to	آتِي
single, alone	فَرْد
love	وُدّ
stubborn opponent	لُدّ
whisper, slightest sound	رِكز

Verbs

to push, confound (with confusion)	أَزَّ – يَؤُزّ
to make haste	عجِل – يَعجَل
to count out, number	عَدَّ – يعُدّ
to drive	ساق – يَسوق
to be on the verge of, almost	كاد – يَكاد
to be torn	تَفَطَّر – يتَفَطَّر
to fall	خَرَّ – يخِرّ
to know, count	أحصَى
to feel, see	أَحَسَّ – يُحِسّ

■ Exercise 1: Verb forms

Identify any ten verbs in the following seven verses, and for each verb:

a.   give the full English translation (of the verb and all affixes),

b.   identify the root, the stem, and the form, using فعل and the form number.

١.   أَلَمْ تَرَ أَنَّا أَرْسَلْنَا الشَّيَاطِينَ عَلَى الكَافِرِينَ تَؤُزُّهُمْ أَزًّا {٨٣}

٢.   لا يَمْلِكُونَ الشَّفَاعَةَ إِلَّا مَنِ اتَّخَذَ عِندَ الرَّحْمَنِ عَهْدًا {٨٧}

٣.   تَكَادُ السَّمَاوَاتُ يَتَفَطَّرْنَ مِنْهُ وَتَنشَقُّ الأَرْضُ وَتَخِرُّ الجِبَالُ هَدًّا {٩٠}

٤.   وَمَا يَنبَغِي لِلرَّحْمَنِ أَن يَتَّخِذَ وَلَدًا {٩٢}

٥.   لَقَدْ أَحصَاهُمْ وَعَدَّهُمْ عَدًّا {٩٤}

٦.   فَإِنَّمَا يَسَّرْنَاهُ بِلِسَانِكَ لِتُبَشِّرَ بِهِ المُتَّقِينَ وَتُنذِرَ بِهِ قَوْمًا لُّدًّا {٩٧}

٧.   وَكَمْ أَهلَكْنَا قَبلَهُم مِّن قَرْنٍ هَل تُحِسُّ مِنهُم مِّنْ أَحَدٍ أَو تَسمَعُ لَهُمْ رِكْزًا {٩٨}

■ Exercise 2: Noun patterns

The following nouns and adjectives appear in the last three parts of سورة مريم.

a.   For each noun or adjective, identify the root, the stem, and the pattern using فعل.

أَشَدّ، شَرّ، شَيئاً، الأَرْض، بِعِبَادَتِهِم، أَعلم، أَولى، عَبداً، خَير، الصالِحات، الشَّفاعة، وارِدها، ثَواباً، مالاً، مَقضِيّاً، الظالِمين، يَوم، الغَيب، بَيِّنات، مَقاماً، نَدِيّاً، المُجرِمين، أَحسن، الجِبال، الرَّحمن، قَوماً، والباقِيات، العَذاب، عَهداً، القِيامة، وأَضعَف، قَرن، الكافِرِين، المُتَّقِين

b.   How many patterns are there? What do the members of each pattern have in common in terms of meaning and/or general function?

■ Exercise 3: Roots and families

The following words are based on 23 roots. Group together the words that are based on the same root, identify the root, and give its general meaning in English.

هُدى، الكِتاب، نَرِث، سَيكفرون، فاتَّبِعني، أَعلم، فَليمدد، سَيجعل، ونَرِثه، فاعبدوه، مَدّاً، وعَدَّهم، فَسيعلمون، خَلقنا، عَدّاً، صِدِّيقاً، يَأتِيك، رَسولاً، تَعبد، لنَحشِرنَّهم، الكافِرِين، صِدق،

خلقناه، صادق، أمراً، عبادنا، فاختلف، نحشر، وعد، اتّخذ، آتي، واتّبعوا، بعبادتهم، مكاناً، يؤمنون، ورداً، واتّخذوا، لأوتينّ، العلم، يأمُر، أرسلنا، نورِث، كفر، اهتدوا، خلف، آتيه، ليكونوا، أهدك، عبداً، وعدُه، آمنوا، يتّخذ، مقاماً، ونمدّ، فخلف، بأمر، ويأتينا، جعلنا، مستقيم، هدينا، يعبدون، وتكونون، نعدّ، سنكتُب، كفروا، الوعد، واردها

■ Words to remember

Write down the meanings of the following words from memory.

....	ضدّ	....	عزّ
....	عَدَّ – يعُدّ	....	عجِل – يَعجَل
....	ساق – يَسوق	....	عَدّ
....	تَفَطَّر – يتَفَطَّر	....	كاد – يَكاد
....	أحصَى	....	خَرَّ – يخِرّ
....	عَدّ	....	عَدَّ
....	وُدّ	....	آتي
		....	أحَسَّ – يُحِسّ

بِسم اللّهِ الرَّحمَنِ الرَّحيم

الر. تِلكَ آياتُ الكِتابِ المُبين {١} إِنّا أَنزَلناهُ قُرآنًا عربيًّا لَعلَّكُم تَعقلون {٢} نَحنُ نَقُصُّ عَلَيكَ أَحسَنَ القَصَصِ بِما أَوحَينا إِلَيكَ هَذا القُرآنَ وَإِن كُنتَ مِن قَبلِهِ لَمِنَ الغَافِلين {٣} إِذ قالَ يوسُفُ لِأبيهِ يا أَبتِ إِنّي رَأَيتُ أَحَدَ عَشَرَ كَوكَبًا والشَّمسَ والقَمَرَ رَأَيتُهُم لي ساجدين {٤} قالَ يا بُنَيَّ لا تَقصُص رُؤياكَ عَلى إِخوَتِكَ فَيَكيدوا لَكَ كَيدًا إِنَّ الشَّيطانَ لِلإِنسانِ عَدُوٌّ مُبين {٥} وَكَذَلِكَ يَجتَبيكَ رَبُّكَ وَيُعَلِّمُكَ مِن تَأويلِ الأَحاديثِ وَيُتِمُّ نِعمَتَهُ عَلَيكَ وَعَلى آلِ يَعقوبَ كَما أَتَمَّها عَلى أَبَوَيكَ مِن قَبلُ إِبراهيمَ وَإِسحَقَ إِنَّ رَبَّكَ عَليمٌ حَكيم {٦} لَّقَد كانَ في يوسُفَ وَإِخوَتِهِ آياتٌ لِلسّائِلين {٧} إِذ قالوا لَيوسُفُ وَأَخوهُ أَحَبُّ إِلى أَبينا مِنّا وَنَحنُ عُصبَةٌ إِنَّ أَبانا لَفي ضَلالٍ مُبين {٨} اقتُلوا يوسُفَ أَوِ اطرَحوهُ أَرضًا يَخلُ لَكُم وَجهُ أَبيكُم وَتَكونوا مِن بَعدِهِ قَومًا صالحين {٩} قالَ قائِلٌ مِّنهُم لا تَقتُلوا يوسُفَ وَأَلقوهُ في غَيابَةِ الجُبِّ يَلتَقِطهُ بَعضُ السَّيّارَةِ إِن كُنتُم فاعلين {١٠} قالوا يا أَبانا ما لَكَ لا تَأمَنّا عَلى يوسُفَ وَإِنّا لَهُ لَناصِحون {١١} أَرسِلهُ مَعَنا غَدًا يَرتَع وَيَلعَب وَإِنّا لَهُ لَحافِظون {١٢}

■ New words

Nouns

stories, narratives	قَصَص
ignorant, heedless	غافِل
star, planet	كوكَب
prostrating	ساجِد
my (dear) son	بُنَيّ
vision	رُؤْيا
brothers	إخوة
Satan	شَيطان
enemy	عَدُوّ
interpretation	تأويل
dreams, events	حديث (ج. أحاديث)
offspring, family	اَل
fathers	أبوين (أبويكَ)
dearer	أَحَبّ
strong group, many	عُصبة
error, aberration	ضَلال
(other) land	أرض
favor	وَجه
folk	قَوم
righteous	صالِح
bottom	غيابة
well, pit	جُبّ
caravan	سيّارة
doing	فاعِل
well-wisher, good friend	ناصِح
tomorrow	غَداً

Verbs

understand	عقل – يعقِل
to relate, narrate	قصّ – يقُصّ
to reveal, inspire	أوحى – يُوحي
to choose, prefer	اجتبى – يجتبِي
to perfect	أتمّ – يُتِمّ
cast out	طرَح – يطرَح
to be all for	خلا – يخلو
throw down, fling	ألقى – يُلقي
to pick up, find	التقَط – يلتَقِط
to trust	أمِن – يأمَن
to enjoy oneself	رتَع – يرتَع
to play	لعِب – يلعَب

Particles

may	لعلّ
even though	إن
thus	كَذَلِكَ
some	بَعض

Expressions

eleven	أحد عَشَر
from before, previously	مِن قَبل

■ Grammar: Form II verbal nouns

One noun pattern derived from verbs is the "verbal noun" (مصدر). Verbal nouns derived from Form I verbs follow too many different patterns to be of practical use in an introductory Arabic book. Verbal nouns derived from other verb forms generally follow one pattern each, with certain derivatives more common than others. One of the more common verbal noun patterns is that based on Form II verbs, which takes the shape تَفعيل as in تكذيب "denying", which is derived from the verb كذّب "to deny".

■ Exercise 1: Verbal nouns

For the following verbal nouns, all derived from Form II verbs, give an English translation and identify the source verb. Follow the example of تكذيب just given.

Source verb	Translation (of verbal noun)	Verbal noun
		تنزيل
		تضليل
		تأويل

■ Exercise 2: Nouns

For the following nouns, provide a full English translation, identify the root, the stem, and the pattern, using فعل, and indicate what meaning or grammatical function is associated with that pattern. Follow the examples.

Function of the pattern	Pattern	Stem	Root	Translation	
AP of FI (Active Participle of Form I)	فاعِل	غافِل	غ.ف.ل	the headless ones	الغافِلين
					ساجدين
VN of FII					تَأويل
					للسائِلين
					صالحين
					قائِل
					فاعِلين
					لَناصِحون
					لَحافِظون

■ Exercise 3: Verbs

Identify all the verbs in the following five verses, and for any ten of them:

a.   give a full English translation,
b.   indicate whether it is perfect or imperfect,
c.   for those verbs in the imperfect, indicate what mood they are in,
d.   identify the root, the stem, and the pattern, using فعل, and the form number.

Follow the examples.

Form and #	Stem	Root	Tense/case	Translation	Verb
فعل، I	قصّ	ق.ص.ص	imperfect/declarative	we narrate	نقُصّ
فعل، IV	أوحى	و.ح.ي	perfect	we revealed	أوحينا

١.   نحن نَقُصُّ عَلَيكَ أَحسَنَ القَصَصِ بِمَا أَوحَينَا إِلَيكَ هَذَا القُرآنَ وَإِن كُنتَ مِن قَبلِهِ لَمِنَ الغَافِلِينَ {٣}

٢.   إذ قَالَ يُوسُفُ لِأَبِيهِ يَا أَبَتِ إِنِّي رَأَيتُ أَحَدَ عَشَرَ كَوكَبًا وَالشَّمسَ وَالقَمَرَ رَأَيتُهُم لِي سَاجِدِينَ {٤}

٣.   وَكَذَلِكَ يَجتَبِيكَ رَبُّكَ وَيُعَلِّمُكَ مِن تَأوِيلِ الأَحَادِيثِ وَيُتِمُّ نِعمَتَهُ عَلَيكَ وَعَلَى آلِ يَعقُوبَ كَمَا أَتَمَّهَا عَلَى أَبَوَيكَ مِن قَبلُ إِبرَاهِيمَ وَإِسحَق إِنَّ رَبَّكَ عَلِيمٌ حَكِيمٌ {٦}

٤.   اقتُلُوا يُوسُفَ أَوِ اطرَحُوهُ أَرضًا يَخلُ لَكُم وَجهُ أَبِيكُم وَتَكُونُوا مِن بَعدِهِ قَومًا صَالِحِينَ {٩}

٥.   قَالَ قَائِلٌ مِّنهُم لَا تَقتُلُوا يُوسُفَ وَأَلقُوهُ فِي غَيَابَةِ الجُبِّ يَلتَقِطهُ بَعضُ السَّيَّارَةِ إِن كُنتُم فَاعِلِينَ {١٠}

■ Exercise 4: Cases

Translate the following four words taken from this part of سورة يوسف, then, with reference to the section on Cases in the Grammar appendix, indicate what case they are in and explain the case assignment: أبانا and ,أبيكم ,أبينا ,أخوه.

Words to remember

Write down the meanings of the following words from memory.

....	عقل – يعقِل	....	لعلّ
....	إنّ	....	أوحى – يُوحي
....	أَبَتِ	....	غافِل
....	كوكَب	....	أحد عَشَر
....	بُنَيَّ	....	ساجِد
....	إخوة	....	رُؤيا
....	عَدُوٌّ	....	شَيطان
....	تأويل	....	كَذَلكَ
....	أتمّ – يُتِمّ	....	حديث (ج. أحاديث)
....	أبوين	....	آل
....	أحَبّ	....	مِن قَبل
....	طرَح – يطرَح	....	ضَلال
....	وَجه	....	أرض
....	صالِح	....	قَوم
....	بَعض	....	ألقى – يُلقي
....	فاعِل	....	سيّارة
....	ناصِح	....	أمِن – يأمَن
....	لعِب – يلعَب	....	غَداً

قالَ إِنّي لَيَحْزُنُني أَن تَذهَبوا بِهِ وَأَخافُ أَن يَأكُلَهُ الذِّئبُ وَأَنتُم عَنهُ غافِلونَ {١٣} قالوا لَئِن أَكَلَهُ الذِّئبُ وَنَحنُ عُصبَةٌ إِنّا إِذًا لَّخاسِرونَ {١٤} فَلَمّا ذَهَبوا بِهِ وَأَجمَعوا أَن يَجعَلوهُ في غَيابَةِ الجُبِّ وَأَوحَينا إِلَيهِ لَتُنَبِّئَنَّهُم بِأَمرِهِم هَذا وَهُم لا يَشعُرونَ {١٥} وَجاؤوا أَباهُم عِشاءً يَبكونَ {١٦} قالوا يا أَبانا إِنّا ذَهَبنا نَستَبِقُ وَتَرَكنا يوسُفَ عِندَ مَتاعِنا فَأَكَلَهُ الذِّئبُ وَما أَنتَ بِمُؤمِنٍ لَّنا وَلَو كُنّا صادِقينَ {١٧} وَجاؤوا عَلى قَميصِهِ بِدَمٍ كَذِبٍ قالَ بَل سَوَّلَت لَكُم أَنفُسُكُم أَمرًا فَصَبرٌ جَميلٌ واللَّهُ المُستَعانُ عَلى ما تَصِفونَ {١٨} وَجاءت سَيّارَةٌ فَأَرسَلوا وارِدَهُم فَأَدلى دَلوَهُ قالَ يا بُشرى هَذا غُلامٌ وَأَسَرّوهُ بِضاعَةً واللَّهُ عَليمٌ بِما يَعمَلونَ {١٩} وَشَرَوهُ بِثَمَنٍ بَخسٍ دَراهِمَ مَعدودَةٍ وَكانوا فيهِ مِنَ الزّاهِدينَ {٢٠} وَقالَ الَّذي اشتَراهُ مِن مِصرَ لِامرَأَتِهِ أَكرِمي مَثواهُ عَسى أَن يَنفَعَنا أَو نَتَّخِذَهُ وَلَدًا وَكَذَلِكَ مَكَّنّا لِيوسُفَ في الأَرضِ وَلِنُعَلِّمَهُ مِن تَأويلِ الأَحاديثِ واللَّهُ غالِبٌ عَلى أَمرِهِ وَلَكِنَّ أَكثَرَ النّاسِ لا يَعلَمونَ {٢١} وَلَمّا بَلَغَ أَشُدَّهُ آتَيناهُ حُكمًا وَعِلمًا وَكَذَلِكَ نَجزي المُحسِنينَ {٢٢} وَراوَدَتهُ الَّتي هُوَ في بَيتِها عَن نَفسِهِ وَغَلَّقَتِ الأَبوابَ وَقالَت هَيتَ لَكَ قالَ مَعاذَ اللَّهِ إِنَّهُ رَبّي أَحسَنَ مَثوايَ إِنَّهُ لا يُفلِحُ الظّالِمونَ {٢٣}

■ New words

Nouns

wolf	ذِئْب
careless, heedless	غافِل
early part of the night, evening	عِشاءً
belongings, things	مَتاع
speaking the truth	صادِق
shirt	قَميص
blood	دَم
false	كَذِب
patience	صَبر
comely	جَميل
whose help can be sought	مُستَعان
water-drawer	وارِد
bucket, pail	دَلو
good news, good luck	بُشرى
boy, youth	غُلام
merchandise, treasure	بِضاعة
price	ثَمَن
low	بَخس
silver coins	دَراهِم
few, number of	معدود
one who attaches little value to	زاهِد
Egypt	مِصر
stay, reception	مَثوى
may be, perchance	عَسى
having full power, predominant	غالِب
wisdom	حُكم
doer of good	مُحسِن
door	باب (ج. أبواب)
evil-doer, wrong-doer	ظالِم

Verbs

to sadden	حَزَن – يحزُن
to inform	نبّأ – يُنبِّى
to know	شعَر – يشعُر
to race with one another	استَبَق – يستَبِق
to leave	تَرَك – يترُك
to make up a tale, beguile	سَوَّل
to describe	وصَف – يصِف
to send	أرسَل
to let down	أدلى
to hide	أسرَّ
to sell	شَرى
to buy, purchase	اشتَرى
make comfortable, make honorable	أكرَم – يُكرِم
to profit, prove useful	نفَع – ينفَع
to adopt	اتّخذ – يتّخِذ
to establish	مَكَّن
to reward	جَزى – يَجزي
to seek to seduce, to ask an evil	راوَد – يُراوِد
to close, bolt	غَلَّق
to be successful, prosper	أفلَح – يُفلِح

Particle

when	لَمّا

Expressions

to attain full manhood, reach his prime	بَلَغَ أَشُدَّه
come on	هَيتَ
I seek refuge in Allah	مَعاذ الله

■ Exercise 1: Nouns

For the following nouns, provide a full English translation, give the case for the nouns whose cells are not marked by an x, identify the root, stem, and the pattern, using فعل. Indicate how many patterns there are and what meaning/grammatical function is associated with each pattern.

Pattern	Stem	Root	Case	Translation	
					غافِلون
					لَخاسِرون
			X		بِمُؤْمِن
			X		جَميل
			X		مَعدودة
					الزاهِدين
			X		غالِب
					المُحسِنين
					الأبوابَ
					الظالِمون
					أَحَبُّ

■ Exercise 2: Verbs

Identify all the verbs in the following six verses, and for any ten of them:

a. give a full English translation,
b. indicate whether it is perfect or imperfect,

c.   for those verbs in the imperfect, indicate what mood they are in,

d.   identify the root, the stem, and the pattern, using فعل, and the form number.

١.   قَالَ إِنِّي لَيَحْزُنُنِي أَن تَذْهَبُوا بِهِ وَأَخَافُ أَن يَأْكُلَهُ الذِّئْبُ وَأَنتُمْ عَنهُ غافِلُون {١٣}

٢.   فَلَمَّا ذَهَبُوا بِهِ وَأَجْمَعُوا أَن يَجْعَلُوهُ فِي غَيَابَةِ الجُبِّ وَأَوْحَينا إِلَيْهِ لَتُنَبِّئَنَّهُم بِأَمرِهِم هَذَا وَهُم لاَ يَشْعُرُون {١٥}

٣.   وَجَاءَت سَيَّارَةٌ فَأَرسَلُوا وَارِدَهُم فَأَدْلَى دَلوَهُ قَالَ يَا بُشرَى هَذَا غُلاَمٌ وَأَسَرُّوهُ بِضَاعَةً وَاللَّهُ عَلِيمٌ بِمَا يَعمَلُون {١٩}

٤.   وَشَرَوْهُ بِثَمَنٍ بَخْسٍ دَرَاهِمَ مَعْدُودَةٍ وَكَانُوا فِيهِ مِنَ الزَّاهِدِين {٢٠}

٥.   وَقَالَ الَّذِي اشْتَرَاهُ مِن مِصرَ لِامرَأَتِهِ أَكرِمِي مَثوَاهُ عَسَى أَن يَنفَعَنَا أَو نَتَّخِذَهُ وَلَدًا وَكَذَلِكَ مَكَّنَّا لِيُوسُفَ فِي الأَرضِ ٦. وَلِنُعَلِّمَهُ مِن تَأوِيلِ الأَحَادِيثِ وَاللَّهُ غَالِبٌ عَلَى أَمرِهِ وَلَكِنَّ أَكثَرَ النَّاسِ لاَ يَعلَمُون {٢١}

٧.   وَرَاوَدَتهُ الَّتِي هُوَ فِي بَيتِهَا عَن نَفسِهِ وَغَلَّقَتِ الأَبوَابَ وَقَالَت هَيتَ لَكَ قَالَ مَعَاذَ اللَّهِ إِنَّهُ رَبِّي أَحسَنَ مَثوَايَ إِنَّهُ لاَ يُفلِحُ الظَّالِمُون {٢٣}

▮ Exercise 3: The verbs اشتراه and شروه

Compare the two verbs شروه and اشتراه and show how the difference in meaning is reflected by the change in verb form. Refer to the verb form table in the Grammar appendix.

▮ Exercise 4: Opposites

Copy each of the words in row ب under its opposite in row أ:

قبل	شَرى	صادِق	كلَّا	تذكَّر	أَضَلَّ	عذَّب	حيّ	هُدى	أ
ضَلال	غفر	هُدى	اشترى	ميت	بعد	كاذِب	بَلى	نسِي	ب

Words to remember

Write down the meanings of the following words from memory.

....	حَزَن – يحزُن		
....	غافِل	....	ذِئب
....	نبّأ – يُنبّى	....	جعَل – يجعَل
....	عِشاءً	....	شعَر – يشعُر
....	مَتاع	....	تَرَك – يترُك
....	قَميص	....	صادِق
....	كَذِب	....	دَم
....	جَميل	....	صَبر
....	بُشرى	....	أرسَل
....	أسرَّ	....	غُلام
....	شَرى	....	بِضاعة
....	دَراهِم	....	ثَمَن
....	اشتَرى	....	معدود
....	أكرَم – يُكرِم	....	مِصر
....	نفَع – ينفَع	....	عَسى
....	مَكّن	....	اتّخذ – يتّخِذ
....	لَمّا	....	غالِب
....	جَزى – يَجزي	....	حُكم
....	راوَد – يُراوِد	....	مُحسِن
....	باب (ج. أبواب)	....	غَلّق
....	أفلَح – يُفلِح	....	مَعاذ الله
		....	ظالِم

وَلَقَد هَمَّت بِهِ وَهَمَّ بِها لَولا أَن رَأى بُرهانَ رَبِّهِ كَذَلِكَ لِنَصرِفَ عَنهُ السّوءَ وَالفَحشاءَ إِنَّهُ مِن عِبادِنا المُخلَصينَ {٢٤} واستَبَقا البابَ وَقَدَّت قَميصَهُ مِن دُبُرٍ وَأَلفَيا سَيِّدَها لَدى البابِ قالَت ما جَزاءُ مَن أَرادَ بِأَهلِكَ سُوءًا إِلّا أَن يُسجَنَ أَو عَذابٌ أَليمٌ {٢٥} قالَ هِيَ راوَدَتني عَن نَفسي وَشَهِدَ شاهِدٌ مِن أَهلِها إِن كانَ قَميصُهُ قُدَّ مِن قُبُلٍ فَصَدَقَت وَهُوَ مِنَ الكاذِبينَ {٢٦} وَإِن كانَ قَميصُهُ قُدَّ مِن دُبُرٍ فَكَذَبَت وَهُوَ مِنَ الصّادِقينَ {٢٧} فَلَمّا رَأى قَميصَهُ قُدَّ مِن دُبُرٍ قالَ إِنَّهُ مِن كَيدِكُنَّ إِنَّ كَيدَكُنَّ عَظيمٌ {٢٨} يوسُفُ أَعرِض عَن هَذا واستَغفِري لِذَنبِكِ إِنَّكِ كُنتِ مِنَ الخاطِئينَ {٢٩} وَقالَ نِسوَةٌ في المَدينَةِ امرَأَةُ العَزيزِ تُراوِدُ فَتاها عَن نَفسِهِ قَد شَغَفَها حُبًّا إِنّا لَنَراها في ضَلالٍ مُبينٍ {٣٠} فَلَمّا سَمِعَت بِمَكرِهِنَّ أَرسَلَت إِلَيهِنَّ وَأَعتَدَت لَهُنَّ مُتَّكَأً وَآتَت كُلَّ واحِدَةٍ مِنهُنَّ سِكّينًا وَقالَتِ اخرُج عَلَيهِنَّ فَلَمّا رَأَينَهُ أَكبَرنَهُ وَقَطَّعنَ أَيدِيَهُنَّ وَقُلنَ حاشَ لِلَّهِ ما هَذا بَشَرًا إِن هَذا إِلّا مَلَكٌ كَريمٌ {٣١} قالَت فَذَلِكُنَّ الَّذي لُمتُنَّني فيهِ وَلَقَد راوَدتُّهُ عَن نَفسِهِ فَاستَعصَمَ وَلَئِن لَم يَفعَل ما آمُرُهُ لَيُسجَنَنَّ وَلَيَكونًا مِنَ الصّاغِرينَ {٣٢}

■ New words

....

Nouns

evidence, argument	بُرهان
evil	سوء
unlawful sexual intercourse, lewdness	فَحشاء
slaves	عِباد
chosen	مُخلَص
back, behind	دُبُر
lord and master, husband	سَيِّد
recompense, reward	جَزاء
front, before	قُبُل
liar	كاذِب
sinful, faulty	خاطِئ
women	نِسوَة
ruler	عَزيز
slave-boy	فَتى
love	حُبّ
accusation, sly talk	مَكر
banquet, a cushioned couch	مُتَّكَأ
knife	سِكّين
hands	أَيدي
man, human being	بَشَر
one who is disgraced, brought low	صاغِر

Verbs

to desire	هَمَّ
to turn away, ward off	صرَف – يصرِف
to tear	قَدَّ
to find, meet	ألفى
to put in prison	سَجَن – يسجن
to bear witness	شَهِد
to turn away	أعرَض – يُعرِض
to ask forgiveness	استغفَر – يستَغفِر
to cause to love violently	شَغَف
to prepare	أعتَد
to give	أتى
to cut	قَطَّع
to blame	لام – يلوم
to refuse, to restrain onself	استعصَم
to order	أمَر – يأمُر

Particles

if not, had it not been	لَولا
at	لَدى
this is	ذلِكُنّ (ذلِك)[1]
if	لَئِن (لإَن)

Expression

God forbid	حاشَ الله

---

[1] The نّ of ذلكُنّ is added for emphasis, a common tool in the language of the Qur'ān in contrast with modern Arabic usage.

Exercise 1: Nouns

a. For the following nouns, provide a full English translation, give the case for
the nouns whose cells are not marked by an x, identify the root, the stem, and the
pattern, using فعل. For case assignments, you might need to refer to the text
of the *sūra* to see what the function of the word is in the sentence.

Pattern	Stem	Root	Case	Translation	
					قميصه (٢٥)
					شاهد (٢٦)
					أهلها (٢٦)
					الكاذبين (٢٦)
			X		لذنبك (٢٩)
			X		نسوة (٣٠)
					ضلال (٣٠)
			X		بشراً (٣١)
					الصاغرين (٣٢)

b. What are the source verbs of the participles المُحسِنين, الظالِمون, المُخلِصين, الكاذِبين
and الصادِقين؟

Exercise 2: Verbs

Identify all the verbs in the following four verses, and for any ten of them:

a. give a full English translation,

b. identify the root, the stem, and the form using فعل skeleton, and the form number.

١. وَاسْتَبَقَا البَابَ وَقَدَّت قَمِيصَهُ مِن دُبُرٍ وَأَلْفَيَا سَيِّدَهَا لَدَى البَابِ قَالَت مَا جَزَاءُ مَن
أَرَادَ بِأَهلِكَ سُوَءًا إِلاَّ أَن يُسجَنَ أَو عَذَابٌ أَلِيم {٢٥}

٢. قَالَ هِيَ رَاوَدَتنِي عَن نَفسِي وَشَهِدَ شَاهِدٌ مِن أَهلِها إِن كَانَ قَمِيصُهُ قُدَّ مِن قُبُلِ
فَصَدَقَت وَهُوَ مِنَ الكَاذِبِينَ {٢٦}

٣. فَلَمَّا سَمِعَت بِمَكرِهِنَّ أَرسَلَت إِلَيهِنَّ وَأَعتَدَت لَهُنَّ مُتَّكَأً وَآتَت كُلَّ وَاحِدَةٍ مِنهُنَّ
سِكِّينًا وَقَالَتِ اخرُج عَلَيهِنَّ فَلَمَّا رَأَينَهُ

٤. أَكْبَرْنَهُ وَقَطَّعْنَ أَيْدِيَهُنَّ وَقُلْنَ حَاشَ لِلّٰهِ مَا هٰذَا بَشَرًا إِنْ هٰذَا إِلاَّ مَلَكٌ كَرِيمٌ {٣١}

٥. قَالَتْ فَذٰلِكُنَّ الَّذِي لُمْتُنَّنِي فِيهِ وَلَقَدْ رَاوَدْتُهُ عَنْ نَفْسِهِ فَاسْتَعْصَمَ وَلَئِنْ لَمْ يَفْعَلْ مَا
آمُرُهُ لَيُسْجَنَنَّ وَلَيَكُونًا مِنَ الصَّاغِرِينَ {٣٢}

■ Exercise 3: Roots and families

The following words are based on 19 roots. Group together the words that are based
on the same root, identify the root, and give its general meaning in English.

كَرِيم، المُحْسِنِين، الصَّادِقِين، العِظَام، الظَّالِمُون، غَفَر، أَرْسَلت، تَصَرَّف، بُشْرى، قَالُوا، لِلسَّائِلِين،
اشْتَراه، أَكْرِمي، حَكِيم، أَتَمَّها، فيكِيدوا، الغْلِفْلِين، قَائِل، نَقُصُّ، كِيدَكُنَّ، بمؤْمِن، فَصَرَف، شَهِد،
أَرْسِله، يسْألُكم، القصص، مُظْلِمون، مَغْفِرة، غافِلون، كِيدَهُنَّ، ويُتِمَّ، تقصص، كِيداً، حُكْماً،
قال، تَأْمَنّا، فَأَرْسِلوا، بشَراً، وشَرَوه، أَحْسَن، لِنَصْرِف، شاهِد، فَصَدَّقَت، عظِيم، واسْتَغْفِري

■ Words to remember

Write down the meanings of the following words from memory.

....	صَرَف – يَصْرِف	....	لَوْلا
....	فَحْشاء	....	سوء
....	مُخْلَص	....	عِباد
....	سَيِّد	....	دُبُر
....	جَزاء	....	لَدى
....	شَهِد	....	سَجَن – يسْجِن
....	كاذِب	....	قُبُل
....	استَغْفَر – يسْتَغْفِر	....	أعْرَض – يُعرِض
....	عَزِيز	....	خاطِئ
....	حُبّ	....	فَتى
....	أتى	....	مَكر
....	قَطَّع	....	سِكِّين
....	بَشَر	....	أيْدي
....	لام – يلوم	....	ذٰلِكُنَّ (ذٰلِك)
....	سِجن	....	أمَر – يأمُر

	الدرس رقم ٣٣	Lesson Thirty Three
	١٢. سورة يوسف ٤	

قالَ رَبِّ السِّجنُ أَحَبُّ إِلَيَّ مِمّا يَدعونَني إِلَيهِ وَإِلّا تَصرِف عَنّي كَيدَهُنَّ أَصبُ
إِلَيهِنَّ وَأَكُن مِنَ الجاهِلين {٣٣} فَاستَجابَ لَهُ رَبُّهُ فَصَرَفَ عَنهُ كَيدَهُنَّ إِنَّهُ هُوَ
السَّميعُ العَليم {٣٤} ثُمَّ بَدا لَهُم مِن بَعدِ ما رَأَوُا الآياتِ لَيَسجُنُنَّهُ حَتّى حين
{٣٥} وَدَخَلَ مَعَهُ السِّجنَ فَتَيانَ قالَ أَحَدُهُما إِنّي أَراني أَعصِرُ خَمرًا وَقالَ
الآخَرُ إِنّي أَراني أَحمِلُ فَوقَ رَأسي خُبزًا تَأكُلُ الطَّيرُ مِنهُ نَبِّئنا بِتَأويلِهِ إِنّا نَراكَ
مِنَ المُحسِنين {٣٦} قالَ لا يَأتيكُما طَعامٌ تُرزَقانِهِ إِلّا نَبَّأتُكُما بِتَأويلِهِ قَبلَ أَن
يَأتيكُما ذَلِكُما مِمّا عَلَّمَني رَبّي إِنّي تَرَكتُ مِلَّةَ قَومٍ لا يُؤمِنونَ بِاللَّهِ وَهُم بِالآخِرَةِ
هُم كافِرون {٣٧} واتَّبَعتُ مِلَّةَ آبائي إِبراهيمَ وَإِسحَقَ وَيَعقوبَ ما كانَ لَنا أَن
نُشرِكَ بِاللَّهِ مِن شَيءٍ ذَلِكَ مِن فَضلِ اللَّهِ عَلَينا وَعَلى النّاسِ وَلَكِنَّ أَكثَرَ النّاسِ
لا يَشكُرون {٣٨} يا صاحِبَيِ السِّجنِ أَأَربابٌ مُتَفَرِّقونَ خَيرٌ أَمِ اللَّهُ الواحِدُ القَهّار
{٣٩} ما تَعبُدونَ مِن دونِهِ إِلّا أَسماءً سَمَّيتُموها أَنتُم وَآباؤُكُم مّا أَنزَلَ اللَّهُ بِها
مِن سُلطانٍ إِنِ الحُكمُ إِلّا لِلَّهِ أَمَرَ أَلّا تَعبُدوا إِلّا إِيّاهُ ذَلِكَ الدّينُ القَيِّمُ وَلَكِنَّ
أَكثَرَ النّاسِ لا يَعلَمون {٤٠}

■ New words

Nouns

prison	سِجن
ignorant, foolish	جاهِل
All-Hearer	سَميع
All-Knower	عَليم
wine	خَمر
bread	خُبز
doer of good	مُحسِن
religion	مِلَّة
fathers	آباء
lords, gods	أرباب
different, diverse	مُتَفَرِّق
Irresistible, Almighty	قَهّار
beside	دون
authority, sanction	سُلطان
straight, right	قَيِّم

Verbs

to invite, urge	دعا – يدعو
turn away, fend off	صرَف – يصرِف
to feel inclined	صَبا – يصبو
to answer (an invocation), to hear (a prayer)	استَجاب
to press	عصَر – يعصُر
to carry	حمَل – يحمِل
to inform, announce	نبّأ – يُنَبِّئ

to give	رزَق – يرزِق
to follow	اتَّبَع
to attribute	أشرَك – يُشرِك
to name	سَمّى

Particles

that is what	ذلِكُما (ذلك + ما)

■ Grammar: Final look at person markers and possessive/object pronouns

Person markers and possessive pronouns corresponding to *he, they* (*m.*), *you* (*m. sg.*), and *I* are much more common in the Qur'ān than persons referring to *you* (*f. pl.*) and *you* (*dual*). However, a few instances of the less common types are found. The following tables include all the person markers and possessive/object pronouns found in the *sūras* introduced in this book:

Person markers

Imperfect	Perfect		
يعبُد	عبد	he	هو
تعبُد	عبدَت	she	هي
تعبُدان	–	they (m. dual)	هُما
يعبدون	عبدوا	they (m.)	هُم
يعبُدن	عبدْنَ	they (f.)	هُنّ
تعبُد	عبدتَ	you (m. sg.)	انتَ
تعبُدان	عبدتُما	you (dual)	انتُما
تعبُدون	عبدتُم	you (m. pl.)	انتُم
–	عبدتُنّ	you (f. pl.)	انتُنّ
أعبد	عبدتُ	I	أنا
نعبُد	عبدنا	we	نحنُ

Possessive/object pronouns

As is the case with person markers, certain possessive/object pronouns are more widespread than others. There are many more instances of pronouns corresponding to my/me, their/them (m.), than pronouns corresponding to dual and feminine plural persons.

The following table includes all the possessive/object pronouns found in the book.

truly, that	on	he sent	wealth		
إنّه	عليه	أرسله	مالُه	his/him/he	هو – ـه
إنّها	عليها	أرسلها	مالها	her/she	هي – ها
إنّهما	عليهما	أرسلهما	مالهما	them/they (m. dual)	هُما – هُما
إنّهم	عليهم	أرسلهم	مالهم	them/they (m.)	هم – هُم
إنّهنّ	عليهنّ	أرسلهنّ	مالهنّ	them/they (f.)	هنّ
إنّكَ	عليكَ	أرسلكَ	مالكَ	you (m. sg.)	انتَ – كَ
إنّكِ	عليكِ	أرسلكِ	مالكِ	you (f. sg.)	انتِ – كِ
إنّكما	عليكما	أرسلكما	مالكما	you (dual)	انتُما – كُما
إنّكم	عليكم	أرسلكم	مالكم	you (m. pl.)	انتُم – كُم
إنّكنّ	عليكنّ	أرسلكنّ	مالكنّ	you (f. pl.)	انتُنّ – نّ
إنّي or إنّني	عليّ	أرسلني	مالي	I	أنا – ي/ني
إنّا or إنّنا	علينا	أرسلنا	مالنا	we	نحن – نا

▨ Exercise 1: Nouns

For each of the following nouns, provide a full English translation, identify the root, the stem, and the pattern, using فعل. Then, with reference to the section on Noun patterns in the Grammar appendix, identify the meaning/grammatical function that is associated with each pattern in general. Some cells are filled in to help you.

Meaning/grammatical function	Pattern	Stem	Root	Translation	
					الجاهِلين
					السَّميع
adjective					العَليم
VN of Form II					بتأويلِه
					المُحسِنين
					كافِرون
					مُتَفَرِّقون
AP of Form I					الواحِد
					القَهّار
	أفعال				أسماء
plural	أفعال				وآباؤُكم

▪ Exercise 2: Verbs

Find all the verbs in the following four verses, and, for any ten of them, give a full English translation, and identify the root, the stem, and the form, using فعل, and the form number.

١. فَاسْتَجَابَ لَهُ رَبُّهُ فَصَرَفَ عَنْهُ كَيْدَهُنَّ إِنَّهُ هُوَ السَّميعُ العَليمُ {٣٤}

٢. قَالَ لَا يَأْتِيكُمَا طَعَامٌ تُرْزَقَانِهِ إِلَّا نَبَّأْتُكُمَا بِتَأْوِيلِهِ قَبْلَ أَن يَأْتِيَكُمَا ذَلِكُمَا مِمَّا عَلَّمَنِي رَبِّي إِنِّي تَرَكْتُ مِلَّةَ قَوْمٍ لَّا يُؤْمِنُونَ بِاللَّهِ وَهُم بِالآخِرَةِ هُمْ كَافِرُونَ {٣٧}

٣. مَا تَعْبُدُونَ مِن دُونِهِ إِلَّا أَسْمَاء سَمَّيْتُمُوهَا أَنتُمْ وَآبَاؤُكُم مَّا أَنزَلَ اللَّهُ بِهَا مِن سُلْطَانٍ إِنِ الْحُكْمُ إِلَّا لِلَّهِ أَمَرَ أَلَّا تَعْبُدُوا إِلَّا إِيَّاهُ ذَلِكَ الدِّينُ القَيِّمُ وَلَكِنَّ أَكْثَرَالنَّاسِ لَا يَعْلَمُونَ {٤٠}

٤. وَقَالَ لِلَّذِي ظَنَّ أَنَّهُ نَاجٍ مِنْهُمَا اذْكُرْنِي عِندَ رَبِّكَ فَأَنسَاهُ الشَّيْطَانُ ذِكْرَ رَبِّهِ فَلَبِثَ فِي السِّجْنِ بِضْعَ سِنِينَ {٤٢}

■ Words to remember

Write down the meanings of the following words from memory.

....	جاهِل	....	صرَف – يصرِف
....	سَميع	....	استجاب
....	حمَل – يحمِل	....	خَمر
....	نبّأ – يُنَبِّئ	....	خُبز
....	رزَق – يرزِق	....	مُحسِن
....	اتَّبع	....	ذلِكُما (ذلك)
....	أشرَك – يُشرِك	....	آباء
....	مُتَفَرِّق	....	أرباب
....	دون	....	قَهّار
....	سُلطان	....	سَمّى

يا صاحِبَيِ السِّجنِ أَمّا أَحَدُكُما فَيَسقي رَبَّهُ خَمرًا وَأَمّا الآخَرُ فَيُصلَبُ فَتَأكُلُ الطَّيرُ مِن رَأسِهِ قُضِيَ الأَمرُ الَّذي فيهِ تَستَفتِيانِ {٤١} وَقالَ لِلَّذي ظَنَّ أَنَّهُ ناجٍ مِنهُما اذكُرني عِندَ رَبِّكَ فَأَنساهُ الشَّيطانُ ذِكرَ رَبِّهِ فَلَبِثَ في السِّجنِ بِضعَ سِنينَ {٤٢} وَقالَ المَلِكُ إِنّي أَرى سَبعَ بَقَراتٍ سِمانٍ يَأكُلُهُنَّ سَبعٌ عِجافٌ وَسَبعَ سُنبُلاتٍ خُضرٍ وَأُخَرَ يابِساتٍ يا أَيُّها المَلَأُ أَفتوني في رُؤيايَ إِن كُنتُم لِلرُّؤيا تَعبُرونَ {٤٣} قالوا أَضغاثُ أَحلامٍ وَما نَحنُ بِتَأويلِ الأَحلامِ بِعالِمينَ {٤٤} وَقالَ الَّذي نَجا مِنهُما وَادَّكَرَ بَعدَ أُمّةٍ أَنا أُنَبِّئُكُم بِتَأويلِهِ فَأَرسِلونِ {٤٥} يوسُفُ أَيُّها الصِّدّيقُ أَفتِنا في سَبعِ بَقَراتٍ سِمانٍ يَأكُلُهُنَّ سَبعٌ عِجافٌ وَسَبعِ سُنبُلاتٍ خُضرٍ وَأُخَرَ يابِساتٍ لَعَلّي أَرجِعُ إِلى النّاسِ لَعَلَّهُم يَعلَمونَ {٤٦} قالَ تَزرَعونَ سَبعَ سِنينَ دَأَبًا فَما حَصَدتُّم فَذَروهُ في سُنبُلِهِ إِلّا قَليلًا مِّمّا تَأكُلونَ {٤٧} ثُمَّ يَأتي مِن بَعدِ ذَلِكَ سَبعٌ شِدادٌ يَأكُلنَ ما قَدَّمتُم لَهُنَّ إِلّا قَليلًا مِّمّا تُحصِنونَ {٤٨} ثُمَّ يَأتي مِن بَعدِ ذَلِكَ عامٌ فيهِ يُغاثُ النّاسُ وَفيهِ يَعصِرونَ {٤٩} وَقالَ المَلِكُ ائتوني بِهِ فَلَمّا جاءَهُ الرَّسولُ قالَ ارجِع إِلى رَبِّكَ فَاسأَلهُ ما بالُ النِّسوَةِ اللّاتي قَطَّعنَ أَيدِيَهُنَّ إِنَّ رَبّي بِكَيدِهِنَّ عَليمٌ {٥٠}

■ New words

Nouns

saved, released	ناجٍ (ناجي)
seven	سبع
cow	بَقَرة
fat	سِمان
lean	عِجاف
ear of corn	سُنبُلة
green	خُضر
other	أُخَر
dry	يابِس
notables	مَلأ
dream, vision	رُؤيا
false, jumbled	أضغاث
dreams	أحلام
man of truth, truthful	صِدّيق
as usual	دَأَب
hard	شِداد

Verbs

to pour out	سَقى – يَسقي
to crucify	صلَب – يصلُب
to judge	قَضى – يقضي
to inquire	استَفتى – يستفتي
to stay	لَبَث
to explain, expound	فَتى – يَفتي
to interpret	عبَر – يعبُر

to be released	نَجا
to remember	ادَّكر
to send	أرسَل – يُرسِل
to sow	زرَع – يزرَع
to leave	وذر – يذر
to guard, store	أحصَن – يُحصِن
to have abundant rain or plentiful crops	أغاث – يُغيث
to bring	أتى بـ

Expression

at length, after a while	بَعد أُمّة

▪ Grammar: The construct (الإضافة)

The phrase صاحِبَي السِّجن in verses 39 and 41 is based on the two words صاحبين (dual of صاحب and السجن). When two nouns are in a relationship like these two, they form a grammatical construction referred to in English as the construct (Arabic إضافة). The English equivalent of the construct generally consists of two nouns joined by the preposition "of" or "possessive s", as in: *the cover of the book* or *the book's cover*.

Some of the examples of the construct that you have seen so far are the following:

(The) Lord of the Universe	ربّ العالمين
The Day of Judgement	يوم الدين
people's breasts	صدور الناس
the weight of an atom	مثقال ذرّةٍ

One important features of the construct is that if its first term ends in the plural suffix ين/ون or the dual suffix ين, then the ن of the suffix is dropped. Hence, صاحبي السجن instead of صاحبين السجن. (More on the construct in the Grammar appendix.)

■ Exercise 1: Nouns

For the following nouns, provide a full English translation, identify the root, the stem, and the pattern, using فعل.

Pattern	Stem	Root	Translation	
فاعَل	أَخَر	أ.خ.ر		الآخَر
				المَلِك
	يابِس			يابِسات
	بَقَرة			بَقَرات
				أضغاث
				أحلام
	عالِم			بعالِمين
				سِمان
				قَليلاً
فِعال				شِداد
فَعل		ع.و.م		عام
		ن.و.س		الناس
				رسول
عَليم				عَليم

■ Exercise 2: Verbs

Final all the verbs in the following three verses, and, for eight of them, give a full English translation, and identify the root, the stem and the form, using فعل, and the form number.

١. وَقَالَ الَّذِي نَجَا مِنْهُمَا وَادَّكَرَ بَعْدَ أُمَّةٍ أَنَا أُنَبِّئُكُم بِتَأْوِيلِهِ فَأَرْسِلُونِ {٤٥}

٢. قَالَ تَزْرَعُونَ سَبْعَ سِنِينَ دَأَبًا فَمَا حَصَدتُّمْ فَذَرُوهُ فِي سُنبُلِهِ إِلاَّ قَلِيلاً مِّمَّا تَأْكُلُونَ {٤٧}

٣. ثُمَّ يَأْتِي مِن بَعْدِ ذَلِكَ سَبْعٌ شِدَادٌ يَأْكُلْنَ مَا قَدَّمْتُمْ لَهُنَّ إِلاَّ قَلِيلاً مِّمَّا تُحْصِنُونَ {٤٨}

■ Words to remember

Write down the meanings of the following words from memory.

ناجٍ (ناجي)	....	سَقى – يَسقي	....
سِجن	....	لَبَث	....
بَقَرة	....	سبع	....
سُنبُلة	....	سِمان	....
أُخَر	....	خُضر	....
فَتى – يَفتي	....	يابِس	....
عبَر – يعبُر	....	رُؤيا	....
ادَّكر	....	نَجا	....
صِدّيق	....	أرسَل – يُرسِل	....
شِداد	....	زرَع – يزرَع	....
		أتى بـ	....

الدرس رقم ٣٥	Lesson Thirty Five
١٢. سورة يوسف ٦	

قَالَ مَا خَطْبُكُنَّ إِذْ رَاوَدتُّنَّ يُوسُفَ عَن نَّفْسِهِ قُلْنَ حَاشَ لِلَّهِ مَا عَلِمْنَا عَلَيْهِ مِن سُوءٍ قَالَتِ امْرَأَةُ الْعَزِيزِ الآنَ حَصْحَصَ الْحَقُّ أَنَا رَاوَدتُّهُ عَن نَّفْسِهِ وَإِنَّهُ لَمِنَ الصَّادِقِينَ {٥١} ذَلِكَ لِيَعْلَمَ أَنِّي لَمْ أَخُنْهُ بِالْغَيْبِ وَأَنَّ اللَّهَ لاَ يَهْدِي كَيْدَ الْخَائِنِينَ {٥٢} وَمَا أُبَرِّئُ نَفْسِي إِنَّ النَّفْسَ لأَمَّارَةٌ بِالسُّوءِ إِلاَّ مَا رَحِمَ رَبِّيَ إِنَّ رَبِّي غَفُورٌ رَّحِيمٌ {٥٣} وَقَالَ الْمَلِكُ ائْتُونِي بِهِ أَسْتَخْلِصْهُ لِنَفْسِي فَلَمَّا كَلَّمَهُ قَالَ إِنَّكَ الْيَوْمَ لَدَيْنَا مِكِينٌ أَمِينٌ {٥٤} قَالَ اجْعَلْنِي عَلَى خَزَائِنِ الأَرْضِ إِنِّي حَفِيظٌ عَلِيمٌ {٥٥} وَكَذَلِكَ مَكَّنَّا لِيُوسُفَ فِي الأَرْضِ يَتَبَوَّأُ مِنْهَا حَيْثُ يَشَاءُ نُصِيبُ بِرَحْمَتِنَا مَن نَّشَاء وَلاَ نُضِيعُ أَجْرَ الْمُحْسِنِينَ {٥٦} وَلَأَجْرُ الآخِرَةِ خَيْرٌ لِّلَّذِينَ آمَنُوا وَكَانُوا يَتَّقُونَ {٥٧} وَجَاء إِخْوَةُ يُوسُفَ فَدَخَلُوا عَلَيْهِ فَعَرَفَهُمْ وَهُمْ لَهُ مُنكِرُونَ {٥٨} وَلَمَّا جَهَّزَهُم بِجَهَازِهِمْ قَالَ ائْتُونِي بِأَخٍ لَّكُم مِّنْ أَبِيكُمْ أَلاَ تَرَوْنَ أَنِّي أُوفِي الْكَيْلَ وَأَنَا خَيْرُ الْمُنزِلِينَ {٥٩} فَإِن لَّمْ تَأْتُونِي بِهِ فَلاَ كَيْلَ لَكُمْ عِندِي وَلاَ تَقْرَبُونِ {٦٠} قَالُوا سَنُرَاوِدُ عَنْهُ أَبَاهُ وَإِنَّا لَفَاعِلُونَ {٦١} وَقَالَ لِفِتْيَانِهِ اجْعَلُوا بِضَاعَتَهُمْ فِي رِحَالِهِمْ لَعَلَّهُمْ يَعْرِفُونَهَا إِذَا انقَلَبُوا إِلَى أَهْلِهِمْ لَعَلَّهُمْ يَرْجِعُونَ {٦٢}

■ New words

Nouns

affair, happening	خَطب
absence, secret	غَيب
betrayer	خائِن
having the inclination	أَمّارة
high in rank, established	مَكين
store-houses	خَزائِن
keeper, guardian	حَفيظ
mercy	رحمة
reward	أجر
not recognizing, not knowing	مُنكِر
to furnish, provide	جَهَّز
provisions	جهاز
measure	كَيل
host	مُنزِل
bags, saddlebags	رِحال

Verbs

to manifest itself	حَصحَص
to betray	خان – يخون
to guide	هدى – يَهدي
to free, exculpate	بَرّأ – يُبَرِّئ
to bestow mercy, have mercy	رَحِم
to attach	استَخلَص – يَستَخلِص
to take possession, be the owner	تَبَوّأ – يتَبَوّأ

to bestow, reach	أصاب – يُصيب
to will	شاء – يشاء
to make lost, lose	أضاع – يُضيع
to fear Allah and keep one's duty to Him	اتّقى – يتّقي
to give in full (measure), fill up	أوفى – يوفي
to come near, draw near	قرِب – يقرَب
to go back	انقلَب
to deny	منَع – يمنَع

■ Exercise 1: Nouns

For each of the following nouns, provide a full English translation, identify the root, the stem, and the pattern, using فعل. Then, with reference to the section on Noun patterns in the Grammar appendix, identify the meaning/grammatical function that is associated with each pattern in general. Some cells are filled in to help you. Ignore the cells with an x.

Meaning/grammatical function	Pattern	Stem	Root	Translation	
x					نفسه
					العزيز
x			ح.ق.ق		الحقّ
					الصادِقين
x					بالغيب
					الخائِنين
					لأَمّارة
					رحيم
x					اليوم
			أ.ر.ض		الأرض
x					غَفور

Meaning/grammatical function	Pattern	Stem	Root	Translation	
			أ.م.ن		أَمِين
					حَفِيظ
					عَلِيم
					بِرحمتنا
X					أجر
					المُحسِنِين
	فاعِل	آخِر			الآخِرة
					مُنكِرون
X					بِجهازهم
X					الكَيل
					المُنزَلِين
					لَفاعِلون
X					بِضاعَتهم
X					أهلهم

▉ Exercise 2: Verbs

a. Find all the verbs in the following five verses, and, for any ten of them, give a full English translation, and identify the root, the stem, and the form, using فعل, and the form number.

b. Find an example each of the declarative, subjunctive, jussive, and imperative moods.

١. ذَلِكَ لِيَعلَمَ أَنِّي لَم أَخُنهُ بِالغَيبِ وَأَنَّ اللّهَ لاَ يَهدِي كَيدَ الخَائِنِين {٥٢}

٢. وَقَالَ المَلِكُ ائتُونِي بِهِ أَستَخلِصهُ لِنَفسِي فَلَمَّا كَلَّمَهُ قَالَ إِنَّكَ اليَومَ لَدَينَا مِكِينٌ أَمِين {٥٤}

٣. وَكَذَلِكَ مَكَّنَّا لِيُوسُفَ فِي الأَرضِ يَتَبَوَّأُ مِنهَا حَيثُ يَشَاء نُصِيبُ بِرَحمَتِنَا مَن نَشَاء وَلاَ نُضِيعُ أَجرَ المُحسِنِين {٥٦}

٤. وَلَمَّا جَهَّزَهُم بِجَهَازِهِم قَالَ ائْتُونِي بِأَخٍ لَّكُم مِّن أَبِيكُمْ أَلَا تَرَوْنَ أَنِّي أُوفِي الْكَيْلَ وَأَنَا خَيْرُ الْمُنزِلِينَ {٥٩}

٥. وَقَالَ لِفِتْيَانِهِ اجْعَلُوا بِضَاعَتَهُمْ فِي رِحَالِهِمْ لَعَلَّهُمْ يَعْرِفُونَهَا إِذَا انقَلَبُوا إِلَى أَهْلِهِمْ لَعَلَّهُمْ يَرْجِعُونَ {٦٢}

■ Words to remember

The following list includes most of the new words in this part of سورة يوسف. Write down their meanings in English from memory.

غَيب	....	خان - يخون	....
خائِن	....	هدى - يَهدي	....
أمّارة	....	بَرّأ - يُبَرِّئ	....
مَكين	....	رَحِم	....
حَفيظ	....	خَزائِن	....
رحمة	....	أصاب - يُصيب	....
أضاع - يُضيع	....	شاء - يشاء	....
اتّقى - يتّقي	....	أجر	....
جهاز	....	جَهَّز	....
قرب - يقرَب	....	كَيل	....
انقَلَب	....	رِحال	....

الدرس رقم ٣٦

١٢. سورة يوسف ٧

Lesson Thirty Six

فَلَمَّا رَجَعُوا إِلَى أَبِيهِمْ قَالُوا يَا أَبَانَا مُنِعَ مِنَّا الكَيْلُ فَأَرْسِلْ مَعَنَا أَخَانَا نَكْتَلْ وَإِنَّا لَهُ لَحَافِظُونَ {٦٣} قَالَ هَلْ آمَنُكُمْ عَلَيْهِ إِلَّا كَمَا أَمِنْتُكُمْ عَلَى أَخِيهِ مِنْ قَبْلُ فَاللَّهُ خَيْرٌ حَافِظًا وَهُوَ أَرْحَمُ الرَّاحِمِينَ {٦٤} وَلَمَّا فَتَحُوا مَتَاعَهُمْ وَجَدُوا بِضَاعَتَهُمْ رُدَّتْ إِلَيْهِمْ قَالُوا يَا أَبَانَا مَا نَبْغِي هَذِهِ بِضَاعَتُنَا رُدَّتْ إِلَيْنَا وَنَمِيرُ أَهْلَنَا وَنَحْفَظُ أَخَانَا وَنَزْدَادُ كَيْلَ بَعِيرٍ ذَلِكَ كَيْلٌ يَسِيرٌ {٦٥} قَالَ لَنْ أُرْسِلَهُ مَعَكُمْ حَتَّى تُؤْتُونِ مَوْثِقًا مِنَ اللَّهِ لَتَأْتُنَّنِي بِهِ إِلَّا أَنْ يُحَاطَ بِكُمْ فَلَمَّا آتَوْهُ مَوْثِقَهُمْ قَالَ اللَّهُ عَلَى مَا نَقُولُ وَكِيلٌ {٦٦} وَقَالَ يَا بَنِيَّ لَا تَدْخُلُوا مِنْ بَابٍ وَاحِدٍ وَادْخُلُوا مِنْ أَبْوَابٍ مُتَفَرِّقَةٍ وَمَا أُغْنِي عَنْكُمْ مِنَ اللَّهِ مِنْ شَيْءٍ إِنِ الحُكْمُ إِلَّا لِلَّهِ عَلَيْهِ تَوَكَّلْتُ وَعَلَيْهِ فَلْيَتَوَكَّلِ المُتَوَكِّلُونَ {٦٧} وَلَمَّا دَخَلُوا مِنْ حَيْثُ أَمَرَهُمْ أَبُوهُمْ مَا كَانَ يُغْنِي عَنْهُمْ مِنَ اللَّهِ مِنْ شَيْءٍ إِلَّا حَاجَةً فِي نَفْسِ يَعْقُوبَ قَضَاهَا وَإِنَّهُ لَذُو عِلْمٍ لِمَا عَلَّمْنَاهُ وَلَكِنَّ أَكْثَرَ النَّاسِ لَا يَعْلَمُونَ {٦٨} وَلَمَّا دَخَلُوا عَلَى يُوسُفَ آوَى إِلَيْهِ أَخَاهُ قَالَ إِنِّي أَنَا أَخُوكَ فَلَا تَبْتَئِسْ بِمَا كَانُوا يَعْمَلُونَ {٦٩} فَلَمَّا جَهَّزَهُمْ بِجَهَازِهِمْ جَعَلَ السِّقَايَةَ فِي رَحْلِ أَخِيهِ ثُمَّ أَذَّنَ مُؤَذِّنٌ أَيَّتُهَا العِيرُ إِنَّكُمْ لَسَارِقُونَ {٧٠}

■ New words

Nouns

measure, load	كَيل
camel	بَعير
easy, light	يسير
solemn oath, undertaking	موثِق
witness, warden	وكيل
different	مُتَفَرِّق
that who trusts, trusting	مُتَوَكِّل
need	حاجة
bowl, drinking-cup	سِقاية
crier	مُؤَذِّن
caravan, camel riders	عير
thief	سارِق

Verbs

to desire, ask	بَغى – يَبغي
to get food, provisions	مار – يمير
to add more, have extra	ازداد – يَزداد
to surround	أحاط – يُحيط
to put one's trust	تَوَكَّل – يتوكَّل
to take to oneself	أَوى
to grieve, sorrow	ابتأس – يبتئِس
to cry	أذَّن

■ Exercise 1: Nouns

For each of the following nouns, provide a full English translation, identify the root, the stem, and the pattern, using فعل. Then, with reference to the section on Noun patterns in the Grammar appendix, identify the meaning/grammatical function that is associated with each pattern in general. Some cells are filled in to help you. Ignore the cells with an x.

Meaning/ grammatical function	Pattern	Stem	Root	Translation	
					لَحافِظون
					حافِظاً
					أرحَم
					الراحِمين
			ي.س.ر		يَسير
X					مَوثِقاً
					وكيل
					مُتَفَرِّقة
			و.ك.ل		المُتَوَكِّلون
X					بجهازهم
X					السِقاية
					مُؤَذِّن
					لَسارِقون

■ Exercise 2: Verbs

a. Find all the verbs in the following four verses, and, for any ten of them, give a full English translation, and identify the root, the stem, and the form, using فعل, and the form number.

b. Find an example each of the declarative, subjunctive, jussive, and imperative moods.

١. فَلَمَّا رَجِعُوا إِلَى أَبِيهِم قَالُوا يَا أَبَانَا مُنِعَ مِنَّا الكَيلُ فَأَرسِل مَعَنَا أَخَانَا نَكتَل وَإِنَّا لَهُ لَحَافِظُونَ {٣٦}

٢. وَقَالَ يَا بَنِيَّ لَا تَدخُلُوا مِن بَابٍ وَاحِدٍ وَادخُلُوا مِن أَبوَابٍ مُتَفَرِّقَةٍ وَمَا أُغنِي عَنكُم مِنَ اللّهِ مِن شَيءٍ إِنِ الحُكمُ إِلَّا لِلّهِ عَلَيهِ تَوَكَّلتُ وَعَلَيهِ فَليَتَوَكَّلِ المُتَوَكِّلُونَ {٦٧}

٣. وَلَمَّا دَخَلُوا مِن حَيثُ أَمَرَهُم أَبُوهُم مَا كَانَ يُغنِي عَنهُم مِنَ اللّهِ مِن شَيءٍ إِلَّا حَاجَةً فِي نَفسِ يَعقُوبَ قَضَاهَا وَإِنَّهُ لَذُو عِلمٍ لِمَا عَلَّمنَاهُ وَلَكِنَّ أَكثَرَ النَّاسِ لَا يَعلَمُونَ {٦٨}

٤. وَلَمَّا دَخَلُوا عَلَى يُوسُفَ آوَى إِلَيهِ أَخَاهُ قَالَ إِنِّي أَنَا أَخُوكَ فَلَا تَبتَئِس بِمَا كَانُوا يَعمَلُونَ {٦٩}

■ Exercise 3: Nouns (cases)

With reference to the section on Cases in the Grammar appendix, indicate what case each of the following nouns is assigned and the reason for the case assignment. The number in parenthesis refers to the number of the verse in سورة يوسف from which the noun is taken.

Reason for case assignment	Case	
governed by the preposition الى	مجرور	أَبِيهِم (٦٣)
		أَبَانَا (٦٣)
		أَخَانَا (٦٣)
		بَاب (٦٧)
		أَبوَاب (٦٧)
		مُتَفَرِّقَة (٦٧)
predicate of إِنَّ		ذو (٦٨)
		أَخَاهُ (٦٩)
		أَخُوكَ (٦٩)

■ Exercise 4: Roots and families

The following words are based on 14 roots. Group together the words that are based on the same root, identify the root, and give its general meaning in English.

فَلْيَتَوَكَّل، الراحمين، فعرفهم، تستفتيان، جَعَل، بتأويله، يرجعون، المتوكّلون، أذّن، لتنبّئهم،
فَتَيان، حافِظاً، موثقهم، توكّلتُ، برحمتنا، نبِّئنا، أرحم، بجهازهم، اجعلوا، نبّأتكما، لفتيانه،
رؤياي، أنبّئكم، وتَرَكنا، رؤيا، حفيظ، تَرَكتُ، مؤذِّن، تأويل، يعرفونها، جهّزهم، افتوني،
لحافظون، رجعوا، موثقاً

■ Learn the new words

The following list includes most of the new words in this part of سورة يوسف. Write
down their meanings in English from memory.

	اكتال – يكتال		منَع – يمنَع
....	ازداد – يَزداد	....	بَغى – يَبغي
....	بَعير	....	كَيل
....	أحاط – يُحيط	....	يسير
....	باب (ج. أبواب)	....	وكيل
....	تَوَكَّل – يتوكَّل	....	مُتَفَرِّق
....	حاجة	....	مُتَوَكِّل
....	مُؤَذِّن	....	أذَّن
....	سارق	....	عير

قالوا وَأَقبَلوا عَلَيهِم ماذا تَفقِدون ﴿٧١﴾ قالوا نَفقِدُ صُواعَ المَلِكِ وَلِمَن جاءَ بِهِ حِملُ بَعيرٍ وَأَنا بِهِ زَعيمٌ ﴿٧٢﴾ قالوا تَاللَّهِ لَقَد عَلِمتُم مّا جِئنا لِنُفسِدَ فِي الأَرضِ وَما كُنّا سارِقينَ ﴿٧٣﴾ قالوا فَما جَزاؤُهُ إِن كُنتُم كاذِبينَ ﴿٧٤﴾ قالوا جَزاؤُهُ مَن وُجِدَ في رَحلِهِ فَهُوَ جَزاؤُهُ كَذَلِكَ نَجزي الظّالِمينَ ﴿٧٥﴾ فَبَدَأَ بِأَوعِيَتِهِم قَبلَ وِعاءِ أَخيهِ ثُمَّ استَخرَجَها مِن وِعاءِ أَخيهِ كَذَلِكَ كِدنا لِيوسُفَ ما كانَ لِيَأخُذَ أَخاهُ في دينِ المَلِكِ إِلَّا أَن يَشاءَ اللَّهُ نَرفَعُ دَرَجاتٍ مِن نَشاءُ وَفَوقَ كُلِّ ذي عِلمٍ عَليمٌ ﴿٧٦﴾ قالوا إِن يَسرِق فَقَد سَرَقَ أَخٌ لَهُ مِن قَبلُ فَأَسَرَّها يوسُفُ في نَفسِهِ وَلَم يُبدِها لَهُم قالَ أَنتُم شَرٌّ مَّكانًا واللَّهُ أَعلَمُ بِما تَصِفونَ ﴿٧٧﴾ قالوا يا أَيُّها العَزيزُ إِنَّ لَهُ أَبًا شَيخًا كَبيرًا فَخُذ أَحَدَنا مَكانَهُ إِنّا نَراكَ مِنَ المُحسِنينَ ﴿٧٨﴾ قالَ مَعاذَ اللَّهِ أَن نَأخُذَ إِلَّا مَن وَجَدنا مَتاعَنا عِندَهُ إِنّا إِذًا لَّظالِمونَ ﴿٧٩﴾ فَلَمّا استَيأَسوا مِنهُ خَلَصوا نَجِيًّا قالَ كَبيرُهُم أَلَم تَعلَموا أَنَّ أَباكُم قَد أَخَذَ عَلَيكُم مَوثِقًا مِنَ اللَّهِ وَمِن قَبلُ ما فَرَّطتُم في يوسُفَ فَلَن أَبرَحَ الأَرضَ حَتَّى يَأذَنَ لي أَبي أَو يَحكُمَ اللَّهُ لي وَهُوَ خَيرُ الحاكِمينَ ﴿٨٠﴾

New words

Nouns

golden (cup)	صُواع
load	حِمل
bound, answerable	زَعيم
bags	أوعِية
degree, grade	دَرَجة
old man, aged	شَيخ
conference	نَجِيّ
eldest	كَبير

Verbs

to turn toward	أقبَل
to lose	فقَد – يفقِد
to make mischief, do evil	أفسَد – يُفسِد
to bring out, produce	استَخرَج
to keep in himself, keep secret	أسَرَّ
to reveal	أبدى – يُبدي
to describe, allege	وصَف – يصِف
take!	خُذ!
to despair	استيأَس
to fail in duty, fail in the case	فَرَّط
to leave, go forth	برَح – يَبرَح

Expression

By Allah	تالله

Grammar: The construct phrase and other types of phrases

It should be remembered that the construct consists of two nouns in a special relationship of possession or something being part of something else; it should not be confused with noun-adjective combinations. Here is an example of each:

Construct

يوم الدين (الفاتحة ٤) the Day of Judgement

Noun-adjective

السراط المستقيم (الفاتحة ٦) the straight path

Exercise 1

The following phrases, all taken from سورة يوسف, include construct as well as adjective phrases. Write next to each one what type it is.

الكتاب المُبِين (١)

قَومًا صالِحين (٩)

غَيابَةِ الجُبِّ (١٥)

تَأويلِ الأَحاديثِ (٢١)

مَلَكُ كَريم (٢٤)

عِبادِنا المُخلَصين (٣٠)

امرَأَةُ العَزيزِ (٣١)

الدّينُ القَيِّمُ (٣٤)

مِلَّةَ قَوم (٣٧)

السَّميعُ العَليم (٤٠)

سُنبُلاتٍ خُضرٍ (٤٦)

خَزائِنِ الأَرضِ (٥٥)

أبوابٍ مُتَفَرِّقَةٍ (٦٧)

نَفسِ يَعقوبَ (٦٨)

■ Exercise 2: Nouns

For each of the following nouns, provide a full English translation, identify the root, the stem, and the pattern, using فعل. Six of the words in the list are participles. Identify their source verbs and give their meanings.

Source verb	Pattern	Stem	Root	Translation	
					بَعير
					زَعيم
					الأرض
he stole سرق					سارقين
					كاذِبين
					رِحلة
					الظالمِين
					عَليم
					مَكاناً
				the Mighty	العَزيز
					شَيخاً
					كَبيراً
					المُحسِنين
					لَظالِمون
					الحاكِمين

■ Exercise 3: Verbs

a. Find all the verbs in the following three verses, and, for any ten of them, give a full English translation, and identify the root, the stem, and the form, using فعل, and the form number.

b. Find an example each of the declarative, subjunctive, and jussive.

١.   قَالُوا تَاللّهِ لَقَد عَلِمتُم مَّا جِئنَا لِنُفسِدَ فِي الأَرضِ وَمَا كُنَّا سَارِقِينَ {٣٧}

٢.   فَبَدَأَ بِأَوعِيَتِهِم قَبلَ وِعَاءِ أَخِيهِ ثُمَّ استَخرَجَهَا مِن وِعَاءِ أَخِيهِ كَذَلِكَ كِدنَا لِيُوسُفَ مَا كَانَ لِيَأخُذَ أَخَاهُ فِي دِينِ المَلِكِ إِلَّا أَن يَشَاءَ اللّهُ نَرفَعُ دَرَجَاتٍ مِن نَشَاءُ وَفَوقَ كُلِّ ذِي عِلمٍ عَلِيمٌ {٧٦}

٣.   قَالُوا إِن يَسرِق فَقَد سَرَقَ أَخٌ لَّهُ مِن قَبلُ فَأَسَرَّهَا يُوسُفُ فِي نَفسِهِ وَلَم يُبدِهَا لَهُم قَالَ أَنتُم شَرٌّ مَّكَانًا وَاللّهُ أَعلَمُ بِمَا تَصِفُونَ {٧٧}

■ Learn the new words

Write down the English meanings of the following words from memory.

....	فقَد – يفقِد	....	أَقبَل
....	زَعِيم	....	حمل
....	أَفسَد – يُفسِد	....	تالله
....	دَرَجة	....	استَخرَج
....	وصَف – يصِف	....	أَسَرَّ
....	أَخَذ – يَأخُذ	....	شَيخ
....	كَبِير	....	استيأس
....	برَح – يَبرَح	....	فَرَّط

الدرس رقم ٣٨	Lesson Thirty Eight
١٢. سورة يوسف ٩	

ارجِعوا إلى أَبيكُم فَقولوا يا أَبانا إِنَّ ابنَكَ سَرَقَ وَما شَهِدنا إِلاَّ بِما عَلِمنا وَما كُنّا لِلغَيبِ حافِظينَ {٨١} واسأَلِ القَريَةَ الَّتي كُنّا فيها والعيرَ الَّتي أَقبَلنا فيها وَإِنّا لَصادِقونَ {٨٢} قالَ بَل سَوَّلَت لَكُم أَنفُسُكُم أَمرًا فَصَبرٌ جَميلٌ عَسى اللَّهُ أَن يَأتِيَني بِهِم جَميعًا إِنَّهُ هوَالعَليمُ الحَكيمُ {٨٣} وَتَوَلّى عَنهُم وَقالَ يا أَسَفى عَلى يوسُفَ وابيَضَّت عَيناهُ مِنَ الحُزنِ فَهُوَ كَظيمٌ {٨٤} قالوا تاللهِ تَفتَأُ تَذكُرُ يوسُفَ حَتّى تَكونَ حَرَضًا أَو تَكونَ مِنَ الهالِكينَ {٨٥} قالَ إِنَّما أَشكو بَثّي وَحُزني إِلى اللَّهِ وَأَعلَمُ مِنَ اللَّهِ ما لاَ تَعلَمونَ {٨٦} يا بَنِيَّ اذهَبوا فَتَحَسَّسوا مِن يوسُفَ وَأَخيهِ وَلاَ تَيأَسوا مِن روحِ اللَّهِ إِنَّهُ لاَ يَيأَسُ مِن روحِ اللَّهِ إِلاَّ القَومُ الكافِرونَ {٨٧} فَلَمّا دَخَلوا عَلَيهِ قالوا يا أَيُّها العَزيزُ مَسَّنا وَأَهلَنا الضُّرُّ وَجِئنا بِبِضاعَةٍ مُزجاةٍ فَأَوفِ لَنا الكَيلَ وَتَصَدَّق عَلَينا إِنَّ اللَّهَ يَجزي المُتَصَدِّقينَ {٨٨} قالَ هَل عَلِمتُم مّا فَعَلتُم بِيوسُفَ وَأَخيهِ إِذ أَنتُم جاهِلونَ {٨٩} قالوا أَإِنَّكَ لأَنتَ يوسُفُ قالَ أَنا يوسُفُ وَهَذا أَخي قَد مَنَّ اللَّهُ عَلَينا إِنَّهُ مَن يَتَّقِ وَيصبِر فَإِنَّ اللَّهَ لاَ يُضيعُ أَجرَ المُحسِنينَ {٩٠}

■ New words

Nouns

suppressing sorrow	كَظيم
weak with old age, with ruined health	حَرَض
dead, perishing	هالك
grief, distress	بَثّ
hard time, misfortune	ضُرّ
poor (quality)	مُزجى

Verbs

to portray as good, tempt	سَوَّل
to never cease	فتأ – يفتأ
to inquire about, ascertain	تَحَسَّس
to give up hope, despair	يئِس – يَيأَس
to hit, touch	مَسَّ – يمَسُّ
to pay, fill	أوفى – يوفي
to be charitable	تصدَّق – يتصدَّق
to fear Allah	اتَّقى – يَتَّقي

Expressions

How grieved I am!	يا أَسفي
his eyes became white, he lost his eyesight	ابيضَّت عيناه

■ Grammar: Form IX

The last verb form to be introduced in this book is Form IX (افعلَّ). It occurs only once in this book, in the verb إبيضَّ "to become white". This form is restricted to colors and defects in the language in general.

Here is the complete verb form table as introduced in this book:

Meaning/ grammatical function	Distinguishing feature	Form	
none	three consonants of the root + short vowels	فعل/يفعل	I
often intensive or causative of I	doubling of the middle consonant	فعَّل/يُفعِّل	II
often associative	inserting ا between the first and second consonants of the root	فاعَل – يُفاعِل	II
often causative of I	prefixing أ before the first consonant of the root in the perfect and replacing it with the subject marker and ضمّة in the imperfect	أفعل/يُفعِل	IV
often passive/ reflexive of II	doubling of the middle consonant of the root, and prefixing ت before the first consonant	تَفَعَّل – يتفعَّل	V
often reflexive of III	adding ا between first and second consonants and prefixing ت before the first consonant	تفاعل/يتَفاعَل	VI
often passive of I	prefixing انا before the first consonant of the root in the perfect and dropping ا in the imperfect	انفعل/ينفعِل	VII
often passive/ reflexive of I	prefixing ا before the first consonant of the root and infixing ت between first and second consonant in the perfect, and dropping ا in the imperfect	افتعل/يفتعل	VIII
restricted to colors and defects	doubling the third consonant of the root	افعَلّ – يَفعَلّ	IX
often passive/ reflexive of IV	prefixing است before the first consonant of the root in the perfect and dropping ا in the imperfect	استفعل/يستفعل	X
none	four consonants of the root + the فتحة – فتحة short vowels	فعلَل – يُفعلِل	Q1

▮ Exercise 1: Nouns

For each of the following nouns, provide a full English translation, identify the root, the stem, and the pattern, using فعل. Four of the words in the list are participles. Identify their source verbs.

Source verb	Pattern	Stem	Root	Translation	
حفِظ to keep					حافِظين
					لَصادِقون
					فَصَبر
					جَميل
					جَميعاً
					العَليم
					الحَكيم
					كَظيم
					الهالِكين
					القَوم
					الكافِرون

▮ Exercise 2: Verbs

a. Find all the verbs in the following six verses, and, for any ten of them, give a full English translation, and identify the root, the stem, and the form, using فعل, and the form number.

b. Find an example each of the declarative, subjunctive, jussive, and imperative.

١. ارجِعُوا إِلَى أَبيكُم فَقُولُوا يَا أَبَانَا إِنَّ ابنَكَ سَرَقَ وَمَا شَهِدنَا إِلاَّ بِمَا عَلِمنَا وَمَا كُنَّا لِلغَيبِ حَافِظِينَ {١٨}

٢. قَالَ بَل سَوَّلَت لَكُم أَنفُسُكُم أَمرًا فَصَبرُ جَميلُ عَسَى اللَّهُ أَن يَأتِيَني بِهِم جَميعًا إِنَّهُ هُوَالعَليمُ الحَكِيمُ {٨٣}

٣. وَتَوَلَّى عَنهُم وَقَالَ يَا أَسَفَى عَلَى يُوسُفَ وَابيَضَّت عَينَاهُ مِنَ الحُزنِ فَهُوَ كَظِيمُ {٨٤}

٤. يَا بَنِيَّ اذهَبُوا فَتَحَسَّسُوا مِن يُوسُفَ وَأَخِيهِ وَلاَ تَيْأَسُوا مِن رُوحِ اللَّهِ إِنَّهُ لاَ يَيْأَسُ
مِن رُوحِ اللَّهِ إِلاَّ القَومُ الكَافِرُونَ ﴿٨٧﴾

٥. فَلَمَّا دَخَلُوا عَلَيهِ قَالُوا يَا أَيُّهَا العَزِيزُ مَسَّنَا وَأَهلَنَا الضُّرُّ وَجِئنَا بِبِضَاعَةٍ مُزجَاةٍ
فَأَوفِ لَنَا الكَيلَ وَتَصَدَّق عَلينَا إِنَّ اللَّهَ يَجزِي المُتَصَدِّقِينَ ﴿٨٨﴾

٦. قَالُوا أَإِنَّكَ لأَنتَ يُوسُفُ قَالَ أَنَا يُوسُفُ وَهَذَا أَخِي قَد مَنَّ اللَّهُ عَلينَا إِنَّهُ مَن يَتَّقِ
وَيصبِر فَإِنَّ اللَّهَ لاَ يُضِيعُ أَجرَ المُحسِنِينَ ﴿٩٠﴾

◼ Learn the new words

Write down the English meanings of the following words from memory.

....	ابيضَّت عيناه	....	يا أَسفي
....	هالك	....	فتأَ – يفتأَ
....	يئِس – يَيأَس	....	تَحَسَّس
....	مَسَّ – يمَسُّ	....	مُنكِر
....	أوفى – يوفي	....	ضُرّ
....	اتَّقى – يَتَّقي	....	تصدَّق – يتصدَّق

قالوا تَاللّهِ لَقَد آثَرَكَ اللّهُ عَلَينا وَإِن كُنّا لَخاطِئينَ {٩١} قالَ لَا تَثْريبَ عَلَيكُمُ
اليَومَ يَغفِرُ اللّهُ لَكُم وَهُوَ أَرحَمُ الرّاحِمينَ {٩٢} اذهَبوا بِقَميصي هَذا فَأَلقوهُ عَلى
وَجهِ أَبي يَأتِ بَصيرًا وَأتوني بِأَهلِكُم أَجمَعينَ {٩٣} وَلَمّا فَصَلَتِ العيرُ قالَ أَبوهُم
إِنّي لَأَجِدُ ريحَ يوسُفَ لَولا أَن تُفَنّدونِ {٩٤} قالوا تَاللّهِ إِنّكَ لَفي ضَلالِكَ القَديمِ
{٩٥} فَلَمّا أَن جاءَ البَشيرُ أَلقاهُ عَلى وَجهِهِ فَارتَدَّ بَصيرًا قالَ أَلَم أَقُل لَكُم إِنّي
أَعلَمُ مِنَ اللّهِ ما لا تَعلَمونَ {٩٦} قالوا يا أَبانا استَغفِر لَنا ذُنوبَنا إِنّا كُنّا خاطِئينَ
{٩٧} قالَ سَوفَ أَستَغفِرُ لَكُم رَبّي إِنَّهُ هُوَ الغَفورُ الرَّحيمُ {٩٨} فَلَمّا دَخَلوا
عَلى يوسُفَ آوى إِلَيهِ أَبَوَيهِ وَقالَ ادخُلوا مِصرَ إِن شاءَ اللّهُ آمِنينَ {٩٩} وَرَفَعَ
أَبَوَيهِ عَلى العَرشِ وَخَرّوا لَهُ سُجَّدًا وَقالَ يا أَبَتِ هَذا تَأويلُ رُؤيايَ مِن قَبلُ قَد
جَعَلَها رَبّي حَقًّا وَقَد أَحسَنَ بَي إِذ أَخرَجَني مِنَ السِّجنِ وَجاءَ بِكُم مِنَ البَدوِ
مِن بَعدِ أَن نَزَغَ الشَّيطانُ بَيني وَبَينَ إِخوَتي إِنَّ رَبّي لَطيفٌ لِما يَشاءُ إِنَّهُ هُوَ
العَليمُ الحَكيمُ {١٠٠} رَبِّ قَد آتَيتَني مِنَ المُلكِ وَعَلَّمتَني مِن تَأويلِ الأَحاديثِ
فاطِرَ السَّماواتِ والأَرضِ أَنتَ وَلِيّي في الدُّنيا والآخِرَةِ تَوَفَّني مُسلِمًا وَأَلحِقني
بِالصّالِحينَ {١٠١}

▪ New words

Nouns

reproach, fear	تَثريب
clear-sighted, able to see	بَصير
to smell, breath	ريح
bearer of glad tidings	بَشير
throne	عَرش
bedouin life, desert	بَدو
courteous, tender	لَطيف
Creator	فاطِر
Protector, Guardian, Lord	وَلِيّ

Verbs

to prefer	آثَر
to forgive	غفَر – يغفِر
to cast, lay	ألقى – يُلقي
to depart	فَصَل
to think of as weak of mind because of old age	فنَّد – يُفنِّد
to go back to a previous state	ارتَدَّ
to ask forgiveness	استغفَر – يستغفِر
to fall (in prostration)	خَرَّ
to sow enmity, make strife	نَزَغ
to cause to die, make die	تَوَفّى
to join to	ألحَق

■ Grammar: The construct and possession

It was mentioned in the discussion of the construct that if the first term ends in the plural suffix ون/ين or the dual suffix ين, the ن of the suffix is dropped, as in the example صاحبي السجن. The same rule applies when a possessive suffix is attached to the noun ending in any of these suffixes. The word أبويه "his parents" is based on أبوين + the possessive suffix ـه. This demonstrates the similarity between construct phrases, which often exhibit a relationship of possession, and nouns + possessive suffixes.

■ Exercise 1: Nouns

For the following five participles and one verbal noun:

a. Provide a full English translation, identify the root, the stem, and the pattern, using فعل.
b. Identify the source verb of each participle or verbal noun and guess its meaning.

The first one is given as an example.

Source verb	Pattern	Stem	Root	Translation	
to be charitable تصدّق	متفعّل	متصدّق	ص.د.ق	the charitable ones	المُتَصَدّقين
					جاهلون
					المُحسِنين
					لَخاطِئين
					تَثريب
					الراحِمين

■ Exercise 2: Parts of speech

Arabic words are traditionally grouped into three categories: *nouns, verbs,* and *particles*. The category of nouns includes adjectives and participles, as well as different types of nouns. Verbs are easy to identify because they follow a limited number of patterns and are conjugated in specific ways. The category of particles includes words not included in the other two categories such as *prepositions, pronouns, conjunctions, the definite article, question words,* etc. While nouns and verbs derive from three- or, less commonly, four-letter roots, particles consist of one, two, or three consonants and vowels. Nouns and verbs come in families, while particles are not related to other words. Particles are sometimes written separately, but are often attached to a preceding or following noun or verb or another particle.

Verse 96 of سورة يوسف includes the following nouns, verbs, and particles, where n = noun, v = verb, p = particle.

p	when	لّا	p	and	ف
v	he came	جاء	p	that	أَن
n	someone who brings good news	بشير	p	the	ال
p	him, it	ه	v	he threw	ألقى
n	face	وجه	p	on	على
p	and	ف	p	his	ه
n	able to see	بصيراً	v	he returned	ارتدّ
p	question particle	أ	v	he said	قال
p	I	أ	p	not (past)	لم
p	to	ل	v	he said	قال
p	that, verily	إنّ	p	you	كُم
p	I	أ	p	I	ي
p	from	مِن	v	he knew	علم
p	that which	ما	n	Allah	الله
p	you (imp. pl.)	ت – ون	p	not	لا

■ Exercise 3

1. Examine the following verse and make three lists that include all the words or parts of words in it grouped into the three categories outlined above. Give the English translation of each word or part of a word you identify.

اذهَبُوا بِقَمِيصِي هَذَا فَأَلْقُوهُ عَلَى وَجهِ أَبِي يَأْتِ بَصِيرًا وَأْتُونِي بِأَهلِكُم أَجمَعِينَ {٩٣}

قَالَ سَوفَ أَستَغفِرُ لَكُم رَبِّيَ إِنَّهُ هُوَ الغَفُورُ الرَّحِيمُ {٩٨}

■ Learn the new words

Write down the English meanings of the following words from memory.

....	غَفَر – يغفِر	....	اَثَر
....	بَصير	....	اَلقى – يُلقي
....	ريح	....	فَصَل
....	ارتَدَّ	....	بَشير
....	استغفَر – يستغفِر	....	بصيراً
....	أبَتِ	....	عَرش
....	لَطيف	....	بَدو
....	وَلِيّ	....	فاطِر
....	ألحَق	....	تَوَفّى

ذَلِكَ مِن أَنباءِ الغَيبِ نوحيهِ إِلَيكَ وَما كُنتَ لَدَيهِم إِذ أَجمَعوا أَمرَهُم وَهُم يَمكُرون {١٠٢} وَما أَكثَرُ النّاسِ وَلَو حَرَصتَ بِمُؤمِنين {١٠٣} وَما تَسأَلُهُم عَلَيهِ مِن أَجرٍ إِن هُوَ إِلّا ذِكرٌ لِّلعالَمين {١٠٤} وَكَأَيِّن مِن آيَةٍ في السَّماواتِ والأَرضِ يَمُرّونَ عَلَيها وَهُم عَنها مُعرِضون {١٠٥} وَما يُؤمِنُ أَكثَرُهُم بِاللهِ إِلّا وَهُم مُشرِكون {١٠٦} أَفَأَمِنوا أَن تَأتِيَهُم غاشِيَةٌ مِن عَذابِ اللهِ أَو تَأتِيَهُمُ السّاعَةُ بَغتَةً وَهُم لا يَشعُرون {١٠٧} قُل هَذِهِ سَبيلي أَدعو إِلى اللهِ عَلى بَصيرَةٍ أَنا وَمَنِ اتَّبَعَني وَسُبحانَ اللهِ وَما أَنا مِنَ المُشرِكين {١٠٨} وَما أَرسَلنا مِن قَبلِكَ إِلّا رِجالاً نوحي إِلَيهِم مِن أَهلِ القُرى أَفَلَم يَسيروا في الأَرضِ فَيَنظُروا كَيفَ كانَ عاقِبَةُ الَّذينَ مِن قَبلِهِم وَلَدارُ الآخِرَةِ خَيرٌ لِّلَّذينَ اتَّقَوا أَفَلا تَعقِلون {١٠٩} حَتّى إِذا استَيأَسَ الرُّسُلُ وَظَنّوا أَنَّهُم قَد كُذِبوا جاءَهُم نَصرُنا فَنُجِّيَ مَن نَشاء وَلا يُرَدُّ بَأسُنا عَنِ القَومِ المُجرِمين {١١٠} لَقَد كانَ في قَصَصِهِم عِبرَةٌ لِأُولي الأَلبابِ ما كانَ حَديثًا يُفتَرى وَلَكِن تَصديقَ الَّذي بَينَ يَدَيهِ وَتَفصيلَ كُلَّ شَيءٍ وَهُدًى وَرَحمَةً لِّقَومٍ يُؤمِنون {١١١}

New words

Nouns

news, tidings	أَنباء
averse, with an averted face	مُعرِض
covering veil, pall	غاشِية
all of a sudden, suddenly	بَغتة
way	سَبيل
sure knowledge	بَصيرة
glorified and exalted	سُبحان الله
men	رِجال
townships	قُرى
end, nature of the consequence	عاقِبة
the home (abode) of the hereafter	دَار الآخِرة
messengers	رُسُل
punishment, wrath	بَأس
criminal, sinner, disbeliever, guilty	مُجرِم
lesson	عِبرة
men of understanding	أولي الألباب
confirmation	تَصديق
detailed explanation	تَفصيل
guide, guidance	هُدى

Verbs

to plot, scheme	مَكَر – يَمكُر
to desire eagerly, try much	حَرَص
to pass by	مَرَّ – يمُرُّ
to perceive, be aware	شَعَر – يشعُر
to invite, call	دَعا – يَدعو
to follow	اتَّبَع
to travel	سار – يَسير
to give up hope, despair	استَيأَس
to rescue, save	نَجّا – يُنَجّي
to ward off	رَدَّ – يَرُدَّ
to forge, invent	افتَرى – يفتَري

Expression

how many signs . . .	كَأَيٍّ (كَأيِّن) مِن آيات . . .

This is a special use of the word أيّ, which generally means "what" or "which". The phrase كَأيِّن, where the ن stands for the genitive case marking (ِ), translates as "how many signs there are . . ."

◼ Exercise 1: Verbal nouns

The following are all verbal nouns derived from Form II verbs. First, give an English translation of the the verbal noun, then identify the verb from which it is derived and guess its meaning.

Source verb and its meaning	Translation	
		تأويل
		تثريب
		تصديق
		تفصيل

■ Exercise 2: Parts of speech

Make three lists that include all the words or parts of words in the following verse grouped into the three categories of *noun*, *verb*, and *particle*, as was shown in the previous part of سورة يوسف. Give the English translation of each word or part of a word in the lists.

أَفَأَمِنُوا أَن تَأْتِيَهُم غَاشِيَةٌ مِن عَذَابِ اللّهِ أَو تَأْتِيَهُمُ السَّاعَةُ بَغْتَةً وَهُم لاَ يَشْعُرُونَ {١٠٧}

■ Exercise 3: Roots and families

The following words are based on 28 roots. Group together the words that are based on the same root, identify the root, and give its general meaning in English.

يَيَأَس، أَكبرنَه، عَليم، أَجمَعوا، بصيراً، تؤتون، وحُزني، بمكرهن، سُجَّداً، تصدَّق، الأحاديث، قُبُل، الرَّاحِمين، لَفاعِلون، اتبعني، نُشرِك، قدَّمتُم، نَجزي، استخرجها، يأكُلهن، كبيرهم، تيأسوا، وعلَّمتني، الحُزن، يسرِق، نفقِد، علِمتُم، مُشرِكون، فارتَدَّ، الجاهِلين، وأقبَلوا، تعلموا، القديم، لتأتِنَّني، عَلِمنا، فتأكُل، يأتِيكما، فَعَلتُم، جاهِلون، لَسارِقون، أقبَلنا، حديثاً، وألقوه، فدخلوا، وأعلم، بصيرة، أوحينا، ودخل، سَرَق، رُدَّت، استيأس، جَميعاً، تعلَمون، جَزاؤُه، قَبل، تَفقِدون، عِلم، أخرجَني، كبيراً، يمكُرون، استيأسوا، المُتَصدِّقين، أجمَعين، أرحَم، نوحيه، ساجِدين، أتوه، ألقاه، ليحزنَني، تأكُل، يأتيني، واتّبعتُ، المُشرِكين

■ Exercise 4: Opposites

Copy each of the words in row ب under its opposite in row أ:

أقبل	أعطى	ادَّكر	عِجاف	أخضَر	جاهِل	دُبُر	سوء	أفلَح	مُحسِن	أ
نَسي	عليم	أدبَر	حُسنى	خاب	منَع	سِمان	ظالِم	يابِس	قُبُل	ب

Learn the new words

Write down the English meanings of the following words from memory.

....	مَكَر – يَمكُر	....	أَنباء
....	ذِكر	....	حَرَص
....	مَرَّ – يمُرُّ	....	كَأَيٍّ
....	غاشِية	....	مُعرِض
....	شَعَر – يشعُر	....	بَغتة
....	دَعا – يَدعو	....	سَبيل
....	اتَّبَع	....	بَصيرة
....	رجال	....	سُبحان الله
....	سار – يَسير	....	قُرى
....	دَار الآخِرة	....	عاقِبة
....	رُسُل	....	استَيأَس
....	رَدَّ – يَرُدّ	....	نَجّا – يُنَجّي
....	مُجرِم	....	بَأس
....	أُولي الألباب	....	عِبرة
....	تَصديق	....	افتَرى – يَفتَري
....	هُدى	....	تَفصيل

Appendix I	*Grammar notes*

This grammar summary is intended as a quick reference, and includes only those areas that will help you understand the *sūras* included in this book. Grammatical points not found in these *sūras* or which occur rarely are not discussed.

1. The definite article and the sun and moon letters
2. Subject-person markers
3. Root types and verb conjugations
4. Pronominal suffixes attached to nouns, verbs, and particles
5. Emphasizing meaning
6. Expressing future time
7. The different functions of ما
8. The plural of nouns and adjectives
9. Roots and patterns
10. Noun patterns regularly derived from the verb forms
11. Other common noun patterns
12. The passive voice
13. Negation
14. Moods of the imperfect verb
15. The case system
16. The construct الإضافة

1. The definite article and the sun and moon letters

Definiteness in Arabic is expressed by attaching the prefix ال [al] "the" to nouns and adjectives:

"whisperer"	وسواس
"the whisperer"	الوسواس

If ال is followed by a *sun* letter, it is assimilated to (becomes the same as) that letter, which results in a doubled consonant in pronunciation but not in writing, as in الناس, which is pronounced *an-nās*. ل remains unchanged before *moon* letters, as in المستقيم "the straight", which is pronounced *al-mustaqīm*.

The following table shows the sun and moon letters:

Sun letters	ت، ث، د، ذ، ر، ز، س، ش، ص، ض، ط، ظ، ل، ن
Moon letters	أ، ب، ج، ح، خ، ع، غ، ف، ق، ك، هـ، و، ي

▪ 2. Subject-person markers

Arabic verbs have two aspects or tenses: the *perfect* and the *imperfect*. The perfect corresponds roughly to the past tense in English, and generally indicates completed action, and the imperfect corresponds to the present tense and indicates actions that have not been completed. Different persons are expressed by attaching different suffixes to the verb in the case of the perfect, and prefixes and suffixes in the case of the imperfect verb. In the case of the third person masculine singular (the one corresponding to: he wrote, he was, etc.), nothing is attached in the perfect.

Prefix (and suffix)	Imperfect	Suffix	Perfect		
يَ –	يعبُد	–	عبد	he	هو
تَ –	تعبُد	عَت	عبدَت	she	هي
ي – ان	يعبُدان	ا –	عبدا	they (m.) dual	هُما
ت – ان	تعبُدان	تا –	عبدتا	they (f.) dual	هُما
ي – ون	يعبدون	وا –	عبدوا	they (m.)	هُم
ي – نَ	يعبُدن	نَ –	عبدْنَ	they (f.)	هُنّ
تَ –	تعبُد	تَ –	عبدتَ	you (m. sg.)	انتَ
ت – ان	تعبُدان	تُما –	عبدتُما	you (dual)	انتُما
ت – ون	تعبُدون	تُم –	عبدتُم	you (m. pl.)	انتُم
تَ – نَ	–	تُنَّ –	عبدتُنّ	you (f. pl.)	انتّن
أَ –	أعبد	تُ –	عبدتُ	I	أنا
نَ –	نعبُد	نا –	عبدنا	we	نحنُ

◼ 3. Root types and verb conjugations

Words in Arabic are generally divided into three main categories: *nouns*, *verbs*, and *particles*. Nouns and verbs are generally based on roots of three or four radicals and come in "families" that are related in form and meaning. Particles, which can be made up of one, two, or three radicals, consist of the limited sets of function words or parts of words, such as the definite article, pronouns, question words, prepositions, conjunctions, exclamations, and certain adverbs. In contrast to verbs and nouns, particles are not regularly or productively derived from other words.

Three-consonant roots are divided into sound roots and weak roots according to their consonant structure, and weak roots are further subdivided into four types. The type of root determines the verb's conjugational pattern.

Sound roots have three consonants in the three root positions, no doubling of any two consonants, and no ا, و, or ي in any of the three consonant positions: ثَقُل – يَثقُل، جَعَل – يجعَل، حَسِب – يحسَب.

Assimilated roots have و (rarely ي) in the first consonant position: ولد – يَلِد, وجد – يجِد, وزن – يزِن.

Hollow roots have و or ي in the second position. The و and ي generally appear as ا in the perfect تاب – يتوب, سار – يسير, كان – يكون.

Lame roots have و or ي as the third consonant. It is generally realized as ى (less frequently ا) in the perfect form of the verb: تَلا – يَتلو, جزى – يَجزي, رضِي – يَرضى.

Doubled roots have identical second and third consonants: رد – يَرُدّ, فَرّ – يفِرّ, حَض – يَحُضّ.

Roots with initial ا (*hamza*) behave for the most part like sound roots. In some instances, particularly the assimilation of ا in the verb اتّخذ and its derivatives and in imperative formation, it behaves like assimilated roots.

The following tables show how verbs based on different root types are conjugated in the different persons in the perfect and the imperfect. (Person pronouns of rare occurrence, such as the dual or the feminine plural are not included in these tables.) Notice in particular the behavior of weak roots. Four-consonant roots behave like sound three-consonant roots in that no changes occur in their consonant structure as a result of adding person-subject markers.

Sound roots

(عبد – يَعْبُدُ "to worship")

Imperfect	Perfect			Imperfect	Perfect	
يعبُدون	عبدوا	هُم		يَعْبُدُ	عبد	هو
				تعبُد	عبدَت	هي
تعبُدون	عبدتُم	انتُم		تَعبُدُ	عبدْتَ	انتَ
				تعبُدين	عبدْتِ	انتِ
نعبُدُ	عبدنا	نحن		أعبُدُ	عبدتُ	أنا

Assimilated roots

(وجَد – يَجِد "to find")

Imperfect	Perfect			Imperfect	Perfect	
يَجِدون	وَجَدوا	هُم		يَجِد	وَجَد	هو
				تَجِد	وَجَدَت	هي
تجِدون	وَجَدْتُم	انتُم		تَجِد	وَجَدْتَ	انتَ
				تَجِدين	وجدْتِ	انتِ
نَجِد	وَجَدْنا	نحن		أجِد	وَجَدْتُ	أنا

Note the disappearance of initial و in the imperfect conjugation of assimilated roots.

Hollow roots

(تاب – يتوب "to repent")

Imperfect	Perfect			Imperfect	Perfect	
يَتوبون	تابوا	هُم		يَتوب	تاب	هو
				تَتوب	تابَت	هي
تَتوبون	تُبتُم	انتُم		تَتوب	تُبتَ	انتَ
نَتوب	تُبْنا	نحن		أتوب	تُبْتُ	أنا

Lame roots

(رمى – يرمي "to throw")

Imperfect	Perfect		Imperfect	Perfect	
يَرمون	رَمَوا	هُم	يَرْمي	رَمى	هو
			تَرْمي	رَمَت	هي
تَرْمون	رَمَيْتُم	انتُم	تَرْمي	رَمَيْتَ	انتَ
			تَرْمين	رَمَيْتِ	انتِ
نَرْمي	رَمَيْنا	نحن	أَرْمي	رَمَيْتُ	أنا

Doubled roots

(رَدَّ – يَرُدُّ "to return [something]")

Imperfect	Perfect		Imperfect	Perfect	
يَرُدّون	رَدّوا	هُم	يَرُدُّ	رَدَّ	هو
			تَرُدُّ	رَدَّت	هي
تَرُدّون	رَدَدْتُم	انتُم	تَرُدُّ	رَدَدْتَ	انتَ
			تَرُدّين	رَدَدْتِ	انتِ
نَرُدّ	رَدَدْنا	نحن	أَرُدُّ	رَدَدْتُ	أنا

Quadriliteral roots

(وَسْوَس – يُوَسْوِس "to whisper")

Imperfect	Perfect		Imperfect	Perfect	
يُوَسْوِسون	وَسْوَسوا	هُم	يُوَسْوِس	وَسْوَس	هو
			تُوَسْوِس	وَسْوَسَت	هي
تُوَسْوِسون	وَسْوَسْتُم	انتُم	تُوَسْوِس	وَسْوَسْتَ	انتَ
			تُوَسْوِسين	وَسْوَسْتِ	انتِ
نُوَسْوِس	وَسْوَسْنا	نحن	أُوَسْوِس	وَسْوَسْتُ	أنا

■ 4. Pronominal suffixes attached to nouns, verbs, and particles

Pronoun suffixes are attached to nouns, verbs, prepositions and particles like إِنّ "that" to convey different meanings and functions. When attached to nouns, they indicate possession; when attached to verbs or prepositions they function as objects of these verbs and prepositions; and when attached to إِنّ (and لَأَنّ، كَأَنّ، لَعَلّ, etc.) they function as the subject of the clause beginning with such particles. The forms of the suffixes are the same in all these cases, with the exception of the first person singular objective suffix noted below.

Nouns

(Note that التَاء المربوطة changes to a regular تاء, when a possessive suffix is added.)

prayer صلاة	wealth مال			
صلاته	مالُه	his	هـ	هو
صلاتها	مالها	her	ها	هي
صلاتهما	مالهما	their (m. dual)	هُما	هُما
صلاتهما	مالهما	their (f. dual)	هُما	هُما
صلاتهم	مالهم	their (m.)	هُم	هُم
صلاتهنّ	مالهن	their (f.)	هنّ	هُنّ
صلاتكَ	مالكَ	your (m. sg.)	كَ	انتَ
صلاتك	مالك	your (f. sg.)	كِ	انتِ
صلاتكما	مالكما	your (m. dual)	كُما	انتُما
صلاتكما	مالكما	your (f. dual)	كُما	انتُما
صلاتكم	مالكم	your (m. pl.)	كُم	انتُم
صلاتكنّ	مالكنّ	your (f. pl.)	كُنّ	انتنّ
صلاتي	مالي	my	ي	أنا
صلاتنا	مالنا	our	نا	نحنُ

Verbs

أرسل he sent			
أرسله	him	ـه	هو
أرسلها	her	ها	هي
أرسلهما	them (m. dual)	هُما	هُما
أرسلهما	them (f. dual)	هُما	هُما
أرسلهم	them (m.)	هُم	هُم
أرسلهن	them (f.)	هنّ	هُنّ
أرسلكَ	you (m. sg.)	كَ	انتَ
أرسلكِ	you (f. sg.)	كِ	انتِ
أرسلكما	you (m. dual)	كُما	انتُما
أرسلكما	you (f. dual)	كُما	انتُما
أرسلكم	you (m. pl.)	كُم	انتُم
أرسلكنّ	you (f. pl.)	كُنّ	انتُنّ
أرسلني	me	ني	أنا
أرسلنا	us	نا	نحنُ

Notes

1. ن is added before the object suffix of the first person singular pronoun.
2. The ألف مقصورة, which is only found at the end of a word, is changed to either ي or ا when a suffix follows. The words أدراك "he made you aware" and ألهاكم "it distracted you (m. pl.)" are derived from أدرى and ألهى, respectively.

Particles (prepositions; إنّ)

that, verily إنّ	on على	to إلى	for, to ل	about عن	from من			
إنَّهُ	عَلَيْهِ	إلَيْهِ	لَهُ	عَنْهُ	منه	him	ـه	هو
إنّها	عَلَيها	إلَيْها	لَها	عَنها	منها	her	ها	هي
إنّهما	عَلَيهِما	إليهِما	لهما	عنهما	منهما	them (m. dual)	هُما	هُما
إنّهما	عَلَيهِما	إليهِما	لهما	عنهما	منهما	them (f. dual)	هُما	هُما
إنّهِم	عَلَيْهِم	إلَيْهِم	لهُم	عَنهُم	منهم	them (m.)	هُم	هُم
إنّهُنّ	عَلَيهِنّ	إليهِنّ	لهنّ	عنهنّ	منهنّ	them (f.)	هنّ	هُنّ
إنّكَ	عَلَيكَ	إلَيْكَ	لكَ	عَنكَ	مِنْكَ	you (m. sg.)	كَ	انتَ
انّك	عليك	اليك	لك	عنك	منك	you (f. sg.)	ك	انت
إنّكما	عَلَيكما	إليكُما	لكما	عنكما	منكما	you (m. dual)	كُما	انتُما
إنّكما	عَلَيكما	إليكُما	لكما	عنكما	منكما	you (f. dual)	كُما	انتُما
إنّكم	عَلَيكُم	إلَيْكُم	لكُم	عَنكُم	مِنكُم	you (m. pl.)	كُم	انتُم
إنّكنّ	عَلَيكنّ	إليكنّ	لكنّ	عنكنّ	منكنّ	you (f. pl.)	كُنّ	انتُنّ
إنّني، إنّي	عَلَيّ	إلَيّ	لي	عَنّي	مِنّي	me	ني	أنا
إنّنا، إنّا	عَلَيْنا	عَلَيْنا	لَنا	عَنّا	مِنّا	us	نا	نحن

Note the change of ألف مقصورة, found at the end of the prepositions إلى and على to ي or when a suffix follows.

Pronunciation of the third person suffix vowel

The vowel of the third person pronominal suffixes (ـه، هما، هم، هنّ) in all the above tables is pronounced either as a كسرة (i) or as a ضمّة (u), depending on the vowel right before the suffix. If it is a كسرة or a ي, then the vowel is pronounced as a كسرة: hi, himā, him, hinna; otherwise, it is pronounced as a ضمّة: hu, humā, hum, hunna.

◼ 5. Emphasizing meaning

Different tools are used to emphasize meaning in the Qur'ān. For example, in سورة الفاتحة, word order is used to emphasize the pronoun "you" in the verse: إيّاك نعبد وإيّاك نستعين. The normal order would be: نعبد إيّاك ونستعين إيّاك, which would be translated as "we worship you and we seek help from you". The order used in the *sura* gives the meaning added weight: "You [and no other] we worship, and you [and no other] we seek help from."

Other commonly used tools are the following: إنَّ "verily, truly", كلّا "nay, definitely not", لـ prefixed to verbs, and نّ suffixed to verbs. The last two are often untranslatable; they simply add emphasis to the meaning. The use of إنّ is demonstrated in the following verse:

Verily we gave you [the] abundance.	إنَّا أعطيناك الكوثر.

The other three are used in the following verse:

Nay, [verily, truly] he will be thrown into the consuming one (fire).	كلّا لينبذنّ في الحطمة.

■ 6. Expressing future time

سوف, as in سوف تعلمون, and the prefix سـ, as in سَيصلى, followed by the imperfect form of the verb, indicate future time. Both are translated as "will". سـ, being a one-letter particle, is attached to the following verb, while سوف is written separately.

■ 7. The different functions of ما

The particle ما has at least four different meanings/grammatical functions:

a. Negative particle	ما أغنى عنه ماله (المسد ٢)	His wealth did not make him self-sufficient
b. What/that which	لا أعبد ما تعبدون (الكافرون ٢)	I do not worship what/ that which you worship
c. Question particle meaning "What?"	وما أدراك ما الحطمة (الهمزة ٤)	And what made you aware of *al-ḥuṭama*?
d. Following words like إنّ, إذا, بعد, قبل. In such cases it has no meaning.	إلّا مِن بَعد ما جاءَتهُمُ البَيِّنَة (البيِّنة ٤)	Except after the proof came to them
	فأمَّا الإنسانُ إذا ما ابتَلاهُ رَبُّه (الفجر ١٥)	As for man, if his Lord tested him . . .
	فإنَّما هِيَ زَجرَةٌ واحِدَة (النازعات ١٣)	So truly it is only one shout

■ 8. The plural of nouns and adjectives

Nouns and adjectives in Arabic can be pluralized in one of two principal ways: by adding a suffix to the word or by changing its internal structure. Plurals formed by the addition of a suffix are called *sound plurals*; those formed by an internal vowel change are called *broken plurals*.

Sound Plurals

Sound plurals are of two types: *masculine* and *feminine*. Masculine sound plurals are formed by adding the suffix ون (nominative), or ين (accusative and genitive)[1] to the singular noun.

disbeliever – disbelievers	كافِر – كافِرون/كافِرين
worshiper – worshipers	عابِد – عابِدون/عابِدين

Feminine sound plurals are formed by adding the suffix ات to the noun. If the noun ends in التاء المربوطة, it is dropped:

blower – blowers (on knots)	نَفّاثة – نفاثات
good deed – good deeds	صالِحة – صالِحات
courser – coursers	عادِية – عادِيات

Broken plurals

These plurals are formed by changing the vowels of the word; the consonants are usually not affected. Think of English words like *goose – geese* and *foot – feet*. Broken plurals follow certain patterns. One of the most common patterns is أفعال, listed as one of the main noun patterns discussed below. Other common broken plural patterns include the following:

فِعال

mountain – mountains	جَبَل – جِبال
generous	كريم – كِرام

فُعول

chest – chests	صَدر – صُدور
generation – generations	قَرْن – قُرون
witness – witnesses	شاهِد – شُهود

■ 9. Roots and patterns

As was pointed out above, most words in Arabic are derived from roots. The overwhelming majority of these roots consist of three consonants, while a minority consists of four. A root has a basic meaning that is shared by all the words derived from it. One thing you need to remember about roots is that the consonants maintain the same order in all derivatives of the same root. For example, the words فليعبدوا and نعبد، أعبد، تعبدون، عابدون، عبدتم، all derive from the same three-consonant root ع.ب.د, which has the basic meaning of "to worship". Here are the meanings of these words:

we worship	نعبد
I worship	أعبد
you (m. pl.) worship	تعبدون
worshipers	عابدون
you (m. pl.) worshiped	عبدتُم
then let them (have them) worship	فليعبدوا

When a child learns his first language or when an adult learns a foreign language, most of their time is spent on learning new words; the set of sounds and their pronunciation is limited, grammatical rules are limited, but the vocabulary is vast.

Arabic has a system of word formation that is particularly helpful in acquiring new vocabulary. It is the system referred to as the *root and pattern system*. A limited number of roots combine with a limited set of patterns to produce the great majority of words.

Roots are the basic elements of meaning, and words derived from them, following the specific patterns, represent extensions or modifications of the basic meaning of the root. For example, the root عبد has the basic meaning of worshiping. The following list includes the words that you have seen or you will see in this book that are derived from this root and their meanings:[2]

he worshiped	عَبَدَ
I worship	أَعبُدُ
you (m. pl.) worship	تعبُدونَ
worshiper	عابِد
slave	عَبْد
bondmen, honored slaves	عِباد
worship	عِبادة

All these derivatives of the root د.ب.ع follow specific patterns. For example, the verb عَبَدَ is created by inserting فتحة after the first and second consonants of the root; the word عابِد is created by inserting ا between the first and second consonants and a كسرة between the second and third consonants; and the word مَعْبود is created by prefixing م to the root and inserting و between its second and third consonants. The verb عَبَدَ is the form used to express past action performed by the third person singular; the word عابِد is referred as the active participle and refers to the doer of the action; the word معبود follows the pattern of the passive participle and refers to the recipient of the action of the verb or its result; the word مَعْبَد, created by inserting the prefix مَ before the first consonant and فتحة between the second and third consonants, and refers to the place where the activity is performed. The same extensions of meaning are found in other roots. So, from the root كتب "to write", the following words, among others, are derived:

he wrote	كَتَبَ
writer	كاتِب
written	مَكتوب
office, place of writing	مَكْتَب

[2] Other words derived from the same root that are not found in the *sūras* discussed in this book are:

place of worship	مَعبَد	worshiped	مَعْبود
slavery	عُبوديّة	places of worship	معابِد
piety, worship	تَعَبُّد	he devoted himself to the service of God	تَعَبَّد
enslavement	اِستِعْباد	he enslaved	اِستعبَدَ
		pious, devout	مُتَعَبِّد

The فَعَل *Skeleton*

When discussing word derivation and word patterns, Arabic grammarians use the three letters ف.ع.ل to refer to the three consonants of the triliteral root and ف.ع.ل.ل to those of a quadriliteral one: ف refers to the first consonant, ع to the second, and ل to the third, and the second ل to the fourth consonant in a four-consonant root. The pattern of a word consists of the root فعل and any consonants or vowels added to it.

Using the skeleton فعل, the above examples can be represented as follows:

فَعَل	عَبَد، كَتَب
فاعِل	عابِد، كاتِب
مَفعول	مَعبود، مَكتوب
مَفْعَل	مَعْبَد، مَكْتَب

Verb patterns

The thousands of Arabic verbs follow a surprisingly small number of patterns, namely 14. Certain forms are more common than others. The most common is the basic form, فعل, exemplified by عبد and كتب.

In place of فعل and its derivatives, Western scholars of Arabic use a system of roman numerals I–X and QI–QIV (for quadriliteral roots) to refer to the different verb forms. According to this system, فَعَل is Form I, أَفعَل is Form IV, etc. The following is a listing of all the forms found in this book in their perfect and imperfect forms with an example of each. It should be noted that the stem vowel, the vowel between second and third consonants of the root in Form I verbs, can be ضمّة, كسرة, or فتحة. There is a certain degree of predictability as to which verbs or groups of verbs have which vowel, but a discussion of this phenomenon is beyond the scope of this introductory book.

Note that linguists use the third person masculine singular conjugation of the verb (perfect and imperfect) as the simplest forms corresponding to the English infinitive. So, خَلَق and يَخْلِق are translated literally as "he created" and "he creates", respectively. Note also that the same prefixes and suffixes are used to indicate the different persons regardless of the form used.

yaf'ul	يفعَل	fa'al	فعَل	
yaf'il	يفعِل	fa'al	فعَل	
yaf'al	يفعَل	fa'il	فعِل	I
yaf'al	يفعَل	fa'al	فعَل	
yaf'ul	يفعُل	fa'ul	فعُل	
yufa''il	يُفَعِّل	fa''al	فَعَّل	II
yufā'il	يُفاعِل	fā'al	فاعَل	III
yuf'il	يُفعِل	'af'al	أفعَل	IV
yatafa''al	يتفَعَّل	tafa''al	تفَعَّل	V
yatafā'al	يتفاعَل	tafā'al	تفاعَل	VI
yanfa'il	ينفعِل	infa'al	انفعل	VII
yafta'il	يفتعِل	ifta'al	افتعل	VIII
yaf'all	يَفعَلّ	if'all	افعَلّ	IX
yastaf'il	يستفعِل	istaf'al	استفعَل	X
yufa'lil	يفَعلِل	fa'lal	فعَلَل	Q1

The derived forms, i.e., those other than Form I and QI, often have clear grammatical or semantic associations. Some common associations are:

II (فعّل)	Transitive/causative of I	علّم "to teach"	from علِم "to learn"
	Denominative (creating a verb from a noun or an adjective)	صَلّى "to pray"	from صلاة "prayer"
	To consider, or think of someone or something as	كذّب "to think that someone is a liar"	from كاذب or كذّاب "liar"
IV (أفعل)	Causative of I	أنْزَل "to make someone or something go down"	from نزل "to go down"
V (تفعّل)	Reflexive of II	تذكّر "to be reminded, remind oneself"	from ذَكّر "to remind"
VI (تفاعَل)	Reciprocal, generally found in the plural with the meaning ". . . one another"	تواصوا "they exhorted one another"	

VII (انفعل)	Passive of I	انشقّ "to be split"	from شقّ "to split"
VIII (افتعل)	Reflexive of I	اكتال "to measure for oneself"	from كال "to measure"
IX (افعلّ)	This form is restricted to colors and defects, with the meaning of "to become (the color)"	إبيضّ "to become white"	from أبيض "white"
X (استفعل)	To think of, or consider oneself, as	استغنى "to think of oneself as rich, independent"	from غني "rich"
	To seek for oneself	استغفر "to seek forgiveness"	from غفر "to forgive"

If you know the form of a given verb and the meaning of its root or of one of its relatives, you can make predictions about its pronunciation and general meaning. For instance, if you know the word أعان "he helped" and you see the word استعان for the first time, you can predict that its meaning is likely to be "he sought help", because you know that one of the basic meanings of verbs that belong to that form is "to ask for/seek what is meant by the root". In addition, knowledge of verb forms is helpful in looking up words in a dictionary. Dictionaries list words as families under the root from which they are derived. The roots are arranged alphabetically. Verbs derived from a certain root are not listed in their full form, but under roman numerals, so you need to know what a Form X verb derived from a specific root looks like. Take as an example the verb استغفر. To look it up in a typical Arabic–English dictionary, you need to know that it derives from the root غفر. Under that root it will be referred to with the roman numeral X; it will not be listed in full as استغفر. Try looking it up in your dictionary.

Some verb forms are easier to recognize than others. This is due mainly to the type of root the verb is derived from. For example, أرسل "to send" is more transparent as a Form IV verb than أدرى "to inform, make aware" is. أرسل is derived from the sound root رسل, while أدرى is derived from the lame root دري.

Assimilated roots in Form VIII and its derivatives

Form VIII verbs and their derivatives (see active and passive participles and verbal nouns) that are based on roots with a weak letter (و, أ, or ي) in initial position undergo a process of assimilation whereby the initial weak letter is assimilated to the ت of Form VIII. This results in a doubled ت. The process can be shown as follows, where three initial-weak roots are contrasted with a sound root.

Final shape	Assimilation	Form VIII افتعل	Roots
اجتنب	none	اجتنب	ج‍.ن‍.ب
اتّخذ	أ changes to ت	اوتخذ	أ.خ.ذ
اتّقى	و changes to ت	اوتقى	و.ق‍.ي
اتّسق	و changes to ت	اوتسق	و.س‍.ق

■ 10. Noun patterns regularly derived from the verb forms

As in the case of verbs, Arabic nouns (and adjectives) follow specific patterns of derivation which share similar meanings or grammatical functions. Whereas the number of verb patterns is limited to 14, the number of noun patterns is much higher. Some noun patterns are more common than others. Some of the most common noun types are participles and verbal nouns, which are derived regularly from certain verb patterns.

Participles and Verbal Nouns

Some of the common noun patterns with regular meaning associations are active participles (اسم فاعل), passive participles (اسم مفعول), and verbal nouns (مصدر). Verbal nouns are generally abstract nouns derived from verbs, which can be translated into gerunds in English, like: تكذيب "denying", تضليل "misguiding". As is the case with active and passive participles, verbal nouns are often lexicalized; i.e., they become substantives, like تنزيل "revelation", which at some point meant revealing or sending down.

Active and passive participles with exercises were introduced in the body of the book, but verbal nouns were not because they are less widespread than participles. Verbal nouns derived from Form I verbs follow too many patterns to be introduced as a useful derivational category in an introductory Arabic book. But verbal nouns derived from the other forms follow regular patterns. The following table lists the active and passive participles and verbal nouns of the different verb forms for which examples are found in the book. An x indicates the absence of that category in the book. Representative examples of forms found in the book are given in the following table.

Verbal noun	Passive participle	Active participle	Verb form	
many patterns	مَفْعُول	فَاعِل	فعل – يفعل	I
تفعيل	مُفَعَّل	مُفَعِّل	فَعَّل – يُفَعِّل	II
x	مُفَاعَل	مُفَاعِل	فَاعَل – يُفَاعِل	III
إفعال	مُفعَل	مُفعِل	أَفْعَل – يُفعِل	IV
x	x	مُتَفَعِّل	تَفَعَّل – يتفعّل	V
x	x	مُتَفَاعِل	تَفَاعَل – يَتَفَاعَل	VI
x	x	مُنفَعِل	انفَعَل – ينفَعِل	VII
افتعال	مُفتَعَل	مُفتَعِل	افتَعَل – يفتَعِل	VIII
x	x	x	افعَلّ – يَفعَلّ	IX
x	مستفعَل	مُستفعِل	استفعَل – يستفعِل	X
x	x	مُفَعلِل	فعلل – يُفعلِل	QI
x	x	مُفَعَلِلّ	x	QIV

Examples

1. فَاعِل (Active participle of FI)	حاسِد "envious person", عابِد "worshiper", كافِر "non-believer"
2. مفعول (Passive participle of FI)	مَأكُول "eaten, devoured", منفوش "carded", مبثوث "scattered"
3. مُفَعِّل (Active participle of FII)	مُطَفِّف "one who give less in measure or weight", مُكَذِّب "one who denies"
4. مُفَعَّل (Passive participle of FII)	مُكَرَّمة "honored", مُطَهَّرة purified, مُقَدَّس "holy, sacred"
5. تفعيل (Verbal noun of FII)	تَضْليل "leading astray", تَكْذيب "denying"
6. مُفَاعِل (Active participle of FIII)	مُلاقِي "someone meeting"

7. مُفاعَل (Passive participle of FIII)	مُبارَك "blessed"
8. مُفعِل (Active participle of FIV)	مُسْلِم "Muslim", مُشرِك "disbeliever", مُخلِص "faithful", مُؤمِن "believer"
9. مُفعَل (Passive participle of FIV)	موقَد "lit", مؤصَد "shut", مُطاع "obeyed"
10. إفعال (Verbal noun of FII)	إطعام "feeding"
11. مُتَفعِّل (Active participle of FV)	مُتفرِّق "dispersed, separate", مُتوكِّل "depending (upon)"
12. مُتَفاعِل (Active participle of FVI)	مُتَنافِس "competing"
13. مُنفَعِل (Active participle of FVII)	مُنفَكّ "ceasing, stopping"
14. مُفتَعِل (Active participle of FVII)	مُعتَدي "transgressor", مُختَلِف "different", مُتَّقي "pious, fearful of Allah"
15. مُفتَعَل (Passive participle of FVIII)	مُنتَهى "end point, term"
16. افتِعال (Verbal noun of FVIII)	ابتِغاء "seeking, desire"
17. مستفعِل (Active participle of FX)	مستقيم "straight", مُستبشِر "seeking good tidings"
18. مُستَفعَل (Passive participle of FX)	مُستَعان "one whose help is sought"
19. مُفَعلِل (Active participle of FQI)	مُصيطِر "dominant"
20. مُفعَلِّ (Active participle of FQIV)	مُطمَئِنّ "content"

◼ 11. Other common noun patterns

1. أفعَل Many words in this form are adjectives with a comparative/superlative meaning	الأكرَم "the most generous", الأشقى "the most wretched", الأعلى "the most high"
2. فعيل Words of this form are generally adjectives	رحيم "merciful", شديد "intense, hard", خبير "knowing, expert", أمين "safe"

3. فَعّال or فعّالة denotes habitual, repetitive, or intensive action	نفّاثة "blower (someone who blows a lot)", حمّالة "carrier (someone who carries a lot or habitually)", تَوّاب "forgiving (someone who forgives a lot)"
4. أفعال Words in this form are generally plural nouns	أفواج "groups, troupes", أثقال "burdens", أشتات "scattered groups", أصحاب "companions"

■ 12. The passive voice

Two types of passive are found in Qur'ānic Arabic: one involves the use of the passive and reflexive verb forms (V, VI, VII, and VIII) and another involves an internal vowel change. The latter type has a distinctive vocalic melody in the perfect and another in the imperfect: in the perfect, the melody is ـُ ـِ, ضمّة then كسرة, and in the imperfect it is ـُ ـَ. ضمّة then فتحة. Note the use of the two types side by side in the two *suras* الانفطار and الانشقاق.

In theory, any transitive verb (a verb that takes an object) in any form can be made passive through this internal vowel change. However, in reality, such passives are found only in certain forms and not in others. For example, occurrences of internal passives in Form VII, generally considered the passive counterpart of Form I, are virtually absent, but are abundant in Forms I and II. In this section, only the verb forms with passive counterparts that you have encountered or will encounter in this book will be shown.

Most of the internal passives found in these *suras* are passives of Forms I and II verbs, with 24 and 11 occurrences, respectively. There is one occurrence of a Form III internal passive, four of Form IV, and two of QI. The following two tables show the active/passive alternations of the forms of verbs which are found in the book with examples.

Passive		Active		
Imperfect	Perfect	Imperfect	Perfect	
يُفْعَل	فُعِل	يفعَل، يفعُل، يفعِل	فعَل، فعِل	I
يُفَعَّل	فُعِّل	يُفَعِّل	فَعَّل	II
يُفاعَل	فوعِل	يُفاعِل	فاعَل	III
يُفْعَل	أُفْعِل	يُفْعِل	أَفْعَل	IV
يُفَعْلَل	فُعْلِل	يُفَعْلِل	فَعْلَل	QI

Examples

	Passive		Active		
	Imperfect	**Perfect**	**Imperfect**	**Perfect**	
to create – sound	يُخْلَق	خُلِق	يخلِق	خلَق	I
to beget – assimilated	يولَد	وُلِد	يَلِد	ولد	
to say – hollow	يُقال	قيل	يقول	قال	
to recite – lame	يُتْلى	تُلي	يَتلو	تلا	
to stretch – doubled	يُمَدُّ	مُدَّ	يَمُدُّ	مَدَّ	
to unite	يُزَوَّج	زُوِّج	يُزَوِّج	زَوَّج	II
to settle an account	يُحاسَب	حوسِب	يُحاسِب	حاسَب	III
to send	يُرْسَل	أُرسِل	يُرسِل	أَرْسَل	IV
to show	يُرى	أُرِي	يُرِي	أَرى	
to give	يُؤْتى	أوتي	يؤتي	اتى	
to be scattered	يُبَعْثَر	بُعْثِر	يُبَعْثِر	بَعْثَر	QI

▪ 13. Negation

Arabic negation rules generally distinguish between two main categories: verbs
and non-verbs (nouns, adjectives, adverbs, and prepositional phrases). However,
this generalization is often violated: particles typically used to negate verbs are
used to negate non-verbal elements, and vice versa. The simplest way to approach
negation may be to list the different negation particles (لا، كلا، ما، لم، لن، ليس، غير)
and illustrate their usage with examples.

1. غير and ليس are used to negate non-verbal elements. غير can be translated as
    not or *other than*, while ليس can be translated as *not*:

Not those that anger fell on them.	غير المغضوب عليهم (الفاتحة ٧)
(There is) not food for them except bitter thorn-fruit.	ليس لهم طعام الا من ضريع (الغاشية ٦)

2. لا and كلا

a. By itself لا can be translated as "no" or "nay". In this usage, it is similar to كلا:

| Nay, I swear by this city. | لا، أقسم بهذا البلد (البلد ١) |
| Nay, if he does not cease, we will seize him by the forelock. | كلا، لإن لم ينته لنسفعن بالناصية (العلق ١٥) |

b. لا is used to negate verbs in the imperfect:

| I do not worship what you worship. | لا أعبد ما تعْبُدون (الكافرون ٢) |
| Does not he know (that) when the contents of the graves are poured forth? | أفلا يعلَم اذا بُعْثر ما في القبور (العاديات ٩) |

c. لا is used in negative commands (prohibition) with the meaning of *do not*:

| Nay, do not obey him, and prostrate yourself and draw near. | كلا، لا تُطِعْه واسجد واقترِب (العلق ١٩) |

d. ولا in conjunction with another negative particle can be translated as *nor*:

| Not those who earn thy anger, nor those who go astray. | غير المغضوب عليهم، ولا الضالين. (الفاتحة ٧) |
| Then he will have no might nor any helper. | فما له من قوّة ولا ناصر (الطارق ١٠) |

3. ما is used mostly to negate verbs in the perfect, but it is also used to negate imperfect verbs and non-verbal elements:

a. Negation of perfect verbs:

| Thy Lord has not forsaken you, nor does he hate you. | ما ودّعك ربّك وما قلى. (الضحى ٣) |

b.   Negation of imperfect verbs:

Which none denies except each criminal transgressor.	وما يكذّب به الا كلّ معتدٍ أثيم (المطفّفين ١٢)
And you will not, unless (it be) that Allah wills, the Lord of Creation.	وما تشاؤون الا أن يشاء الله ربّ العالمين (التكوير ٢٩)

c.   Negation of verbless phrases:

Then he will have no (does not have) might nor any helper.	فما له من قوّة ولا ناصر (الطارق ١٠)
And your comrade is not mad.	وما صاحبكم بمجنون (التكوير ٢٢)

3.   لم is generally followed by the imperfect form of the verb, but the reference is for past tense. It is the equivalent of English *did not*:

He did not beget and was not begotten.	لم يلِد ولم يولَد (التوحيد ٣)
Did not we cause your bosom to dilate?	ألم نشرَح لك صدرك (الشرح ١)

4.   لم sometimes appears as لّا:

Nay, but he has not done what He commanded him.	كلّا لّا يقضِ ما أمره. (عبس ٢٣)

5.   لن is used to negate verbs with a future reference. It can be translated into English *will not*:

Does he think that no one can (will) overcome him?	أيحسب أن لن يقدر عليه أحد (البلد ٥)
We will not increase (anything) for you except torment.	فلن نزيدنّكم الا عذاباً (النبأ ٣٠)

■ 14. Moods of the imperfect verb

Four main moods of the imperfect verb are recognized in Qur'ānic Arabic: *declarative* or *indicative* (المرفوع), *subjunctive* (المنصوب), *jussive* (المجزوم), and the *imperative* (الأمر). Each mood is marked by certain endings, modifications of the vowels of a verb, or the loss of certain elements. The shapes that the verbs assume are directly related to the type of root they are derived from. Examples that represent the different root types will be used in the tables below.

Declarative (المرفوع)

The indicative mood is the neutral one. It is used when no special meanings or functions are imposed on the verb, and is marked by a ـُ (*damma*) at the end of verbs in the singular and ون at the end of verbs in the plural. This mood is the one used in the imperfect forms of verbs in the section on Root types and verb conjugations.

Subjunctive (المنصوب)

The subjunctive is marked by a ـَ (فتحة) at the end of verbs in the singular and deletion of the ن of the indicative in the plural and its replacement by ا, which is not pronounced. It is used after certain particles, of which the following are found in this book:

to	لِ
to, that	أَن
will not	لَن

Examples

١. فذوقوا فلن نزيدَكم الا عذاباً (النبأ ٣٠)

٢. وما تشاءون الا أن يشاءَ الله ربِّ العالمين (التكوير ٢٩)

٣. وما أُمِروا الا لِيعبدوا الله (البيّنة ٥)

Jussive (المجزوم)

The *jussive* mood is used mainly after the particle لم "did not" (and its variant لمّا), after لا of prohibition, and in conditional sentences. It is marked differently on different types of verbs in the singular person, but in the same way for the plural, where it is identical to the subjunctive form. In verbs derived from sound, assimilated, and quadriliteral roots, it is marked by a ـْ (سكون) at the end of the verb. In verbs derived from hollow roots, it is marked by a shortening of the long vowel and a سكون on the last consonant of the verb. In verbs derived from lame roots, it is marked by a shortening of the long final vowel; and in verbs derived from doubled roots, it is marked by a فتحة (as in the subjunctive).

١. ألم يعلَمْ بأنّ الله يرى (العلق ١٤)

٢. ولم يكُن له كفواً أحد (التوحيد ٤)

٣. ألم ترَ كيف فعل ربّك بأصحاب الفيل (الفيل ١)

٤. لم يلبثوا الا عشيّة أو ضحاها (عبس ٤٦)

٥. إنّ الذين فتنوا المؤمنين والمؤمنات ثمّ لم يتوبوا (البروج ١٠)

٦. ألم يروا كم أهلكنا قبلهم من القرون (يس ٣١)

Imperative (الأمر)

The imperative mood is used to give commands. Verbs in the imperative can be divided into three categories:

a. Ordinary commands given in the second person

The English equivalent would be verbs like *Stop*, *Write*, *Go*, etc. The second person is implied (*You stop, You write, You go*).

Ordinary commands are formed in the following way:

1. Starting with the *jussive* form of the verb, remove person prefixes.
2. If the removal of such prefixes results in a two-consonant cluster, prefix a ا to the verb. The ا appears in sound and lame verbs of Form I and in Forms VII, VIII, and X.

١. اقرأ باسم ربّك الذي خلق (العلق ١)

٢. قُل هو الله أحَد (التوحيد ١)

٣. وأمّا بنعمة ربّك فحدِّث (الضحى ١١)

٤. فصلِّ لربّك وانحَر (الكوثر ٢)

٥. كلا لا تطِعْه واسجُد واقترب (العلق ١٩)

٦. ارجعي الى ربّكِ راضية مرضيّة. وادخُلي في عِبادي وادخُلي جنّتي. (الفجر ٢٨-٣٠)

b. Commands given in the third person

The English equivalent would be: *Let him stop, Let them write*, etc. The form of the verb used here is the *jussive* preceded by لِ or فلِ:

١. فلْيَنْظُرِ الانسان مِمّ خُلِق (الطارق ٥)

٢. فليعبُدوا ربّ هذا البيت (قريش ٣)

c. Prohibition

The verb is in the *jussive* form and is generally preceded by the negative particle لا. In English, these are the negative counterparts of the commands in a. above: *Don't stop*, *Don't write*, etc.

١. فأمّا اليتيم فلا تقهَر، وأمّا السائل فلا تنهَر. (الضحى ٩–١٠)

٢. كلا لا تُطِعْه واسجد واقترب. (العلق ١٩)

The energetic mood

This is the least common of all moods. It consists of suffixing the consonant ن to the verb in the declarative. There are two variants, one with a شدّة followed by a فتحة on ن and another with سكون:

١. كلا لينبَذَنَّ في الحطمة. (الهمزة ٤)

٢. كلا لئن لم ينتهِ لنَسفَعَن بالناصية. (العلق ١٥)

The following tables show a representative sample of verbs conjugated in the different persons in the *declarative*, *jussive*, *imperative*, and *subjunctive* moods.

1. Verbs derived from sound roots

Subjunctive	Imperative	Jussive	Declarative	
يَعْبُدَ		يَعْبُدْ	يَعْبُدُ	هو
تَعْبُدَ		تَعْبُدْ	تَعْبُدُ	هي
يَعْبُدوا		يَعْبُدوا	يَعْبُدون	هم
تَعْبُدَ	اعبُدْ	تَعْبُدْ	تَعْبُدُ	انتَ
تعبُدي	اعبُدي	تعبُدي	تَعبُدين	انتِ
تعبُدوا	اعبُدوا	تعبُدوا	تعبُدون	انتُم
أَعْبُدَ		أَعْبُدْ	أَعبُدُ	أنا
نعبُدَ		نعبُدْ	نَعبُدُ	نحنُ

2. Assimilated roots

Subjunctive	Imperative	Jussive	Declarative	
يَرِثَ		يَرِثْ	يَرِثُ	هو
تَرِثَ		تَرِثْ	تَرِثُ	هي
يرِثوا		يرِثوا	يَرِثون	هم
تَرِثَ	رِثْ	تَرِثْ	تَرِثُ	انتَ
تَرِثِي	رِثِي	ترِثي	تَرِثين	انتِ
ترِثوا	رِثوا	ترِثوا	ترِثون	انتم
أَرِثَ		أَرِثْ	أَرِثُ	أَنا
نرِثَ		نَرِثْ	نَرِثُ	نحنُ

The verbs أكل and أخذ follow the conjugation pattern of sound verbs except in the imperative, where they behave like assimilated verbs, as shown in the following table:

كُل	خُذ	انتَ
كُلِي	خُذِي	انتِ
كُلوا	خُذوا	انتم

3. Hollow roots

Subjunctive	Imperative	Jussive	Declarative	
يقولَ		يقُلْ	يَقولُ	هو
تقولَ		تقُلْ	تَقولُ	هي
يكونوا		يكونوا	يَكونون	هم
تقولَ	قُلْ	تَقُلْ	تَقولُ	انتَ
تكوني	كوني	تكوني	تَكونين	انتِ
تكونوا	كونوا	تكونوا	تكونون	انتُم
أقولَ		أقولْ	أَقولُ	أَنا
نقولَ		نَقولْ	نَقولُ	نحنُ

4. Lame roots

Subjunctive	Imperative	Jussive	Declarative	
يرميَ		يرمِ	يرمي	هو
ترميَ		ترمِ	ترمي	هي
يرموا		يرموا	يرمون	هم
ترميَ	ارمِ	ترمِ	ترمي	انتَ
ترمي	ارمي	ترمي	ترمين	انتِ
ترموا	ارموا	ترموا	ترمون	انتم
أرميَ		أرمِ	أرمي	أنا
نرميَ		نرمِ	نرمي	نحنُ

5. Doubled root

Subjunctive	Imperative	Jussive	Declarative	
يعدَّ		يرُدّ	يَرُدّ	هو
تَرُدّ		تَرُدّ	تَرُدُّ	هي
يرُدّوا		يرُدّوا	يرُدّون	هم
تَرُدّ	رُدّ	تَرُدّ	تَرُدُّ	انتَ
ترُدّي	رُدّي	ترُدّي	ترُدّين	انتِ
ترُدّوا	رُدّوا	ترُدّوا	ترُدّون	انتم
أرُدَّ		أرُدّ	أرُدُّ	أنا
نَرُدَّ		نرُدّ	نرُدُّ	نحن

The Verb رأى "to see"

The following table shows the conjugation of the highly irregular verb رأى "he saw" in the perfect and imperfect indicative, jussive, and subjunctive. It is not used in the imperative; the sound verb نظر "to look" is used instead.

Subjunctive	Jussive	Indicative	Perfect	
يرى	يَرَ	يَرى	رأى	هو
ترى	تَرَ	تَرى	رأَت	هي
يرَوْا	يَرَوا	يَرَوْن	رأوا	هم
تَرى	تَرَ	تَرى	رأَيْتَ	انتَ
تَرَيْ	تَرَي	تَرَيْن	رأيتِ	انتِ
تَرَوا	تَرَوا	تَرَوْن	رأيتُم	انتم
أرى	أَرَ	أرى	رأيتُ	أنا
نَرى	نَرَ	نَرى	رأينا	نحن

لم يكُ/لم يكُن

As a verb derived from a hollow root, the imperfect verb يكون "he is, will be" loses its و in the jussive mood. This is a general rule of Qur'ānic Arabic. This word and its related forms are further shortened by the loss of final ن in some instances. There is no rule for this type of shortening. Just remember that لم يكُ is a shortened form of the more common لم يكُن.

One final note about verb moods. The examples given in the tables above demonstrate the behavior of Form I verbs, the most common verb form, in the different moods. It should be noted, however, that, in general, derived verbs (Forms II–X) based on weak roots, which are less regular than verbs based on sound roots, tend to be more regular with respect to mood assignment than the basic Form I. Compare the conjugation of the Form I verb أورث "to give as inheritance" to that of the Form I verb ورث, shown above.

Subjunctive	Imperative	Jussive	Declarative	
يورِثَ		يورِثْ	يورِثُ	هو
تورِثَ		تورِثْ	تورِثُ	هي
يورِثوا		يورِثوا	يورثون	هم
تورِثَ	أورِثْ	تورِثْ	تورِثُ	انتَ
تورِثي	أورِثي	تورِثي	تورِثين	انتِ
تورِثوا	أورِثوا	تورِثوا	تورثون	انتم
أورِثَ		أورِثْ	أورِثُ	أنا
نورِثَ		نورِثْ	نورِثُ	نحنُ

For more on this, see (references): Wright's *Grammar of the Arabic Language*, Grammar of Classical Arabic.

◼ 15. The case system

Nouns and adjectives in Arabic may have one of three cases, depending on their function in the sentence: *nominative* (المرفوع), *accusative* (المنصوب), or *genitive* (المجرور).

The three cases are indicated by certain endings, which vary according to the following factors: first, whether the noun or adjective is definite or indefinite; second, whether it has a sound plural or a dual ending (ان/ين, ات, or ين/ون); and third, whether it ends in التاء المربوطة. These endings are shown in the following table:

Singular and broken plural

		Nominative	Accusative	Genitive	
indefinite	masculine	كِتابٌ	كِتاباً	كِتابٍ	book
	feminine	آيةٌ	آيةً	آيةٍ	Qur'ānic verse
definite	masculine	الكِتابُ	الكِتابَ	الكِتابِ	the book
	feminine	الآيةُ	الآيةَ	الآيةِ	the Qur'ānic verse
indefinite	Broken plural	كُتُبٌ	كُتُباً	كُتُبٍ	books
definite		الكُتُبُ	الكُتُبَ	الكُتُبِ	the books

Sound plural

		Nominative	Accusative/genitive
indefinite	masculine	كافِرونَ	كافِرينَ
	feminine	آياتٌ	آياتٍ
definite	masculine	الكافِرونَ	الكافِرين
	feminine	الآياتُ	الآياتِ

Dual

		Nominative	**Accusative/genitive**
indefinite	masculine	اثنان	اثنَين
	feminine	اثنتان	اثنتَين
definite	masculine	الاثنان	الاثنين
	feminine	الاثنتان	الاثنتين

The endings ـٌ, ـٍ (or اً), and ـ are called *nunation*. *Nunation* is mutually exclusive with the definite article; if the noun or adjective has the definite article, then it cannot be *nunated*. Similarly, *nunation* is absent when the noun or adjective is the first term of an إضافة construction (see الإضافة) or ends in a pronominal suffix. So whereas الكِتابُ and كِتابُهم are acceptable, الكتابٌ* and كتابُهمٌ* are not.

Rules of case assignment

Nominative

a. Subject of a verb:

ما أَغنى عنه مالُه وما كسب (المسد ٢)

فأمّا مَن ثقُلَت موازينُه فهو في عيشة راضية (القارعة ٦)

يشهدُه المقرّبون (المطفّفين ٢١)

b. Subject of an equational (verbless) sentence:

الحمدُ لله ربّ العالمين (الفاتحة ٢)

في جيدِها حبلٌ من مسد (المسد ٦)

رسولٌ من الله يتلو صحفاً مطهّرة (البيّنة ٢)

c. Predicate of an equational sentence:

وأنتَ حِلٌّ بهذا البلد (البلد ٢)

جزاؤُهم عند ربِّهم جنّاتُ عدن تجري من تحتها الأنهار (٨)

ليلةُ القدرِ خيرٌ من ألف شهر (القدر ٣)

d. Subject of كان and its sisters (ليس):

يوم يكون الناسُ كالفَراش المبثوث، وتكون الجبالُ كالعهن المنفوش (القارعة ٤-٥)

ليس لهم طعامٌ الا من ضريع. (الغاشية ٦)

e. Predicate of إنّ and its sisters (أنّ):

ألا يَظنّ أولئك أنّهم مبعوثون (المطفّفين ٤)

Genitive

a. *Object of a preposition* (ك, على ,من ,في ,ب ,لـ):

الحمد لله ربِّ العالَمين (الفاتحة ٢)

فويلٌ للمصلِّين، الذين هم عن صلاتِهم ساهون (الماعون ٤–٥)

قُل أعوذُ بِرَبِّ الناس (الناس ١)

وهم على ما يفعلون بالمؤمنين شهود (البروج ٧)

من شرِّ الوسواس الخنّاس (الناس ٤)

الذي يوسوس في صدورِ الناس (الناس ٥)

ولا يحضّ على طعام المسكين (الماعون ٣)

فجعلهم كعصفٍ مأكول (الفيل ٥)

b. *Second term of* الإضافة *construction (see* الإضافة *below):*

مالكِ يوم الدين (الفاتحة ٤)

من شرِّ **الوسواس** الخنّاس (الناس ٤)

من شرِّ **النفّاثاتِ** في العُقد (الفلق ٤)

ومن شرِّ **حاسدٍ** اذا حسد (الفلق ٥)

Accusative

a. *Object of a verb:*

اهدنا السراطَ المستقيم (الفاتحة ٦)

فليعبدوا ربَّ هذا البيت (قريش ٣)

الذي جمع مالاً وعدّده (الهمزة ٢)

ويُقيموا الصلاةَ ويؤتوا الزكاةَ (البيّنة ٥)

يومئذٍ تحدّث أخبارَها (الزلزلة ٤)

فمهِّل الكافرين أمهلهم رُويداً. (الطارق ١٧)

إنّ الذين فتنوا المؤمنينَ والمؤمناتِ ثمّ لم يتوبوا (البروج ١٠)

b. *Predicate of* كان:

إنّه كان توّاباً (النصر ٣)

لم يكن الذين كفروا من أهل الكتاب والمشركين منفكّين حتى تأتيهم البيّنة (البيّنة ١)

إنّه كان في أهله مسروراً (الانشقاق ١٣)

c. *Subject of* إنّ *and* أنّ:

إنّ شانئَك هو الأبتر (الكوثر ٣)

إنّ الينا إيابَهم، ثمّ إنّ علينا حسابَهم (الغاشية ٢٥ – ٢٦)

إنّ ربَّهم بهم يومئذٍ لخبير (العاديات ١١)

أيحسب أنّ مالَه أخلده (الهمزة ٣)

d. المفعول المطلق

This category of accusatives refers to verbal nouns derived directly from verbs in the same sentence. The English equivalent, much less common than in Arabic, is found in sentences like: *He laughed a big laugh.*

تأكلون التراث أكلاً لمّاً (الفجر ١٩)

وتحبّون المال حُبّاً جمّاً (الفجر ٢٠)

إنّهم يكيدون كيداً، وأكيد كيْداً (الطارق ١٥–١٦)

فسوف يُحاسَب حساباً يسيراً (الانشقاق ٨)

e. *The vocative*

يا أختَ هارون (مريم ٢٨)

General remarks about the case system

1. Case assignment is a grammatical function that has no bearing on the meaning. In other words, كافرين and كتابُ, كتابٌ, and كتاب, all mean "book", and كافرون and كافرين both translate as "disbelievers".

2. The system of case and mood endings is called collectively إعراب. Arab grammarians distinguish between إعراب بالحروف) إعراب with letters) and إعراب بالحركات) إعراب with diacritics or short vowels). In general, the short vowels associated with إعراب are optionally dropped at the end of a phrase, and what is called "pause forms" are used.

3. Nouns and adjectives joined by a conjunction share the same case:

الذي له ملكُ السماواتِ والأرضِ (البروج:٩)

فأنبتنا فيها حبّاً. وعنباً وقضباً (عبس: ٢٧–٢٨)

4. An adjective agrees in case with the noun it modifies (unless it serves as the predicate of كان and its sisters or the predicate of إنّ and its sisters).

قُل أعوذُ بربِّ الناسِ، ملكِ الناسِ، الهِ الناسِ، من شرِّ الوسواسِ الخنّاسِ (الناس: ١–٤)

فسوف يُحاسَب حساباً يسيراً (الانشقاق: ٨)

5. Case is marked on the words أب "father" and أخ "brother" with letters rather than diacritics when possessive pronouns are attached to these words, as shown in the following table:

	Nominative	Accusative	Genitive
his father	أبوه	أباه	أبيه
your (m. sg.) brother	أخوه	أخاه	أخيه

The word ذو and its derivatives ذي and ذات (as well as ذوي and ذوات) can be translated into English as "of", "with", or "characterized by":

ذو العرش the one with the throne

ذي حِجر the one characterized by, or the one with the mind or understanding

ذات العِماد the one (f.) with the columns

The difference between ذو and ذي is a difference of case, ذو is in the nominative case, and ذي is in the genitive case. The difference between both forms and ذات is that the latter refers to feminine nouns.

6. Indefinite nouns and adjectives ending in ي lose it in the nominative and genitive cases, and show genitive *nunation* in its place:

Examples	Indefinite in the nominative or genitive case	Original form
والفجر وليالٍ عشر. (الفجر: ١)	ليالٍ	ليالي
وما يكذّب به الا كلّ معتدٍ أثيم. (المطففين: ١٢)	معتدٍ	مُعتدي

◾ 16. The construct الإضافة

When two or more nouns are closely associated, as in the case of possession or something being part of something else, they form a special grammatical construction called the construct (إضافة). This is shown in the following examples:

(the) Lord of the Universe	ربّ العالمين
the Day of Judgement	يوم الدين
people's breasts	صدورِ الناس
the weight of an atom	مثقال ذرّةٍ

Important features of الإضافة:

1. The first term of إضافة is never *nunated* (ending in ـاً, ـٌ, or ـٍ) and never has the definite article; the second term may have either.

2. If the first term of a construct ends in التاء المربوطة (the feminine ending ـة), التاء المربوطة is pronounced as a regular ت. In other words, the pause form is never used in the first term of the construct. A common example is the word سورة followed by the name of a Qur'ān chapter, as in سورة يوسف or سورة مريم. The ة of سورة is never dropped in the pronunciation of such phrases.

3. If the first term of إضافة is a masculine plural or dual noun ending in ين, ـيْن, ون, or ان, the final ن is dropped. For example, in the verse يا صاحبي السجن يوسف (Yūsuf: 39) the word صاحبي was originally صاحبين. The same thing happens when a pronominal suffix is attached to the noun. The word أبويه (Yūsuf: 100) is based on أبوين "two parents" and the possessive suffix ـه.

4. The first term of an إضافة construction may have any of the three cases, but the second is always in the genitive case, as shown in the following three verses:

ليلةُ القدرِ خيرٌ من ألف شهرٍ (القدر ٣)

In ليلة القدر, ليلة is in the nominative case because it is the subject of an equational sentence, القدر is in the genitive case because it is the second term of إضافة.

فمن يعمل مثقال ذرّةٍ خيراً يره. (الزلزلة ٧)

In مثقال ذرّة, مثقال is in the accusative case because it is the object of the verb يعمل, ذرّةٍ is in the genitive case because it is the second term of إضافة.

مالك يوم الدين (الفاتحة ٤)

مالك يوم الدين has two construct phrases يوم الدين and مالك يوم الدين. مالك is in the genitive case because it modifies a preceding noun in the genitive case (لك), يوم is in the genitive case because it is the second term of إضافة in the phrase مالك يوم, and الدين is in the genitive case because it is the second term of إضافة in the phrase يوم الدين.

yes/no question particle		أ
posterity, house of		آل
(Qur'ānic) verse, revelation	آية (ج. آيات)	آية
father	أب (ج. آباء)	أب
parents	أبوين	
(O) my father	(يا) أبَتِ	
grasses, herbage	أبّ	أبب
for ever		أبداً
swarms	أبابيل	أبل
camels	إبِل	
child	ابن (ج. بَني، بنين)	أبن
Abu/Abi Lahab	أبو/أبي لَهَب	أبو
to come	I (أتى – يأتي)	أتي
to give	IV (آتى – يؤتي)	
to be given	IV (أُوتِي – يُؤتى)	
coming	آتِي	
to bring	أتى بـ	
they were given	أوتوا	
fulfillment will come to pass, sure of fulfillment	مَأتِيّ	
goods, gear	أثاث	أثث
to stir up	IV (أثَار – يُثير)	أثر
to choose, prefer	IV (آثَر – يؤثر)	

traces, footprints	آثار	
sinner, criminal	أَثيم	أثم
reward	أجر	أجر
brothers	إخوة	أخ
to take	I (أَخَذ – يَأخُذ)	أخذ
to adopt, seek	VIII (اتّخذ – يتّخِذ)	
to leave behind	II (أَخَّر – يُؤخِّر)	أخر
latter portion, Afterlife	آخِرة	
other	أُخَر	
terrible, evil, disastrous thing	إدّ	أدد
to listen and obey, be attentive	I (أَذِن – يأذَن)	أذن
to cry, call	II (أَذَّن)	
permission	إذْن	
crier	مُؤَذِّن	
then	إذَن	أذن
earth, land	أرْض	أرض
thrones, couches	أرائك	أرك
to push, confound	I (أَزَّ – يَؤُزّ)	أزز
my grief	يا أَسَفي	أسف
horizon	أُفُق	أفق
to eat	I (أكل – يأكُل)	أكل
eating, greed	أكل	
eaten, devoured	مأكول	
not to be	أن لا	ألّا
thousand	أَلْف	ألف
thick foliage, thick growth	ألفاف	ألف
painful	أليم	ألم

god	اله (ج. اَلِهة)	أله
By Allah	تالله	
as for		أمّا
to be ordered	I (أُمِر – يؤمر)	أمر
to order, enjoin	I (أَمَر – يأمُر)	
to be inclined, enjoined	أمّارة	
event, command, decree, decision	أمر	
mother	أمّ	أمم
book	إمام	
to trust	I (أَمِن – يأمَن)	أمن
to believe, to make safe	IV (آمَن – يؤمن)	
if	إذ	
that not	ألاّ = أنْ لا	أن
that, when, because	أنْ	
I		أنا
you (m. pl.)		أنتُم
female	أُنثى	أنث
mankind	إنسان	أنس
human being, mortal	إنسيّ	
mankind	ناس	
how		أنّى
boiling	آني	أني
people	أهل	أهل
return	إياب	أوب
home, dwelling place	مآب	
ancients, men of old	أوّل (ج. أوّلين)	أول
first, former, this life	أولى	

men of understanding	أولي الألباب	
interpretation	تأويل	
those		أولئك
to take to oneself	I (أَوى – يأوي)	أوى
to offer shelter	IV (آوى – يُؤوي)	
O you (f. sg.)	أيّتها	أيّ
you (m. sg.)	إيّاك	أيّا
when	أيّان	أين
O you (m. sg.)		أيّها
name of place		إرم
except		إلّا
either, whether		إمّا
that, lo, though, verily		إنّ
you are only . . . , you are nothing but . . .		إن أنتُم الاّ . . .
and surely, everyone of them; but all, without exception		إن كُلٌّ لَّا جَميع
truly that		إنّما
if, when		اذا
name	سم، اسم	اسم
the		ال
that, which (f. sg.)		الّتي
that, who		الّذي
those who		الّذين
in		بِ
to grieve, sorrow	VIII (ابتأس – يبتئس)	بأس
punishment, wrath	بَأس	بأس
one without posterity	أَبتَر	بتر

grief, distress	بَثّ	بثث
spread, scattered	مَبثوث	
sea	بَحر (ج. بِحار)	بحر
low	بَخس	بخس
to hoard (be miserly)	I (بَخِل – يبخَل)	بخل
to begin, produce, reveal	IV (أبدأ – يُبدِئ)	بدأ
bedouin life, desert	بَدو	بدو
to free, exculpate	II (بَرَّأ – يُبَرِّئ)	برأ
mansions (of the stars), big stars	بُروج	برج
to leave, go forth	I (بَرَح – يَبرَح)	برح
dutiful, righteous, obedient	بَرّ (ج. أبرار، بَرَرة)	برر
created beings	بَرِيّة	برأ
to stand forth, to be made apparent in full view	بُرِّز	برز
blessed	مُبارَك	برك
evidence, argument	بُرهان	برهن
to give tidings to, announce	II (بَشَّر – يُبَشِّر)	بشر
human beings	بَشَر	
good news, good luck	بُشرى	
bearer of glad tidings	بَشير	
rejoicing at good news	مُستَبشِر	
to see	IV (أبصَر – يُبصِر)	بصر
eyes	أبصار	
clear-sighted, seer	بَصير	
looking, beholding	بصير	
sure knowledge	بَصيرة	
to see	IV (أبصَر – يُبصِر)	

merchandise, treasure	بِضاعة	بضع
punishment	بَطش	بطش
to raise up, out of	I (بَعَثَ – يبعث)	بعث
to break forth	VII (انبَعَثَ – ينبعِث)	
resurrected	مَبعوث	
to be scattered, turned upside down	QI (بُعثِرَ – يُبعثر)	بعثر
(henceforth, still)	بَعْد	بعد
after	بَعْد	
at length, after a time	بَعد أُمَّة	
camel	بَعير	بعر
some	بَعض	بعض
all of a sudden, suddenly	بَغتة	بغت
seeking	ابتِغاء	بغو/بغي
to desire, ask	I (بَغى – يَبغي)	
to be (suitable) for	VII (إنبَغى – يَنبَغي)	
unchaste	بَغِيّ	
cow	بَقَرة	بقر
more lasting	أبقى	بقي
morning, break of day	بُكرة	بكر
weeping	بُكِيّ	بكي
land, country	بَلَد	بلد
conveying (of a message)	بلاغ	بلغ
to attain, to reach	I (بَلَغَ – يبلُغ)	
to be examined	I (بُلِيَ – يُبلى)	بلو
to try, put to the test	VIII (ابتَلى – يبتلي)	بلو
yes, indeed		بَلى
my (dear) son	بُنَيّ	بن

to build	I (بَنَى – يَبني)	بني
to take possession, be the owner	V (تَبَوَّأ – يَتَبَوَّأ)	بوأ
door, gate	باب (ج. أبواب)	بوب
house	بَيت	بيت
his eyes became white, he lost his eyesight	ابيضَّت عيناه	بيض
before, between the hands	بَين أَيدي	بين
clear	بَيِّن	
proof	بَيِّنة	
clear	مُبين	
to perish	I (تبّ)	تبب
to follow	I (تبِع – يتبَع)	تبع
to follow	VIII (اتَّبَع – يَتَّبِع)	
under		تَحْت
of equal age	أتراب	ترب
ribs	تَرائب	
dust	تُراب	
misery	مَترَبة	
inheritance	تُراث	ترث
to leave	I (تَرَك – يترُك)	ترك
to fear, be dutiful towards Allah, ward off (evil)	VIII (اتّقى – يتّقي)	تقو
righteous	أتْقى	
piety	تَقْوى	
righteous, devout	تَقِيّ	
to read, recite	I (تلا – يتلو)	تلو
to follow	I (تَلا/تلى – يتلو)	
to be recited	I (تُلِي – يُتلى)	

to perfect	IV (أَتَمَّ – يُتِمّ)	تمم
to repent	I (تاب – يتوب)	توب
one who is ready to show mercy	تَوّاب	
fig	تين	تين
destruction	ثُبور	ثبر
abundant	ثَجّاج	ثجج
reproach, fear	تَثريب	ثرب
piercing	ثاقِب	ثقب
burdens	أثقال	ثقل
to be heavy	ثَقُل	
weight	مِثقال	
third	ثالِث	ثلث
and then	ثُمَّ	
fruit	ثَمَر	ثمر
price	ثَمَن	ثمن
Thamūd (name of a tribe)		ثَمود
two	اثنَين	ثني
to be paid for	II (ثُوِّب – يُثَوَّب)	ثوب
reward	ثَواب	
stay, reception	مَثوى	ثوي
well, pit	جُبّ	جبب
arrogant	جَبّار	جبر
mountains	جِبال	جبل
multitude	جِبِلّ	
to choose, prefer	VIII (اجتبى – يجتبي)	جبي
on their knees, crouching	جِثِيّ	جثو
hell-fire	جَحيم	جحم

graves	أجداث	جدث
trunk	جِذع	جذع
to commit a crime	IV (أجرَم – يُجرِم)	جرم
criminal, disbeliever, sinner, wicked, guilty	مُجرِم	
to flow	I (جَرى – يَجري)	جري
running, gushing	جاري	
to reward	I (جزى – يَجزي)	جزي
recompense, reward	جَزاء	
to make, throw, place	I (جعَل – يجعَل)	جعل
to be resplendent	V (تَجَلّى – يتجلّى)	جلو/جلي
to reveal	II (جَلّى – يجلّي)	
gathering	جَمْع	جمع
he collected	جَمَع	
comely	جَميل	جمل
much, in abundance	جَمّ	جمم
to be made to avoid	I (جُنِّب – يُجَنَّب)	جنب
to be avoided	V (تَجَنَّب – يَتَجَنَّب)	
side, slope	جانِب	
host	جُند (ج. جنود)	جند
the Garden of Eden	جنّة (ج. جنّات) عَدْن	جنن
jinn	جِنّة	
mad	مجنون	
fresh; ripe	جَنِيّ	جني
what is apparent	جَهر	جهر
to furnish, provide	II (جَهَّز – يُجهِّز)	جهز
provisions	جِهاز	

ignorant, foolish	جاهِل	جهل
hell		جَهَنَّم
to cut, cleave	I (جاب – يجوب)	جوب
to answer (an invocation), to hear (a prayer)	X (استجاب)	
stars, planets	جَواري	جور
hunger	جوع	جوع
to come	I (جاء – يجيء)	جيء
to be brought	I (جيء ب)	
to drive to, bring to	IV (أجاء – يُجي)	
neck	جِيد	جيد
how perfect is Allah, God forbid, Allah blameless	حاشَ الله	حاش
to like, love	IV (أحبّ – يُحِبّ)	حبب
dearer	أحَبّ	
love	حُبّ	
rope	حَبل	حبل
decree, ordinance	حَتم	حتم
until		حَتّى
screen, seclusion	حِجاب	حجب
covered, veiled	مَحجوب	
stones	حِجارة	حجر
thinking, mind	حِجر	
to tell, relate	II (حَدّث – يُحَدِّث)	حدث
dreams, events	حديث (ج. أحاديث)	
gardens	حَدائق	حدق
praying place, sanctuary	مِحراب	حرب
to desire eagerly, try much	I (حَرَص – يحرِص)	حرص

weak with old age, with ruined health	حَرَض	حرض
burning fire	حَريق	حرق
sects	أحزاب	حزب
to grieve, sadden	I (حَزِن – يحزَن)	حزن
to think	I (حسِب – يحسَب)	حسب
to settle an account	III (حاسَب – يُحاسِب)	
reckoning	حِساب	
to envy	I (حَسَد – يحسِد)	حسد
envier	حاسِد	
alas, anguish	حَسرة	حسر
to find, see	IV (أحَسَّ – يُحِسّ)	حسس
inquire about, ascertain	V (تَحَسَّس – يتحسَّس)	
best	أحسَن	حسن
goodness	حُسْنى	
doer of good	مُحسِن	
to be gathered, herded together	I (حَشِر – يُحشَر)	حشر
to gather together, assemble	I (حَشَر – يَحشُر)	
to come out, become manifest	حَصحَص	حصحص
to be brought out, made known	II (حَصَّل – يُحصِّل)	حصل
to guard, store	IV (أحصَن – يُحصِن)	حصن
to know, record	IV (أحصَى – يُحصي)	حصو
to bring, make ready	IV (أحضَر – يُحضِر)	حضر
brought	مُحضَر	
to urge	I (حضّ – يَحُضّ)	حضض
to urge one another	VI (تَحاضّ – يتحاضّ)	
wood	حَطَب	حطب
consuming one	حُطَمة	حطم

first state, former state	حافِرة	حفر
protector, guardian	حافِظ	حفظ
keeper, guardian	حَفيظ	
guarded, preserved	مَحفوظ	
gracious	حَفِيّ	حفو
ages	أحقاب	حقب
to be afraid, to be obligated to do	I (حُقّ – يُحَقّ)	حقق
truth	حَقّ	
to prove true	I (حَقَّ – يحِقّ)	
wise, full of wisdom	حَكيم	حكم
most conclusive	أَحْكَم	
judge	حاكِم	
wisdom	حُكم	
indweller	حِلّ	حلل
dreams	أحلام	حلم
praise	حَمد	حمد
to carry	I (حمَل – يحمِل)	حمل
carrier	حمّال	
load	حِمل	
to bear	I (حَمَل – يحمِل)	
boiling water	حَميم	حمم
hot	حامي	حمي
upright (pl.)	حُنَفاء	حنف
sympathy, mercy, compassion	حَنان	حنن
need	حاجة	حوج
to return	I (حار – يحور)	حور
to surround	IV (أحاط – يُحيط)	حوط

encompassing	مُحيط	
dark	أَحوى	حوي
living, alive	حَيّ	حيي
to bring to life	IV (أحيا – يُحيي)	
for a while	الى حين	حين
news, chronicles	أخبار	خبر
knowing, perfectly informed	خَبير	
bread	خُبز	خبز
to seal up	I (خَتَم – يختِم)	ختم
seal, last part of	خِتام	
sealed	مَختوم	
ditch	أُخدود	خدد
to bring out	IV (أخرَج – يُخرِج)	خرج
to bring out, produce	X (استَخرَج – يستخرج)	
to fall	I (خَرَّ – يخِرّ)	خرر
store-houses	خَزائن	خزن
to give less	IV (أخسَر – يُخسِر)	خسر
vain, losing	خاسِر	
state of loss	خُسر	
downcast, humiliated	خاشِع	خشع
to fear	I (خَشِي – يخشى)	خشي
to dispute	II (خَصَّم – يَخِصِّم)	خصم
opponent	خَصيم	
green	أخضَر	خضر
sinful, faulty	خاطِئ	خطأ
conversing, speaking	خِطاب	خطب
affair, happening	خَطب	

English	Arabic	Root
was light	خَفّ	خفف
to be hidden	I (خَفِي – يَخفى)	خفي
secret	خَفِيّ	
to render immortal	IV (أَخلد – يُخلد)	خلد
everlasting	خالد	
to attach	X (استَخلَص – يَستَخلِص)	خلص
chosen	مُخلَص	
pure, faithful	مُخلِص	
to differ	VIII (اختَلَف – يَختلِف)	خلف
behind	خَلف	
posterity, later generation	خَلف	
to succeed	خَلَف	
to be created	I (خُلِق – يُخلَق)	خلق
to create	I (خلق – يخلُق)	
Creator	خَلّاق	
creating, creation	خَلق	
to be all for	I (خلا – يخلو)	خلو
to become empty	V (تَخَلّى – يتَخَلّى)	
still (dead, destroyed), extinct	خامِد	خمد
wine	خَمر	خمر
sneaking	خَنّاس	خنس
planets (that recede)	خُنَّس	
labor, pain of childbirth	مَخاض	خود
to dread, fear	I (خاف – يَخاف)	خوف
fear	خَوف	
to betray	I (خان – يخون)	خون
betrayer	خائِن	

to be a failure	I (خاب – يخيب)	خيب
good, better	خَيْر	خير
wealth, goods	خَيْر	
as usual	دَأَب	دأب
to turn away, turn his back	IV (أَدبَر – يُدبِر)	دبر
back, behind	دُبُر	
one who governs, arranges	مُدَبِّر	
to spread	I (دَحا – يدحو)	دحو
to enter	I (دخل – يدخُل)	دخل
degree, grade	دَرَجة	درج
to overtake	IV (أَدرَك – يُدرِك)	درك
silver coins	دَراهِم	درهم
to convey to, inform	IV (أَدرى – يُدري)	دري
to stunt	II (دَسّى – يدسّي)	دسي
to repel	I (دعّ – يَدُعُّ)	دعع
to call upon, invite, invoke	I (دعا – يدعو)	دعو
to ask (for)	VIII (ادّعى – يَدَّعي)	
invocation, prayer	دُعاء	
gushing forth	دافِق	دفق
to be ground	I (دُكَّ – يُدَكّ)	دكك
grinding	دَكّ	
to let down	IV (أَدلى – يُدلي)	دلو
bucket, pail	دَلو	
blood	دَم	دم
to doom	QI (دَمْدَم – يدمدم)	دمدم
full	دِهاق	دهق
the home (abode) of the hereafter	دَار الآخِرة	دور

as long as	I (ما) دام – يَدوم	دوم
besides, in place of		دون
Day of Judgement; religion	دين	دين
town, city	مَدينة	
wolf	ذِئب	ذأب
atom	ذَرّة	ذرر
offspring	ذُرِّيّة	
to leave	I (ذرى – يذري)	ذري
to remind	II (ذَكَّر – يُذَكِّر)	ذكر
to be reminded, remember	V (تَذَكَّر – يتَذَكَّر)	
to remember	VIII (ادَّكر)	
mention, reminder (the Qur'ān)	ذِكْر	
fame	ذِكْر	
male	ذَكَر	
remembrance, reminder	ذِكرى	
that	ذلك	ذلك
this is	ذلِكُما، ذلِكُنّ	
thus	كَذَلِكَ	
to subdue, humiliate	II (ذَلَّ – يُذلِّ)	ذلل
sin	ذَنْب	ذنب
of, characterized by		ذو
to taste	I (ذاق – يذوق)	ذوق
head	رَأس	رأس
to see	I رأى – يرى (يَرَ)	رأي
to show off	III (راءى – يُراءي)	
to show	IV (أرى – يري)	
dream, vision	رُؤيا	

outward appearance	رِئِيّ	
they (m.) will be shown	يُرَوا	
lord, god	رَبّ (ج. أرباب)	ربّ
to enjoy oneself	I (رتَع – يرتَع)	رتع
to bring back	I (رَجَع – يرجِع)	رجع
to return (someone or something)	IV (أرجَع – يُرجِع)	
rain that returns again and again	رَجع	
return	رُجعى	
to resound, to shake violently	I (رجَف – يرجُف)	رجف
the first trump, the earth and the mountains	راجِفة	
legs, feet	أرجُل	رجل
men	رِجال	
to stone	I (رجَم – يرجُم)	رجم
outcast, worthy to be stoned	رَجيم	
to look for	I (رَجا – يَرجو)	رجو
pure wine	رَحيق	رحق
bags, saddlebags	رِحال	رحل
trip, journey	رِحلة	
to bestow mercy, have mercy	I (رَحِم – يرحَم)	رحم
beneficent	رَحمن	
merciful	رَحيم	
pity	مَرحَمة	
mercy	رَحمة	
to reduce, return, ward off	I (رَدّ – يرُدّ)	ردد
to become again	VIII (ارتَدَّ – يَرتِدّ)	
resort	مَرَدّ	

one who is restored	مَردود	
second (blowing of the Trumpet)	رادِفة	ردف
to perish	V (تَرَدّى – يتردّى)	ردي
to give	I (رزَق – يرزِق)	رزق
means of life	رِزق	
to send	IV (أَرسَل – يُرسِل)	رسل
messenger	رسول (ج. رُسُل)	
messenger, one who is sent	مُرسَل	
to make fast, fix firmly	IV (أرسى – يُرسي)	رسو
port, appointed hour	مَرسى	
watchful	بالمِرصاد	رصد
ambush	مِرصاد	
to be content	I (رَضِي – يَرْضى)	رضي
well-pleased, pleasant	راضِي	
well-pleased, acceptable	رَضِيّ	
pleased with	مَرضِي	
dates	رُطَب	رطب
pasturage	مَرعى	رعو
to please	I (رغِب – يرغَب)	رغب
rejecting	راغِب عَن	
to raise, exalt	I (رَفَع – يرفَع)	رفع
raised high	مَرفوع	
slave (neck)	رَقَبة	رقب
place of sleep	مَرقَد	رقد
inscribed, written	مَرقوم	رقم
to ride	I (ركِب – يَركَب)	ركب
to cast, put together	II (ركَّب – يركِّب)	

English	Arabic	Root
riding	رُكوب	
whisper, slightest sound	رِكز	ركز
dust, something that has rotted away	رَميم	رمم
to pelt, throw	I (رَمى – يرمي)	رمي
to veil, cover	I (رهَق – يرهَق)	رهق
spirit; Gabriel or another angel	روح	روح
to smell, breath	ريح	
to seek to seduce, to ask an evil	III (راوَد – يُراوِد)	رود
to will, intend, wish	IV (أراد – يُريد)	
a while	رُوَيداً	
to be covered with sins and evil deeds	I (ران – يران)	رون
henchmen	زَبانية	زبن
shout	زَجرة	زجر
poor (quality)	مُزجى	زجي
to add more, have extra	VIII (ازداد – يَزداد)	زدد
rich, silken carpets	زَرابي	زرب
to sow	I (زرَع – يزرَع)	زرع
bound, answerable	زَعيم	زعم
alms	زَكاة	زكو/زكي
to cause to grow	II (زكّى – يزكّى)	
to become pure, grow in goodness	V (تزكّى – يتزكّى)	
righteous, faultless	زَكِيّ	
to be shaken	QI (زُلزِل)	زلزل
shaking, earthquake	زِلزال	
to be brought near	VII (أُزلِف – يُزلَف)	زلف
one who attaches little value to	زاهِد	زهد
to be reunited, joined together	II (زُوِّج – يُزَوَّج)	زوج

English	Arabic	Root
pair	زَوج (ج. أزواج)	
to visit	I (زَارَ – يزور)	زور
olive	زَيْتون	زيت
to increase	I (زاد – يزيد)	زيد
to be asked, questioned	I (سُئِل – يُسأَل)	سأل
to ask one another	VI (تساءل – يتساءل)	
beggar, someone asking for help	سائِل	
repose, rest	سُبات	سبت
to exalt, glorify	II (سَبَّح – يسَبِّح)	سبح
lone star, that which swims along	سابِحة	
swimming, floating	سَبح	
glorified and exalted	سُبحان الله	
float	I (سَبَح – يَسبَح)	
seven	سبع	سبع
to struggle, race with one another	X (استَبَق – يستَبِق)	سبق
that (angel) which hastens, presses forward	سابِقة	
hastening, pressing forward	سَبق	
outstripping	سابِق	
way, path	سَبيل	سبل
to prostrate, kneel, worship	I (سَجَد – يَسجُد)	سجد
prostrating	ساجِد	
prostrate, adoring	سُجَّد	
to become like blazing fire, overflow, rise	II (سُجِّر – يُسَجَّر)	سجر
baked clay	سِجّيل	سجل
to put in prison	I (سَجَن – يسجِن)	سجن
prison	سِجن	

to be still	سَجَى	سجي
barrier	سَدّ	سدد
mirage	سَراب	سرب
lamp	سِراج	سرج
to keep secret, conceal	IV (أَسَرَّ – يُسِرّ)	سرر
secrets	سَرائِر	
couches, thrones	سُرُر	
transgressing all bounds, forward	مُسرِف	سرف
thief	سارِق	سرق
to depart	I (سَرى – يسري)	سري
stream, rivulet	سَرِيّ	
to be spread out	I (سُطِح – يُسَتَح)	سطح
tales, fables	أساطير	سطر
lighted, to be kindled to a fierce blaze	II (سُعِّر – يُسَعَّر)	سعر
blazing, scorching fire	سَعير	
to hasten, strive hard	I (سَعى – يسعى)	سعي
effort, endeavor	سَعي	
hunger	مَسغَبة	سغب
scribes (angels)	سَفَرة	سفر
bright	مُسفِر	
we seize	نَسْفَعَن	سفع
lowest	أسفَل	سفل
low	سافِل	
to let fall, cause to fall	III (ساقَط – يُساقِط)	سقط
to pour out	I (سَقى – يَسقي)	سقي
golden bowl, (drinking-cup)	سِقاية	سقي
drinking, giving water to drink	سُقيا	

to be given to drink	I (سُقِي – يُسقى)	
knife	سِكِّين	سكن
needy	مِسكين	
to withdraw, strip	I (سَلَخ – يسلَخ)	سلخ
authority, sanction	سُلطان	سلطن
peace	سَلام	سلم
to name	II (سَمَّى – يسمّي)	سم/سمي
name	سم، اسم	
of the same name	سَمِيّ	
All-Hearer	سَميع	سمع
height	سَمك	سمك
to nourish	IV (أَسمَن – يُسمِن)	سمن
fat	سِمان	
heaven	سَماء	سمو
ear of corn	سُنبُلة	سنبل
awakened, alive	ساهِرة	سهر
heedless	ساهون	سهو
adultery, wickedness, evil	سوء	سوء
lord and master, husband	سَيِّد	سود
disaster, different kinds	سَوط	سوط
the Hour (of Doom)	(ال) ساعة	سوع
will		سَوفَ
to drive	I (ساق – يَسوق)	سوق
to make up a tale, beguile	II (سَوَّل – يُسوِّل)	سول
to perfect	II (سَوّى – يسوّي)	سوي
the same	سَواء	
complete, in all respects, perfect	سَوِيّ	

to travel	I (سار – يَسِير)	سير
to be set in motion, be moved away	II (سُيِّر – يُسيَّر)	
caravan	سيّارة	
warder, dictator	مُسَيطِر	سيطر
left hand	مَشأَمة	شأم
concern	شَأن	شأن
scattered groups	أشتات	شتت
dispersed	شتّى	
winter	شِتاء	شتو
tree	شَجَر	شجر
laden	مَشحون	شحن
harder, more difficult	أشَدّ	شدد
hard, strong	شِداد	
intense	شَديد	
to drink	I (شرِب – يشرَب)	شرب
drink	شَراب	
drinks	مَشارِب	
to dilate, open up	I (شَرَح – يشرَح)	شرح
evil	شَرّ	شرر
east, facing east	شَرقي	شرق
to attribute	IV (أشرَك – يُشرِك)	شرك
idolater, polytheist	مُشْرِك	
to sell	I (شَرى – يشري)	شري
to buy, purchase	VIII (اشتَرى – يشتري)	
to perceive, be aware	I (شَعَر – يشعُر)	شعر
poetry	شِعر	
to spread, shine	VIII (اشتَعَل – يَشتغِل)	شعل

to cause to love violently, to smite to the heart	I (شَغَفَ – يشغَف)	شغف
busy	في شُغُل	شغل
intercession	شَفاعة	شفع
even	شَفع	
afterglow of sunset	شَفَق	شفق
two lips	شَفَتَين	شفه
to split	I (شَقّ – يشُقّ)	شقق
to be split asunder	VII (انشَقّ – ينشَقّ)	
splitting	شَقّ	
unblest, (most) wretched	أَشْقى	شقي
to give thanks	I (شَكَر – يشكُر)	شكر
sun	شَمْس	شمس
to attest, bear witness	I (شَهِد – يشهَد)	شهد
witness, witnessing day (Friday)	شاهِد (ج. شُهود)	
Worthy of Praise, witness	شَهيد	
meeting	مَشهَد	
witnessed day (the day of Arafat)	مَشهود	
month	شَهْر	شهر
lust	شَهوة	شهو
to point	IV (أَشار – يُشير)	شور
to will	I (شاء – يشاء)	شيء
gray hair	شَيب	شيب
old man, aged	شَيخ	شيخ
Satan, the devil	شَيطان	شيطن
sect	شيعة	شيع
insulter	شانِئ	شين

to pour	I (صَبّ – يصُبّ)	صبب
pouring	صَبّ	
morning	صُبح	صبح
to be constant and patient, steadfast	VIII (اصطَبَر – يَصطبِر)	صبر
endurance, patience	صَبر	
to feel inclined	I (صَبا – يصبو)	صبو
child, young boy	صَبِيّ	صبي
companion, owner, person of	صاحب (ج. أصحاب)	صحب
wife	صاحِبة	
pages, scriptures	صُحُف	صحف
the Shout, Day of Resurrection's second blowing of Trumpet	صاخّة	صخخ
rock	صَخر	صخر
to issue forth	I (صَدَر – يصدُر)	صدر
breast, chest, heart	صدر (ج. صُدور)	
splitting (with the growth of trees and plants)	صَدع	صدع
to speak the truth	I (صَدَق – يصدُق)	صدق
to believe	II (صَدّق – يُصدِّق)	
to be charitable	V (تصدَّق – يتصدَّق)	
confirmation	تَصديق	
speaking the truth	صادِق	
man of truth, saint	صِدِّيق	
to pay regard, to attend	V (تصدّى – يتصَدّى)	صدي
shout, help	صَريخ	صرخ
path	صراط	صرط
to turn away, ward off	I (صرَف – يصرِف)	صرف
one who is disgraced, brought low	صاغِر	صغر

arrayed, in rows	صَفّ	صفف
in rows	صَفّ	
ranged, in rows	مصفوف	
to crucify	I (صلَب – يصلُب)	صلب
backbone	صُلب	
righteous	صالح	صلح
good deed	صالحة	
to pray	II (صَلّى – يصلّي)	صلو
prayer	صَلاة	
worshiper	مُصَلّ(ي)	
to endure, be exposed to heat	I (صلي – يَصْلى)	صلي
burned	صالي (ج. صالون)	
to burn	I (صلى – يصلى)	
being burned	صِلِيّ	
the eternally besought of all	صَمَد	صمد
to bestow, reach	IV (أصاب – يُصيب)	صوب
right	صَواب	
Trumpet	صور	صور
form	صورة	
golden (cup)	صُواع	صوع
fast	صَوم	صوم
shout	صَيحة	صيح
summer	صَيف	صيف
snorting	ضَبْح	ضبح
brightness, morning hours	ضُحى	ضحو
opponent	ضِدّ	ضدد
to put forward a similitude	I (ضرَب – يضرِب مثَلا)	ضرب

hard time, harm, misfortune	ضُرّ	ضرر
bitter thorn-fruit	ضَريع	ضرع
false, jumbled	أضغاث	ضغث
to lead astray	IV (أضَلَّ – يُضِلّ)	ضلل
(comes to) nothing	تضليل	
gone astray	ضالّ (ج. ضالّون)	
one who goes astray	ضالّ	
error, aberration	ضلال، ضلالة	
avid, withholding knowledge	ضَنين	ضنن
to make lost, lose	IV (أضاع – يُضيع)	ضيع
stage, plane	طَبَق	طبق
to spread	I (طَحى – يطحو)	طحو/ي
cast out	I (طرَح – يطرَح)	طرح
night-comer (the bright star)	طارِق	طرق
to feed	IV (أطعَم – يُطعم)	طعم
feeding	إطعام	
feeding	طَعام	
to transgress, be rebellious	I (طغا – يَطغى)	طغو/طغي
rebellious pride	طَغوى	
rebellious, transgressor	طاغي	
he who gives less in measure and weight	مُطَفِّف	طفف
to leap	VIII (اطّلع – يطّلِع)	طلع
to know, to peruse	VIII (اطّلَع – يطلِّع)	
the time (of rising)	مَطلَع	
content, satisfied	مُطمَئنّ	طمأن
to wipe out, blind, quench	I (طمَس – يطمس)	طمس
disaster, catastrophe	طامّة	طمم

purified	مُطَهَر	طهر
mount	طُور	طور
Mount Sinai	طور سينين	
to obey	IV (أطاع – يُطيع)	طوع
obeyed	مُطاع	
to see an evil omen	V (تَطَيَّر – يَتَطَيَّر)	طير
evil omen	طائر	
birds, flying things	طير	
pleasant shade	ظِلال	ظلل
evil-doer, wrong-doer	ظالِم	ظلم
in darkness	مُظلِم	
back	ظَهْر	ظهر
'Aad (a tribe)		عاد
to worship	I (عَبَد – يعبُد)	عبد
worshiper, worshiping	عابِد	
bondmen, honored slaves	عِباد	
slave	عَبْد	
to interpret	I (عَبَر – يعبُر)	عبر
lesson, instructive admonition	عِبرة	
to frown	I (عَبَس – يَعبِس)	عبس
to prepare	IV (أعتَد – يُعتِد)	عتد
obstinate, stubborn in rebellion	عِتِيّ	عتو
extremity, infirmity	عِتِيّاً	
lean	عِجاف	عجف
to make haste	I (عجِل – يَعجَل)	عجل
to count, number	I (عَدَّ – يعُدّ)	عدد
to count	II (عَدّد – يعدِّد)	

English	Arabic	Root
counting, numbering	عَدّ	
number, sum	عدد	
few, counted as few	معدود	
to give due proportion	I (عَدَل – يعدِل)	عدل
coursers, runners	عاديات	عدو
enemy, foe	عَدُوّ	
transgressor	مُعتَد(ي)	
torture, torment	عَذاب	عذب
to punish, torture	II (عذّب – يعذِّب)	
dried, curved date stalk, shriveled palm-leaf	عُرجون	عرج
throne, dais	عَرش	عرش
to turn away	IV (أعرَض – يُعرِض)	عرض
averse, with an averted face, turning away	مُعرِض	
to reinforce	II (عزَّز – يُعزِّز)	عزز
power	عِزّ	
Almighty, ruler	عزيز	
to turn away from, withdraw	VIII (اعتزَل – يعتزِل)	عزل
hardship	عُسْر	عسر
adversity	عُسْرى	
to depart, close	I (عَسعس – يُعَسعِس)	عسعس
may be, perchance	عَسى	عسي
pregnant she-camels	عِشار	عشر
early part of the night, evening	عِشاءً	عشي
afternoon, evening	عَشِيّ	
evening, fall of night	عَشِيّاً	
evening, afternoon	عَشِيّة	

strong group, many	عُصبَة	عصب
to press	I (عصَر – يعصُر)	عصر
declining day, mid-afternoon	عَصر	
rainy cloud	مُعصِرة	
green crops	عَصف	عصف
to refuse, to prove continent	X (استعصَم – يستعصم)	عصم
to disobey	عَصى	عصي
disobedient, rebellious	عَصيّ	
to be neglected, abandoned	II (عُطِّل – يُعَطَّل)	عطل
to give	IV (أعطى – يُعطي)	عطو
gift	عَطاء	عطو
bone	عَظم (ج. عِظام)	عظم
awful, mighty, great	عَظيم	
ascent	عقَبة	عقب
end, nature of the consequence	عاقِبة	
sequel, what comes after	عُقْبى	
knots	عُقَد	عقد
to hamstring	I (عَقَر)	عقر
barren	عاقِر	
understand	I (عقل – يعقِل)	عقل
clot	عَلَق	علق
may	لعلّ	علل
to know	I (عَلِم – يعلَم)	علم
to teach	II (عَلَّم – يعلِّم)	
worlds	عالَمين	
knowledge	عِلم	
All-Knower	عَليم	

to reveal, proclaim	IV (أعلَنَ – يُعلِن)	علن
most high	أعْلى	علي
high	عَليّ	
on me, for me	عَلَيَّ	
highest place	عِلّيِّين، عِلّيّون	
on, over	على	
columns	عَمَد، عِماد	عمد
to have a long life, to go into old age	II (عَمَّرَ – يُعَمِّرُ)	عمر
to do	I (عمِل – يعمَل)	عمل
deeds	أعمال	
toiling	عامِل	
of, about, from	عَن	عن
about what	عَمَّ = عن ما	
grapes	عِنَب	عنب
at, with		عِند
necks	أعناق	عنق
to command, charge	I (عهِدَ – يَعهَد)	عهد
wool	عِهن	عهن
to return	I (عاد – يعود)	عود
to repeat, reproduce	IV (أعاد – يُعيد)	
to seek refuge	I (عاذ – يعوذ)	عوذ
(I) seek refuge in Allah	مَعاذ الله	
destitute	عائِل	عول
to seek help	X (استعان – يستعين)	عون
whose help can be sought	مُستَعان	
caravan, camel riders	عير	عير
life	عيشة	عيش

livelihood	مَعاش	
spring	عَين	عين
vision	عَين	
two eyes	عَينَين	
springs of water	عُيون	
dust	غَبَرة	غبر
stubble	غُثاء	غثي
tomorrow	غَداً	غدو
to make (someone) careless	I (غَرّ – يَغُرّ)	غرر
to drown	IV (أغرَق – يُغرِق)	غرق
destruction, with great violence	غَرق	
darkness	غاسِق	غسق
paralyzing cold, dirty wound discharges	غَسّاق	
to enshroud	I (غَشِي – يَغشى)	غشي
to cover	IV (أغشى – يُغشي)	
covering veil, overwhelming (Day of Resurrection)	غاشية	
having earned the anger of	مَغضوب	غضب
to make dark, cover with darkness	IV (أغطَش – يُغطِش)	غطش
to forgive, pardon	I (غَفَر – يغفِر)	غفر
to ask forgiveness	X (استغفَر – يستَغفِر)	
forgiving	غَفور	
forgiveness	مَغفِرة	
careless, heedless	غافِل	غفل
a state of carelessness	غَفلة	
having full power, predominant	غالِب	غلب
of thick foliage, dense	غُلب	

to close, bolt	II (غَلَّق – يُغلِّق)	غلق
iron collars	أغلال	غلل
boy, youth	غُلام	غلم
to wink to one another	VI (تغامَز – يتغامَز)	غمز
to make rich, independent, careless or heedless	IV (أغنى – يُغني)	غني
to deem oneself independent	X (استَغنى – يستغني)	
to have abundant rain or plenteous crops	IV (أغاث – يُغيث)	غوث
raiding	مُغيرات	غور
deception	غَيّ	غوي
bottom	غيابَة	غيب
absence, secret, unseen	غَيب	
not, other than	غير	غير
then, and	فَ	
hearts	أفئِدة	فأد
to never cease	I (فتأ – يفتأ)	فتأ
conquest	فَتح	فتح
to persecute, put to trial	I (فتَن – يفتِن)	فتن
slave-boy	فَتى	فتو
to explain, expound	I (فَتى – يَفتي)	فتي
to inquire	X (استَفتى – يستفتي)	
to be poured forth, burst forth	II (فُجِّر – يُفَجَّر)	فجر
to cause to gush forth	II (فَجَّر – يُفجِّر)	
disbelievers, sinners, evil-doers	فُجّار	
dawn	فَجْر	
disbelievers, wicked	فَجَرة	
immorality	فُجور	

unlawful sexual intercourse, lewdness	فَحشاء	فحش
alone	فَرد	فرد
to flee	II (فَرَّ – يفِرّ)	فرر
moths	فَراش	فرش
to fail in duty, fail in the case	II (فَرَّط – يُفرِّط)	فرط
Pharaoh		فِرعون
to relieve	I (فَرَغ – يفرُغ)	فرغ
to be divided	V (تَفَرَّق – يَتَفرَّق)	فرق
group, party	فَريق	
different, diverse	مُتَفرِّق	
mighty, amazing	فَريّاً	فري
to forge, invent	VIII (افتَرى – يفتَري)	
to make mischief, do evil	IV (أَفسَد – يُفسِد)	فسد
mischief, iniquity	فَساد	
detailed explanation	تَفصيل	فصل
decision, something conclusive, that which separates truth from falsehood	فَصل	
to depart	فَصَل	
to be torn	V (تَفَطَّر – يَتَفَطَّر)	فطر
to be cleft asunder	VII (انفطر – ينفطِر)	
Creator	فاطِر	
to create	I (فَطَر – يفطُر)	
to do	I (فَعَل – يفعَل)	فعل
doing	فاعِل	
doer	فَعّال	
to lose	I (فقَد – يفقد)	فقد
freeing	فَكّ	فكك

happy, joyful	فاكِه	فكه
fruit	فاكِهة	
jesting	فَكِه	
to be successful, prosper	IV (أفلَح – يُفلِح)	فلح
daybreak	فَلَق	فلق
ship, orbit	فَلَك	فلك
to think of as weak of mind because of old age	II (فنَّد – يُفنِّد)	فند
troops	فوج (ج. أفواج)	فوج
success	فَوز	فوز
achievement, success	مَفاز	
mouths	أفواه	فوه
in		في
elephant	فيل	فيل
to put in the grave	IV (أقبَر – يُقبِر)	قبر
grave	قَبر (ج. قُبور)	
graves	مَقابِر	
to turn toward	IV (أقبَل – يُقبِل)	قبل
front, before	قُبُل	
from before	مِن قَبل	
darkness	قَتَرة	قتر
to be cursed, destroyed	I (قُتِل – يُقتَل)	قتل
to attempt	VIII (اقتحَم – يقتحِم)	قحم
sparks	قَدْح	قدح
to tear	I (قَدَّ – يقُدّ)	قدد
be able to	I (قدِر – يقدِر)	قدر
to measure, to appoint	II (قَدَّر – يُقدِّر)	

able	قادِر	
to straiten, tighten	قَدَر	
decree, measuring	تَقدير	
to send forward, before	II (قَدَّم – يُقَدِّم)	قدم
to read	I (قرأ – يقرأ)	قرأ
to make (someone) recite	IV (أقرأ – يُقرِئ)	
to come near, draw near	I (قرِب – يقرَب)	قرب
to make (someone) draw near	II (قَرَّب – يُقرِّب)	
to draw near	VIII (اقتَرَب – يقْتَرِب)	
that who is nearest, brought near	مُقَرَّب	
near of kin	مَقرَبة	
to be happy, be consoled	II (قرَّ – يَقرَّ)	قرر
fixed course, resting-place	مُستَقَرّ	
calamity	قارِعة	قرع
generations	قُرون	قرن
townships	قُرى	قري
town, city	قَرية	
Quraysh (a tribe)		قُرَيش
to swear	IV (أقسَم – يُقسِم)	قسم
oath	قسَم	
to relate, narrate	I (قصّ – يقُصّ)	قصص
stories, narratives	قَصَص	
far	قَصِيّ	قصو
farthest part	أقصى	
green fodder, clover plants	قَضب	قضب
to do, decree, judge	I (قضى – يقضي)	قضي
decreed, ordained	مَقضِيّ	

to cut	II (قَطَّع – يُقَطِّع)	قطع
people sitting	قُعود	قعد
to return	VII (انقَلَب – ينقَلِب)	قلب
pen	قَلَم	قلم
to hate	I (قَلى – يقلو)	قلي/قلو
with heads raised up, stiff-necked	مُقمَح	قمح
moon	قَمَر	قمر
shirt	قَميص	قمص
to oppress	I (قهَر – يقهَر)	قهر
Irresistible, Almighty	قَهّار	
to say	I (قال – يقول)	قول
word	قَول	
to establish	IV (أَقام – يُقيم)	قوم
to walk straight	X (استقام – يستَقيم)	
stature	تقويم	
folk	قَوم	
straight, right	قَيِّم	
straight	مُستَقيم	
(place of standing), position	مَقام	
fast, with strength	بقُوّة	قوي
power	قُوّة	
like		كَ
cup	كَأس	كَأس
in affliction	كَبَد	كبد
old age	كِبَر	كبر
eldest	كَبير	
writing down	كاتِب	كتب

book, record, register	كِتاب (ج. كُتُب)	
increase	تَكاثُر	كثر
abundance	كَوثَر	
working, returning	كادِح	كدح
work, return	كَدح	
to fall	VII (انكَدَر – ينكَدِر)	كدر
to deny, think something as a lie	II (كذّب – يُكذّب)	كذب
denial	تَكذيب	
liar, lying	كاذِب	
denying, belying strongly	كِذّاب	
false	كَذِب	
that who denies	مُكذِّب	
proceeding, return	كَرّة	كرر
honored	مُكرَم	كرم
to honor, make comfortable, honorable	IV (أكرَم – يُكرِم)	
most bounteous, generous	أكرَم	
honorable, noble, generous	كَريم (ج. كِرام)	
to earn	I (كسَب – يكسِب)	كسب
to be stripped off, torn away	I (كُشِط – يُكشَط)	كشط
suppressing sorrow	كَظيم	كظم
young, full-breasted or mature (maidens)	كَواعِب	كعب
to disbelieve	I (كَفَر – يكفِر)	كفر
ungrateful	أكفَر	
unbeliever	كافِر	
one who is comparable	كُفُو	كفو/كفي
every	كُلّ	
nay	كَلّا	

to talk to	II (كَلَّم – يُكَلِّم)	كلم
ingrate	كَنود	كند
that which moves swiftly and hides itself, that rises and sets	كُنَّس	كنس
cups, goblets	أَكواب	كوب
to be on the verge of, almost	I (كاد – يَكاد)	كود
to be wound around, lose its light, and be overthrown	II (كُوِّر – يُكَوَّر)	كور
star, planet	كوكَب (ج. كواكِب)	كوكَب
to be	I (كان – يكون)	كون
you were not	لَم تَكُ (لم تكُن)	
to plot	I (كاد – يَكيد)	كيد
plot, evil planning	كَيد	
how		كَيفَ
to give by measure	I (كال – يكيل)	كيل
to get the measure	VIII (اكتال – يكتال)	
measure, load	كَيل	
for, unto, to, in order to		لِ
verily		لَ
if		لَئِن (لإِن)
not, nor		لا
to stay, tarry	I (لَبَث – يلبَث)	لبث
abiding	لابِث	
vast	لُبَد	لبد
cloak, covering	لِباس	لبس
to join to	IV (ألحَق – يُلحِق)	لحق
most quarrelsome, forward	لُدّ	لدد
Yourself, Your presence		لَدُنك

before, at	لَدى	لدي
tongue	لِسان	لسن
most courteous, tender	لَطيف	لطف
to flame	V (تلَظّى – يتَلَظّى)	لظي
to play	I (لعِب – يلعَب)	لعب
idle speech	لاغِية	لغو
vain discourse; dirty, false, evil talk	لَغو	
to find, meet	IV (ألفى – يُلفي)	لفي
surely		لَقَد
to pick up, find	VIII (التقَط – يلتَقِط)	لقط
to meet	I (لَقِي – يَلقى)	لقي
throw down, fling, cast	IV (ألقى – يُلقي)	
meeting	مُلاقي	
devouring		لَمّ
you were not, she was not	لَم تَك (لم تكُن)	لم
did not		لَم/لِّا
when		لِّا
fault-finder, back-biter	لِمَزة	لُمَز
flame	لَهَب	لهب
to inspire	IV (ألهَم – يلهِم)	لهم
to distract	IV (ألهى – يُلهي)	لهو/لهي
to be neglectful, distracted	V (تلَهّى – يتلهّى)	
if		لَو
if not, had it not been		لَولا
tablet	لَوح	لوح
to blame	I (لام – يلوم)	لوم
if only	لَيتَ	ليت

would that I	يا ليتَني	
night	لَيْل	ليل
Night of Predestination, Power	ليلة القَدْر	
you are only . . .	ما أنتُم الا . . .	ما
did not		ما
that which		ما
belongings, things, enjoyment, comfort	مَتاع	متع
to appear, assume the likeness of	V (تَمثَّل – يَتمثَّل)	مثل
like	مِثل	
glorious	مَجيد	مجد
to extend, prolong	I (مَدَّ – يمُدّ)	مدد
to be stretched	I (مُدّ – يُمَدّ)	
extending	مَدّ	
outstretched, extended	ممَدَّد	
town, city	مَدينة	مدن
man	امرأً، مَرء، امرىٔ	مرء
wife	امرأة	مرأ
to pass by	I (مَرَّ – يمُرُّ)	مرر
to doubt or dispute	VIII (امترى – يَمتَري)	مرو
mixing	مِزاج	مزج
to transform into animals, objects	مَسَخ	مسخ
palm-fiber	مَسَد	مسد
to hit, touch, befall, overtake	I (مَسَّ – يمَسُّ)	مسس
musk	مِسك	مسك
Egypt	مِصر	مصر
going forward	مُضِيّ	مضي
small kindness	ماعون	معن

to plot, scheme	I (مَكَر – يَمكُر)	مكر
accusation, sly talk	مَكر	
high in rank, established	مَكين	مكن
to establish	II (مَكَّن – يُمكِّن)	
notables	مَلأ	ملأ
to possess	I (ملَك – يملِك)	ملك
master, owner	مالك	
angels	ملائكة	
angel(s)	مَلَك	
king	مَلِك	
religion	مِلَّة	ملل
safely; for a long while	مَلِيّ	ملو
from what	مِمَّ = مِن ما	
from	مِن	
who	مَن	
to deny, refuse	I (منَع – يمنَع)	منع
failing	مَمنون	منن
cradle	مَهد	مهد
an expanse, bed	مِهاد	
to give a respite	II (مَهَّل – يُمَهِّل)	مهل
to deal gently	IV (أَمهَل – يُمهِل)	
to cause to die	IV (أَمات – يُميت)	موت
dead (pl.)	مَوتى	
dead	مَيت	
wealth	مال	مول
water	ماء	موه
to get food, provisions	I (مار – يمير)	مير

to be apart, distinguished	VIII (إمتاز – يمتاز)	ميز
to inform, announce	II (نبّأ – يُنَبِّئ)	نبأ
news, tidings	أَنباء	
to produce, grow	IV (أَنبَت – يُنبِت)	نبت
to be flung	I (نُبِذ – يُنبَذ)	نبذ
to withdraw in seclusion	VIII (انتَبَذ – يَنتبِذ)	
to be dispersed, scattered	VII (انتثَر – ينتَثِر)	نثر
the parting of the mountain ways	نجدين	نجد
star	نَجم (ج. نُجوم)	نجم
to be released	I (نَجا – ينجو)	نجو
to save, rescue	II (نَجّى – يُنَجِّي)	
talk, communion, conference	نَجِيّ	
escaping, being released	ناجٍ (ناجي)	نجي
to sacrifice	I (نحَر – ينحر)	نحر
crumbled	نَخِر	نخر
palm-tree	نَخلة (ج. نخل)	نخل
to summon, cry out	III (نادى – ينادي)	ندو
call, cry	نِداء	
station, imposing	نَدِيّ	ندي
to vow	I (نَذَر – ينذِر)	نذر
to warn	IV (أَنذَر – يُنذِر)	
warner	مُنذِر	
to drag out, pluck out	I (نَزَع – يَنزِع)	نزع
those who drag forth, pull out	نازعة	
to sow enmity, make strife	I (نَزَغ – ينزِغ)	نزغ
revelation, (something) sent down	تَنزيل	نزل
to reveal, bring down	IV (أَنزَل – يُنزِل)	

to descend	V (تَنَزَّل – يتنزَّل)	
mansions	مَنازِل	
host, sending down	مُنزِل	
to come out quickly	I (نَسَل – يَنسِل)	نسل
women	نِسوَة	نسو
to forget	I (نَسِي – يَنسى)	نسي
forgotten	مَنسِيّ	
forgetful	نَسِيّ	
nothing	نَسِيّ	
to create, produce	IV (أَنشَأَ – يُنشِئ)	نشأ
to be laid open	I (نُشِر – يُنشَر)	نشر
to bring to life, resurrect	IV (أَنشَر – يُنشِر)	نشر
meteor, one who takes out	ناشطة	نشط
taking out	نَشط	
to be set up	I (نُصِب – يُنصَب)	نصب
to toil, work hard	I (نصَب – ينصُب)	
weary	ناصِب	
well-wisher, good friend	ناصِح	نصح
to help	I (نَصَر – يَنصُر)	نصر
helper	ناصِر	
help, succor, triumph	نَصر	
forelock	ناصِية	نصي
brightness, radiance	نضرة	نضر
drop of seed, semen drop	نُطفة	نطف
to favor	IV (أنعَم – يُنعِم)	نعم
to be gracious to, to give gifts to	II (نعَّم – ينعِّم)	
cattle	أنعام	

calm, joyful	ناعِم	
bounty, blessing	نِعمة	
pleasure	نَعيم	
blowers	نَفّاثات	نفث
to be blown	I (نُفِخ – يُنفَخ)	نفخ
to blow	I (نفَخ – ينفُخ)	نفخ
to brighten, to breathe	V (تنَفَّس – يتنفَّس)	نفس
to strive	VI (تنافس – يتنافس)	
that who strives	مُتَنافِس	
soul	نَفْس	
carded	مَنفوش	نفش
to profit, prove useful	I (نفَع – ينفَع)	نفع
benefits	مَنافِع	
to spend	IV (أَنفَق – يُنفِق)	نفق
someone leaving	مُنفَكّ	نفكك
to save	IV (أَنقَذ – يُنقِذ)	نقذ
to weigh down	أنقَض	نقض
dust	نَقع	نقع
to have against	I (نَقَم – ينقِم)	نقم
not recognizing, not knowing	مُنكِر	نكر
to reverse	II (نكَّس – يُنَكِّس)	نكس
example, punishment	نَكال	نكل
cushions	نَمارِق	نمرق
to repulse	I (نهَر – ينهَر)	نهر
rivers	أنهار	
day	نَهار	
to dissuade	I (نَهى – ينْهى)	نهي

to cease, put an end	VIII (اِنتَهى – يَنْتَهي)	
term	مُنتَهى	
to restrain	I (نَهى)	
fire	نار	نور
mankind	ناس	نوس
she-camel	ناقة	نوق
to depart, get away from	I (هَجَر – يهجُر)	هجر
in ruins	هَدّ	هدد
to guide, show, lead in the right direction	I (هَدى – يهدي)	هدي
to walk aright	VIII (اهتَدى – يَهتَدي)	
rightly guided	مُهتَدي	
guidance	هُدى	
to mock	X (استَهزأ – يستَهزِئ)	هزأ
to shake	I (هزّ – يهُزّ)	هزز
amusement, pleasantry	هَزل	هزل
to destroy	IV (أهلَك – يُهلِك)	هلك
dead, perishing	هالك	
they (m.)		هُم
slanderer	هُمَزة	همز
to desire	I (هَمَّ – يهُم)	همم
he		هو
easy	هَيِّن	هون
bereft and hungry	هاوي	هوي
lust, evil desires	هَوى	
she		هي
come on!		هَيتَ!
to humiliate	IV (أهان)	هين

English	Arabic	Root
and		وَ
girl-child buried alive	مَوؤُودة	وأد
bulwarks, pegs	أوتاد	وتد
odd	وَتر	وتر
to be bound	IV (أوثَق – يوثِق)	وثق
solemn oath, undertaking	موثِق	
binding	وِثاق	
to find	I (وَجَد – يَجد)	وجد
that which beats painfully, that which shakes with fear and anxiety	واجِف	وجف
face, favor, purpose	وَجه (ج. وُجوه)	وجه
one	أَحَد	وحد
eleven	أحد عَشَر	
wild beasts	وُحوش	وحش
to reveal, inspire	IV (أوحى – يُوحي)	وحي
love	وُدّ	ودد
full of love	وَدود	
to forsake	II (ودّع – يُودِّع)	ودع
vale, valley	واد(ي)	ودي
to leave	I (وذر – يَذَر)	وذر
to inherit	I (وَرِث – يَرِث)	ورث
to cause to inherit, give as inheritance	IV (أورَث – يورِث)	
passing over, approaching, water-drawer	وارِد	ورد
in a thirsty state; weary herd	وِرد	
striking, lighting	موريات	وري
burden	وِزر	وزر
to weigh	I (وزن – يزِن)	وزن

scales	مَوازين	
to cleave	I (وَسَط)	وسط
to be at the full	VIII (اتّسَق – يتّسِق)	وسق
to gather in darkness, to enshroud	I (وَسَق)	
to whisper	QI (وسوَس – يُوَسوِس)	وسوس
whisperer	وَسواس	
closed	مُوَّصَد	وصد
to describe, allege	I (وصَف – يصِف)	وصف
to enjoin	IV (أوصى – يوصي)	وصي
to exhort one another	VI (تواصى – يتواصى)	
bequest	تَوصِية	
to put down, ease	I (وَضَع – يضع)	وضع
set at hand	موضوع	
to promise	I (وَعَد – يَعِد)	وعد
promised (Day of Resurrection)	مَوعود	
promise	وَعد	
to gather, hide	IV (أوعى – يوعي)	وعي
bags	أوعِية	
(like a) delegation, goodly company	وَفد	وفد
proportioned, exact	وِفاق	وفق
to give in full (measure), fill up	IV (أوفى – يوفي)	وفي
to cause to die, make die	V (تَوَفّى – يَتوفّى)	وفي
to demand full measure	X (استوفى – يستوفي)	
to become intense	I (وَقَب)	وقب
fixed time	مِيقات	وقت
to kindle	IV (أوقَد – يُوقِد)	وقد
kindled, lit	موقَد	

English	Arabic	Root
fuel	وَقود	
banquet, a cushioned couch	مُتَّكَأ	وكأ
reclining	مُتَّكِئ	
to put one's trust	V (تَوَكَّل – يتوَكَّل)	وكل
that who trusts, trusting	مُتَوَكِّل	
witness, warden	وكيل	
to be born	I (وُلِد – يولَد)	ولد
to beget, give birth to	I (وَلَد – يلِد)	
begetter, father	والِد	ولد
taming	ايلاف	ولف
to turn away, go away, not to heed	V (تَوَلَّى – يتولَّى)	ولي
most worthy	أَوْلى	
relatives, kinfolk	مَوالي	
heir, successor	وَلِيّ	
Protector, Guardian, Lord	وَلِيّ	
to give	I (وَهَب – يهَب)	وهب
dazzling, shining	وَهّاج	وهج
to grow feeble	I (وَهَن – يهِن)	وهن
woe	وَيْل	ويل
to give up hope, despair	X (استَيْأَس – يَسْتيئِس)	يأس
to give up hope, despair	I (يئِس – يَيْأَس)	
O, you		يا
dry	يابِس	يبس
orphan	يَتيم	يتم
hand	يَد (ج. أَيدي)	يد
to ease, make easy	II (يَسَّر – يُيَسِّر)	يسر
ease	يُسْر	

state of ease	يُسْرى	
easy, light	يسير	
sure, certainty	يَقين	يقن
right (side)	أَيمَن	يمن
right hand	مَيمَنة	
day	يَوم	يوم
that day	يَومَئِذٍ	

Subject index